# Mamluk Economics

# *Mamluk Economics*

A STUDY AND TRANSLATION OF AL-MAQRĪZĪ'S *IGHĀTHAH*

Adel Allouche

University of Utah Press
Salt Lake City

⊗ Printed on acid-free paper

LIBRARY OF CONGRESS CATALOGING-IN-PUBLICATION DATA

Maqrīzī, Aḥmad ibn ʿAlī, 1364–1442.
[Ighāthat al-ummah bi-kashf al-ghummah. English]
Mamluk economics : a study and translation of al-Maqrīzī's Ighāthah / Adel Allouche.
p. cm.
Includes bibliographical references (p. ) and index.
ISBN 0-87480-431-0 (alk. paper)
1. Egypt—Economic conditions—1250–1517. 2. Egypt—History—1250–1517. 3. Famines—Egypt—History. I. Allouche, Adel. II. Title.
HC830.M3613 1994
330.962'02—dc20 93-42723

TO THE MEMORY OF MY PARENTS

# *Contents*

# *Preface*

Chronicles contemporaneous with the rule of the Circassian Mamluks in Egypt abound in criticism of the maladministration and unorthodox financial practices of these rulers. Their authors complain about the general decline of the country, particularly the suffering of the lower classes and the poor, and often attribute it to the lack of adherence to moral and religious precepts by the state. The religious education of these historians leads them, in typically medieval fashion, to link morality, piety, and economics. Among these authors, the Shafiʿite Taqī al-Dīn Aḥmad ibn ʿAlī al-Maqrīzī (d. 845/1442) stands out as the most vocal critic of the Circassian monetary policy, which he blames for the impoverishment of the country. The targets for his attack were the excessive coinage of the copper *fulūs*, the cessation of silver coinage, and the adoption in 1403 of a money of account: the dirham of *fulūs*. Although several attempts were made later to reintroduce silver coinage, the dirham of *fulūs* remained the unit of account until the fall of the Circassians and the beginning of Ottoman rule in Egypt. The immediate effect of this new monetary system was an acute economic crisis dominated by an inflationary trend. This was worsened by a plague and an epizootic, thus strengthening the belief in a divine punishment. This situation prompted al-Maqrīzī to present his views of the causes of the crisis in a separate monograph appropriately entitled *Ighāthat al-ummah bi-kashf al-ghummah* [Helping the Community (or the Nation) by Examining the Causes of Its Distress]. This work became a reference for students of the medieval economic history of Egypt and its importance did not escape the attention of the erudite Gaston Wiet, who published in 1962 a French translation based on the 1940 Cairo edition, the same edition that is followed in the present translation.

The study of the economic history of the Middle East in the Middle Ages is still in its formative years and it is natural that Wiet's translation, published over thirty years ago, reflects the knowledge of his time. In this respect, the quotations from Wiet's translation in the introduction to the present work are not meant to diminish the worth of his endeavor. Rather, they are a justification for an updated rendering of al-Maqrīzī's work in light of the expansion of our knowledge of the economic history of Egypt under the Circassians and an attempt to draw the reader's attention to the difficulty of the text as well as the complexity of the monetary issues of the period.

While al-Maqrīzī blames the adoption of the dirham of *fulūs* for the economic chaos in his time, modern historians may have the right to blame the Circassians for the designation of this unit of account and for the difficulty it has created in comprehending the monetary data of the Circassian period! The several uses of the term "dirham," together with the variation in the weight of the copper *fals* (which may equal one dirham, as was the case in 879/1474–75) throughout the Circassian period, have led to the same confusion among specialists of Mamluk history regarding the nature of the dirham of *fulūs* and its relation to the copper coins and caused some to limit the scope of their research.

This book is not an exhaustive study of the economic and monetary conditions of Egypt under the Circassian Mamluks, a complex topic that still needs further research and debate. It is an attempt to present a careful translation of *Ighāthat al-ummah* that may eventually contribute to a reassessment of al-Maqrīzī's ideas and a better comprehension of the Circassian monetary system. The reader is provided with a brief introduction that is limited to the presentation and explanation of a number of relevant issues. The inclusion of additional documentation, particularly the appendices, provides a handy reference. With regard to the translation, additions to facilitate the reading of the text are shown in brackets. Dates of death, reign, or tenure in office of important persons are added in parentheses. The rendering of Qur'ānic verses is based on Abdullah Yusuf Ali's translation. The often repetitive traditional laudatory utterances found in the original text have been eliminated in order not to distract the reader from the focus of the work. Throughout the translation, an effort has been made to give both the Hijrī and the corresponding Gregorian date. The transliteration of names and technical terms conforms to the system of the Library of Congress.

This project has been made possible by a grant from the National

Endowment of the Humanities, Washington, D.C. I have also benefited from the advice of several colleagues and friends to whom I would like to pay tribute. Professors Donald P. Little (McGill) and Ulrich Haarmann (Kiel) read and commented on earlier drafts. More recently, Dr. Michael L. Bates, of the American Numismatic Society, New York, made valuable comments and offered extensive explanations that helped me clarify the subtle details of the numismatic data. A number of my graduate students criticized earlier versions and were generous with their time and suggestions, particularly Dr. Devin Stewart (Emory University), and Mr. Asim Memon (University of Pennsylvania). Finally, I would like to express my deep appreciation for the patience of my children (Jeanette, Adam, and Alexander) and the assistance of my wife, Ann Kuhlman, who helped me through the several stages of this project, particularly with her computer skills, despite the demands of her own work.

Adel Allouche

# *Translator's Introduction*

The Mamluks gained control of Egypt and Syria in 648/1250, following their overthrow of the waning dynasty of the Ayyubids. The rule of this caste of manumitted slaves who were initially imported from the Kipchak plain to Egypt for military service continued until 784/1382, when the Circassian Mamluks (military slaves brought from the Caucasus) took over the Mamluk sultanate. This second period of Mamluk history, which is the focus of the present essay, lasted until 922/1517, the date of the Ottoman conquest of Egypt and Syria. These two consecutive periods of Mamluk history are designated, within the Orientalist tradition, as the Baḥrī (or "Turkish" in contemporary Arabic sources) and Burjī (or "Circassian") periods, corresponding respectively to the years 1250–1382 and 1382–1517.

Unlike their Circassian successors, the Baḥrī Mamluks generally receive praise in the chronicles of their contemporaries. They were able to respond successfully to several threats and to consolidate the military position of the state. Baḥrī sultans led their armies to victory against the Mongols at ʿAyn Jālūt in 1260, expanded their suzerainty to Lesser Armenia in 1274, and drove the crusaders from their last enclave in Acre in 1291. Three years after the fall of Baghdad to the Mongols in 1258, the Mamluks revived the Abbasid Caliphate in Cairo, their own capital, thus enhancing their prestige as protectors of Islam and its institutions. Moreover, the long hereditary rule of Sultan Qalāwūn and his two sons, al-Ashraf Khalīl and al-Nāṣir Muḥammad (678–741/1279–1340), gave the kingdom a degree of stability for most of this period.[1]

The principle of hereditary rule was largely ignored by powerful military commanders and their respective factions during the Circassian period. With a few exceptions, Circassian rulers belonged to the military elite and ascended the throne after successful plots. Thus, they had to reckon with increasing factionalism. They also had to secure the allegiance of their military commanders by all means and improve their chances of survival through the purchase of more slaves who would join the ranks of their own royal mamluks.

In addition to this inherent weakness of the Circassian system, important geopolitical factors contributed to the political and financial instability of the kingdom. The campaigns of Tīmūr (Tamerlane, d. 807/1405) against Syria in 1400–1401 and against the Ottomans in Asia Minor in 1402 resulted in the destabilization of the Mamluks' northern borders and the relative weakening of the central government's hold over its Syrian province. Mamluk expeditions sent to subdue unruly Turkoman vassals in Asia Minor or an occasionally rebellious governor in Syria depleted available resources and monies. Later, the geopolitical impact of the fall of Constantinople to the Ottomans in 1453 placed further military and financial strains on the Mamluks, who were then compelled to dispatch a number of expeditions to the Taurus area in a futile attempt to check the Ottoman threat. In 922/1516–17, the Ottomans inflicted a crushing blow to the Mamluks in two decisive battles and annexed their domains in Syria and Egypt.[2]

## CONTEMPORARY VIEWS OF THE EARLY CIRCASSIANS

The rule of the Circassian Mamluks in Egypt was beset by a series of severe economic crises that were symptomatic of a general state of decline. Our knowledge of these conditions relies primarily on the quantitative data supplied by contemporary sources. Data on coinage, exchange rates, and the price of foodstuffs, as well as occasional references to the financial conditions of the Circassian state, are given in a fairly detailed fashion down to the year 877/1472–73.[3] This information has served, particularly from the 1960s on, as the basis for a number of pioneering studies on the social, economic, and monetary history of Egypt in the later Middle Ages.[4] The unavailability of Mamluk archival documentation, such as mint records, official rescripts, financial accounts or business ledgers, or detailed tax registers (the type of documentation that a Europeanist generally has at hand), hinders research on the economy of Mamluk Egypt. The researcher can make use of data contained in European, especially Italian, archival materials of the period,[5] but the scope of these sources is essentially limited to the nature and prices of goods exchanged between Egypt and Syria and their trade partners across the Mediterranean. Therefore, heavy reliance on Mamluk chronicles and on recent numismatic studies,[6] notably those focusing on the fineness of coinage,[7] is dictated by the absence of succinct and more quantitative source materials.[8]

Contemporary Mamluk chronicles blame the economic and monetary policy of the Circassians for the pauperization of Egypt and for driving the state into bankruptcy. With no important exceptions, they describe a chaotic monetary situation and a treasury that was perennially short of funds. They also decry the prevailing injustice, embodied in the government's predatory fiscal policy, as well as widespread bribery and venality and the acceptance of protection money by high officials.[9] In the fashion of the time and in a style laced with religious discourse, they blame the injustice of the Circassian regime for the frequency of dearth, plague, and pestilence, seeing in these natural disasters divine punishment.[10] Referring to new monetary regulations set by the Circassians in 806/1403–4, the same year that drought and plague struck Egypt, Ibn Taghrī Birdī (d. 874/1470), who was closely associated with the Mamluk administration, comments on these events as follows:

> During this year [A.H. 806] there was a vast extent of uninundated land in Egypt, and extreme scarcity resulted, followed by the plague. And this year was the beginning of a series of events and trials in which most of Egypt and its provinces were ruined, not only because of the failure of the inundation [of the Nile] but also because of the lack of harmony in the government and the frequent change of officials in the provinces, as well as other causes.[11]

Such views are shared by most fifteenth-century historians of Egypt, many of whom also held important positions within the Circassian administration at the judicial and bureaucratic levels. Of these, the most outspoken critic of the Circassians was the famous Taqī al-Dīn al-Maqrīzī (d. 845/1442), a prolific author who also served as *muḥtasib* (market supervisor) of Cairo on at least three separate occasions: 11 Rajab to 1 Dhū'l-Ḥijjah 801/19 March to 4 August 1399; 18 Jumādā I to 10 Shaᶜbān 802/16 January to 6 April 1400; and 22 Shawwāl to 21 Dhū'l-Qaᶜdah 807/23 April to 21 May 1405.[12] His disagreement with official policy is implied in a statement that he accepted the last appointment unwillingly and only upon the insistence of the then ruling sultan, Faraj (801–15/1399–1412).[13] Al-Maqrīzī is one of only two fifteenth-century historians who had firsthand experience in monetary matters as *muḥtasib* of Cairo, the other being Badr al-Dīn al-ʿAynī (d. 855/1451).[14] According to Ibn Khaldūn (d. 808/1406), the *muḥtasib*

> has authority over everything relating to fraud and deception in connection with food and other things and in connection with weights and measures. He investigates abuses and applies the appropriate punishments and corrective measures. He sees to it that people act in accordance with the public interest in the town under his supervision.[15]

The elimination of fraud and the implementation of government regulations regarding prices, coin weights, and currency exchange rates are therefore the most important duties of the *muḥtasib*.

The tenure of the *muḥtasib*s of Cairo is a significant indicator of the general economic conditions of the kingdom: under the Baḥrī Mamluks, thirty appointments were made from 1265 to 1382, at an average interval of approximately four years. The Circassian period offers a drastically different picture: from 1382 to 1517, a total of 155 appointments to the *ḥisbah* of Cairo were made, at an average tenure of only ten and a half months. These general statistics already point to the relative economic instability of Circassian Egypt. During crises, the turnover of *muḥtasib*s increased in proportion to the depth of each crisis: seventy appointments were made from the death of Sultan Barqūq in 1399 to the year 1416, at an average tenure of about two and a half months.[16] The year 808/1405–6 holds the record with eleven appointments, excluding a three-week period when the function of *muḥtasib* of Cairo was assumed by the sultan, because of the reluctance of qualified persons to accept the position and abide by his demands.[17]

## THE DATE OF AL-MAQRĪZĪ'S *IGHĀTHAH*

French Orientalists were first to recognize the importance of al-Maqrīzī's works: parts of *Sulūk* that dealt with the 1249–50 crusade of St. Louis against Egypt were translated by D. D. Cardonne and published in 1761 and 1819.[18] In 1796, Silvestre de Sacy (d. 1838) published a translation of *Shudhūr al-ʿuqūd fī dhikr al-nuqūd* under the title *Traité des monnoies musulmanes.*[19] Three years later, he published *Le traité des poids et mesures légales des musulmans*, a translation of *Kitāb al-awzān wa'l-akyāl al-sharʿīyah.*[20] In *Shudhūr*, al-Maqrīzī refers on one occasion to his previous work, *Ighāthat al-ummah bi-kashf al-ghummah*, a title that de Sacy translates as "Remède offert au public contre le chagrin," but he admits that he was unaware of its content.[21] Four decades later, E. de Quatremère (d. 1857) gave a brief synopsis of *Ighāthah*, in the introduction to his translation of the first sections of *Sulūk* that dealt with the years 648–708/1250–1309, but without mentioning the original title of the work, referring to it only as "Le traité des famines."[22] In 1962, Gaston Wiet (d. 1971) published a translation of *Ighāthah*, based on the 1940 Cairo edition by Muḥammad Muṣṭafā Ziyādah and Jamāl al-Dīn al-Shayyāl. Wiet preferred to keep the popular title "Le traité des famines de Maqrīzī" because it "has the advantage of clearly defining its object."[23] As will be shown later, the common view that *Ighāthah* is primarily a treatise on the history of famines in Egypt perpetuates the initial impression of Quatremère and fails to account for the essence and scope of the work.

It is commonly held that al-Maqrīzī completed *Ighāthah* in the month of Muḥarram in A.H. 808 (July 1405). This is in conformity with the information contained in the colophon, where it is stated that this monograph was composed and revised "in a single night" of Muḥarram 808, a date that coincides with the month mentioned by al-Maqrīzī in the text.[24] This date is accepted by the editors of the Arabic text, although they believe that it corresponds to the final revision of the work, rather than to the actual composition, and by Gaston Wiet.[25] Internal evidence, however, points to the possibility that this work may have been completed at a later date. In the text, al-Maqrīzī explains the causes of higher prices as follows:

> Increases in the prices of those few exceptions would be caused by . . . a disaster that strikes a natural product and causes its scarcity: such was the case with beef following the sweeping death that hit cattle in 808/1405.[26]

The precise date of this event can be established with some accuracy: contemporary sources place it toward the middle of A.H. 808. In *Sulūk*, al-Maqrīzī mentions the height of this epizootic among the events of Jumādā I 808/October–November 1405.[27] The same passage contains another clue that strengthens the hypothesis of a later date for the completion of *Ighāthah*: during the same month (Jumādā I 808) the price of mutton reached 15 dirhams of account per *raṭl*, the same price quoted in *Ighāthah*.[28] Appendix 8 shows that the price of mutton jumped from 12 to a record 15 dirhams of account, also in Jumādā I 808. In the last month of 808 (Dhū'l-Ḥijjah), the reader of *Sulūk* finds an example showing the impact of the epizootic on cattle prices: the sale of an ox at 13,000 dirhams of account, a twofold increase from Rabīᶜ I of the same year.[29] In addition, both al-Maqrīzī and Ibn Taghrī Birdī refer to the effect of this disease in the preamble to their narration of the events of 809/1406–7 among their comments on general conditions in Egypt.[30]

These pieces of evidence show that the epizootic in question occurred after the first month (Muḥarram) of the year 808 and point to an anachronism: the stated date of the composition of *Ighāthah* is Muḥarram 808. This is further complicated by al-Maqrīzī's mention of two exchange rates for the *mithqāl* (the legal weight of the dinar): first, he gives it at 150 dirhams of account,[31] but he states later that "one *mithqāl* is calculated by the [present] administration to be the equivalent of 140 dirhams of account" and comments that "this is the exchange rate of the dinar in dirhams of account at this time."[32] In *Sulūk*, the rate of 150 is given for mid-Rabīᶜ I 808 and for 28 Muḥarram 809,[33] and 140 for the first of Muḥarram 808 and for 27 Rabīᶜ I 808.[34] The inclusion of the rate of 150 dirhams of account per *mithqāl* in *Ighāthah* indicates that the relevant passages could have been written no earlier than mid-Rabīᶜ I 808, or two months after the stated date of Muḥarram 808. However, the fact remains that the other rate of 140 per *mithqāl* did exist in Muḥarram 808 (which also coincides with the stated date in the colophon of *Ighāthah*) and at the end of Rabīᶜ I of the same year. Since the manuscripts used for the preparation of the edition of *Ighāthah* are of a much later date, one may posit, in light of the preceding, that al-Maqrīzī had initially composed *Ighāthah* in Muḥarram 808, as stated in the colophon, but amended it on a number of occasions in 808/1404–5 and probably as late as Muḥarram 809.

This last date is suggested by *Sulūk*, where the chronology of Muḥarram A.H. 809 begins (in addition to the mention of the exchange rate of 150 dirhams of account per dinar) with comments on the economic and monetary difficulties of Egypt and includes al-Maqrīzī's statement that he discussed these issues in a monograph entitled *Ighāthat al-ummah bi-kashf al-ghummah*, without stating that he had composed the work within the year.[35] Nevertheless, this does not eliminate the possibility that the final revision of *Ighāthah* did occur in that year, for it is customary among medieval historians to insert sparse autobiographical information in the corresponding years of their chronicles. In the case of al-Maqrīzī, the reader of *Sulūk* learns, for instance, the dates of the author's appointments to the *ḥisbah* of Cairo,[36] the dates and titles of some his other works,[37] the year he returned from pilgrimage,[38] and so forth. The fact that the notice on *Ighāthah* is included among the events of Muḥarram A.H. 809 may be an indication that the final revisions to the original manuscript were made in the same month. At any rate, the generally accepted date of the composition of *Ighāthah* (Muḥarram 808) is untenable on account of internal evidence: the anachronistic reference to the epizootic, the different exchange rates of the dinar, and especially the price quoted for mutton (section 6 of this translation). In light of this, the earliest date would be Jumādā I 808/October–November 1405.

## THE NOTION OF *GHALĀ'*

Wiet's translation was published at a time when studies on specific aspects of the monetary, economic, and social conditions of Mamluk Egypt were still in their infancy, which caused him to neglect a number of erroneous quantitative data in the Arabic text. Wiet's unfamiliarity with the subject matter resulted in an inadequate rendering of a number of key concepts. Therefore, his translation is primarily literary and literal, and his confusion of monetary matters makes the last sections of the work unreliable. This is especially true for the sections corresponding to pages 70 onward of Wiet's translation, where a number of serious mistakes and misinterpretations occur. Although some of these can be blamed on the state of relevant scholarship at the time of the translation, the fact remains that Wiet's lack of awareness of the details of the Circassian monetary system, and especially of the nature of the dirham of account (or trade dirham in William Popper's terminology),[39] has resulted occasionally in an inadequate and at times erroneous rendering of the text. For instance, on page 70 of Wiet's translation, al-Maqrīzī describes the monetary situation in Egypt at the death of Sultan Barqūq in 1399:

> Le *mithqāl* d'or se changeait à cent cinquante fels. Le poids d'un dirhem d'argent valait cinq dirhems de cuivre par pièce frappée, et chaque dirhem était changé à vingt-quatre pièces de cuivre. Le *mithqāl* d'or valait à Alexandrie trois cents pièces de cuivre . . .

This short passage contains a number of serious errors: first, one *mithqāl* of gold was not exchanged for 150 *fals* (a *fals* being a copper coin), but for 150 dirhams of account. Second, one dirham was not worth 24 copper coins, but one dirham of account was equivalent to a weight of 24 dirhams of copper coins (*fulūs*). In this case, the *mithqāl* of gold would be exchanged for a weight of 3,600 dirhams or for a similar number of copper coins weighing one dirham each. Moreover, if the value of the dirham of account was a weight of 24 dirhams of copper coins, the value of one *raṭl* of these coins (i.e., a weight of 144 dirhams) would be 6 dirhams of account. This coincides exactly with the rate already mentioned in *Ighāthah*. Second, one *mithqāl* of gold in Alexandria was not worth 300 copper coins, but 300 dirhams of account, which if converted to copper coins would be equivalent to a weight of 7,200 dirhams. Therefore, this passage should be translated as follows:

> One *mithqāl* of gold [i.e., one dinar] was equivalent to one hundred and fifty dirhams [of account]; one silver dirham was equivalent to five dirhams [of account]. One dirham [of account] corresponded to [a weight of] twenty-four [dirhams of copper]. [Therefore, one *raṭl* of *fulūs* was valued at six dirhams of account.] In Alexandria, one *mithqāl* of gold was equivalent to three hundred dirhams [of account].[40]

Another passage is rendered by Wiet (p. 76) as follows:

> Chaque qantar de ces pièces équivaut en poids à cent *raṭl*s égyptiens, et, en compte, à six cents dirhems, alors que réellement le *raṭl* équivaut en poids à cent quarante-quatre dirhems, soit le poids de six dirhems (d'argent).

Here Wiet attempts to interpret al-Maqrīzī's statement by presuming that the value of the *raṭl* of copper *fulūs* (a weight of 144 dirhams) must be 6 dirhams of silver, which is in fact wrong, since the reference is to the dirham of account. This passage should be rendered as follows:

> Each *qinṭār* of *fulūs*—a weight equivalent to one hundred Egyptian *raṭl*s—corresponds to six hundred dirhams [of account]. Therefore, one [Egyptian] *raṭl* [of copper *fulūs*], a weight of one hundred forty-four dirhams, corresponds to six dirhams [of account].[41]

The importance of these two excerpts lies in the explanation of the Circassian monetary system from 806/1403–4 onward, when a unit of account was adopted following the shortage of silver. Hence, an erroneous interpretation of key passages dealing with monetary matters will affect the reader's comprehension of the rest of the work, especially in light of the fact that al-Maqrīzī (as demonstrated later in this introduction) considers the monetary policy of the Circassians to be the major contributing factor to the economic difficulties of his time. Suffice it to say here that a misrendering of the frequent monetary data contained in *Ighāthah* will ultimately lead to a misconception regarding the scope of the work itself.

The view that *Ighāthah* is a treatise on famines in Egypt originates with the assumption that *ghalā'*, the key concept throughout the text, is synonymous with famine or dearth. Such a view is not altogether incorrect: medieval Arabic sources often speak of *ghalā'* during years of famine.[42] This, however, does not necessarily mean that *ghalā'* denotes famine or dearth only. The subtle nuances of *ghalā'* will be explained later, but the following excerpt from Wiet's translation (p. 47) will suffice to illustrate the confusion resulting from the common reduction of *ghalā'* to famine or to similar terms:

> Telle avait été la situation, comme nous venons de le dire, sous le règne de Ẓāhir Barqūq jusqu'à la famine de l'année 796 (1394), dont nous avons parlé. Le dommage pour la population fut partiel et non total pour deux raisons: la première, c'est que le peuple possédait encore des ressources qui l'aidaient à supporter la disette; la seconde réside dans la multiplicité des aumônes du Sultan Ẓāhir, de ses généreuses attentions pendant la famine de l'année 797 (1395) au point que cette année-là personne ne mourut de faim.

According to this translation, a two-year famine swept over Egypt without causing a single death, which is hardly believable. From Mamluk sources, one learns that this period corresponded to a grain shortage that led to a steep increase in food prices, thus limiting the purchasing power of the poor. Sultan Barqūq first ordered the poor to be given food; but when he learned that a number of them later sold their ration of bread, he decided to distribute money instead, allowing fifty dirhams each.[43]

An early Islamic conception of *ghalā'* is explained by Abū Yūsuf (d. 182/798), a disciple of Abū Ḥanīfah (d. 150/767) and one of the founders of the Ḥanafite school of law. In his *Kitāb al-kharāj*, a treatise on taxation written at the request of the Abbasid caliph Hārūn al-Rashīd (170–93/786–809), *ghalā'* and *rukhṣ* are antonyms: Abū Yūsuf states that "*rukhṣ* is not the result of plentiful foodstuffs, nor is *ghalā'* the result of scarcity . . . foodstuffs may be plenty but expensive [*qad yakūnu al-ṭaʿāmu kathīran ghāliyan*], or scarce and cheap [*wa yakūnu qalīlan rakhīṣan*]."[44] This statement indicates that the two notions of *ghalā'* and *rukhṣ* are tied to high and low prices, respectively. He later quotes a *ḥadīth* according to which people addressed the Prophet Muḥammad telling him that prices had increased, asking him to set the prices (the equivalent of price controls in modern times). Muḥammad responded that the *ghalā'* and *rukhṣ* of prices are in God's hand and added that he wanted to meet God without having to answer for some injustice that he might commit in this respect: *inna al-siʿra ghalā'uhu wa rukhṣuhu bi-yadi 'llāh, wa innī urīdu an alqā Allāha wa laysa li-aḥadin ʿindī maẓlamatun yaṭlubunī bi-hā.*[45] The North African Ibn Manẓūr (d. 711/1312) defines *ghalā'* as "the increase and the exceeding of a limit."[46]

Mamluk sources offer a similar view of *ghalā'*, which is more often opposed to *rakhā'* (prosperity) than to *rukhṣ*. In *al-Taysīr wa'l-iʿtibār* (completed in 855/1451), the Syrian al-Asadī devotes a section to "the causes of *ghalā'* and of price increases." This author traces existing high prices (*ghalā'*) to the imposition of protection money and to hoarding and speculation. He also states that *ghalā'* especially affects the poor and gives this example: if one *raṭl* of bread is sold at one dirham, this is called *rakhā'* (low price, or Abū Yūsuf's *rukhṣ*), but if the same measure is sold at two dirhams, this price constitutes *ghalā'* (*yakūnu al-siʿru ghalā'an*).[47]

In a section of the *Muqaddimah* dealing with hoarding, Ibn Khaldūn states: "Intelligent and experienced people in the cities know that it is inauspicious to hoard grain and to wait for high prices."[48] In this passage, Franz Rosenthal appropriately translates *ghalā'* as "high prices," since Ibn Khaldūn himself opposes it in the following section to *rukhṣ* (low prices).[49] To my knowledge, Ibn Khaldūn is first to use the term *majāʿāt* (sing.: *majāʿah*) for famines, a term that is now standard in modern Arabic but, Ibn Khaldūn excepted, is absent in Mamluk sources. There the usual reference to a famine is *ghalā'* that causes *jūʿ* (hunger) and *mawt* or *mawtān* (death).[50] The causal link between famines or epidemics and high grain prices was expounded by Ibn Khaldūn but not fully accepted by his contemporaries. In his analysis of the decline of dynasties, the Tunisian-born author states: "In the later (years) of dynasties, famines and pestilences become numerous. As far as famines are concerned, the reason is that most people at that time refrain from cultivating the soil,"[51] a phenomenon that he traces to oppressive taxation by the state and to the existence of frequent rebellions.[52] He goes on: "Therefore, as a rule, little grain is stored. . . . Still, for their food requirements, people put their trust in what it is possible to store. If nothing is stored, people must expect famines. The price of grain rises [*ghalā al-zarʿ*]. Indigent people are unable to buy any and perish. If for some years nothing is stored, hunger will prevail."[53] He also sees a correlation between the frequency of famines and pestilence, although he also refers to the miasmic theory of pestilence that was prevalent in his time.[54]

It is clear that in medieval Arabic and especially Mamluk sources *ghalā'* coincides with the excessively high prices of basic foodstuffs or grain. As such, it corresponds to a steep increase in prices regardless of the inherent cause and can refer to shortages, famine, or any economic factor that causes prices to rise. In other words, medieval Arabic chronicles regard prices as an economic, social, and demographic indicator, and, in the case of Ibn Khaldūn, as a political factor as well.

In light of this, the mention of *ghalā'* corresponds to high prices that coincide with either seasonal or long-lasting and rampant inflation. In the case of Egypt, *ghalā'* and its antonyms *rakhā'* and *rukhṣ* are most frequently mentioned in Mamluk sources in connection with prices at the time of the plenitude of the Nile. The Nilometer of the Island of al-Rawḍah, between Cairo and Giza, records the water-level: the Nile reaches plenitude at sixteen cubits, the average needed to open the irrigation canals. According to al-Maqrīzī, the ideal level is between seventeen and eighteen cubits.[55] Most often, the Nile reaches plenitude in the Coptic month of Misrā (August). The statistical data collected by Amīn Sāmī show the chronological distribution of the plenitude of the Nile to be as follows:[56]

| | |
|---|---|
| July | 16.9% |
| August | 75.4% |
| September | 6.7% |
| October | 1 % |
| Total | 100 % |

The plenitude of the Nile affects the prices of foodstuffs, especially of grain, in three distinct ways. First, if the Nile reaches the plenitude level on time, grain prices remain stable and may even come down because of the certainty that there will be bountiful harvest. Thus, we hear of *rakhā'* or *rukhṣ*.[57]

Second, if there is a delay in the timing of the plenitude, this causes a *ghalā'*, which translates into a short-lived but sharp increase in the prices of grain and its derivatives. However, prices usually tumble shortly after the Nile reaches its plenitude-level and irrigation begins. This phenomenon occurs so frequently that the fifteenth-century historian al-Ṣayrafī (d. 900/1495) reports the common usage of a specific expression for the abrupt rise and fall in grain prices, *kadhdhābah* (hoax, false alarm), to distinguish it from a longer inflationary trend.[58]

Third, if the Nile-level is either too high or too low, a deficient crop is anticipated, which results in a sharp increase in grain prices lasting until the maturity of the next abundant crop.[59] In the words of al-Maqrīzī: "this is characteristic of Egypt since ancient times: whenever the Nile delays in flooding, prices continue to increase for two years."[60] Under these conditions, the hoarding of grain by suppliers, brokers, and high officials who double as large fief-holders and are thus able to "corner the market" causes prices to rise steadily.[61] The heavy financial burden that this places on the poor, in addition to the scarcity of grain, may lead to famine conditions, especially in urban areas. During this type of *ghalā'*, the intervention by the sultan, who is also the largest grain holder, can stave off catastrophe: a decision to release grain from the royal silos and to order high officials to do the same will lower prices. Feeding the poor or distributing money among them to help them purchase victuals is another common remedy.[62]

## THE SCOPE OF *IGHĀTHAH*

Al-Maqrīzī's *Ighāthat al-ummah bi-kashf al-ghummah* [Helping the Community by Examining the Causes of Its Distress] is a critique, if not an outright indictment, of the Circassian administration's economic and monetary policy. It is a polemical work written by a former official of the *ḥisbah* that focuses on the etiology of a specific economic crisis, in opposition to the legal and theoretical manuals on the *ḥisbah* and related topics, such as the questions of prices, weights and measures, and other relevant matters.[63] In this respect, al-Maqrīzī's *Ighāthah* and al-Asadī's *al-Taysīr wa'l-iʿtibār* (written in 855/1451) are the only two known works of the Circassian period that deal exclusively with economic and monetary topics.

The composition of *Ighāthah* was prompted by the economic crisis of 806–8/1403–6 in Egypt, a crisis that began only two months after al-Maqrīzī's dismissal from the *ḥisbah* of Cairo. This crisis was an opportunity for al-Maqrīzī to address what he believed were the underlying causes of the decline of Egypt. From the outset, he comments:

> Whoever reflects on this occurrence from its beginning to its end and knows its origin and development realizes that what has befallen the population is caused solely by the malfeasance of the leaders and rulers and their negligence with regard to the public interest. [He also realizes that it] is different from past periods of inflation and from bygone disastrous years. But this [conclusion] needs clarification and elucidation and requires explanation and demonstration. Therefore, I have decided to indicate the causes of this catastrophe and the way in which this terrible calamity has persisted in the country and afflicted the people.[64]

Al-Maqrīzī's purpose was to prove that the *ghalā'* of 806–8 was different from previous periods of *ghalā'* that Egypt had known throughout its history. Following a brief section (section 1) where he states the general principle that the perception of suffering is relative, al-Maqrīzī devotes section 2 to a review of grain shortages or famines, starting with Pharaonic times and ending with the famine of 776/1374 that occurred during the rule of the Baḥrī sultan al-Ashraf Shaʿbān (764–78/1363–76). The primary cause of these crises was the failure of the Nile to reach its plenitude-level. This usually led to diminished crops and possibly to a shortage of grain. Moreover, a low Nile-level, spanning several years, resulted in famine conditions due to the exhaustion of grain reserves. In either case, this would be an opportunity for speculators to seek profit through the hoarding of grain.

Al-Maqrīzī makes an effort to show that, in addition to the common practice of helping or feeding the poor, the state intervenes and takes measures to alleviate the impact of the crisis. This is carried out by compelling the speculators to release grain and by imposing strict price controls, or by bringing grain from unaffected areas, in order to lower prices. Despite his claim that these crises were the result of natural causes, as stated in the beginning of section 3, he shows on a few occasions that political chaos intensifies the crisis. This is true of his narrative of the last years of the Ikhshidid period, following the death of Kāfūr in 357/968, and of the events that took place after the death of al-Yāzūrī in 450/1058, during the rule of the Fatimid al-Mustanṣir (427–87/1036–94).

Al-Maqrīzī also describes in fair detail the role of currency instability in worsening an already bad situation. This is exampled by the crisis of 395–97/1044–7, which started with a drought but coincided with the well-known devaluation of the silver dirham under al-Ḥākim (386–411/996–1021): "the dirhams which were in circulation then were called *muzāyadah* and *qiṭa*ʿ. The populace suffered from these coins: the dinar was equivalent to twenty-six of these dirhams, but this ratio increased to one dinar for thirty-four dirhams in the year 397/1006–7, thus leading to soaring prices and increased confusion among the people, who grew reluctant to change their money. As a result, matters came to a halt."[65] Al-Maqrīzī also blames the monetary policy of the Baḥrī sultan Kitbughā (694–96/1295–97) and of his vizir Fakhr al-Dīn ibn al-Khalīlī, who resorted to confiscation, allowed bribes and protection money, and flooded the market with copper *fulūs*, which aggravated the already critical conditions created by famine.[66]

Following this exposé of previous periods of *ghalā'* in Egypt, which were primarily the result of natural causes, al-Maqrīzī presents the main theme of *Ighāthah*, to which he devotes the second half of the book: analysis of the 806–8/1403–6 crisis. He traces its roots to the political, economic, and monetary instability that followed the death of the Circassian sultan Barqūq in 801/1399. He also blames the

Circassian administration for leading the country to ruination because of ill-advised economic measures. Describing the situation of Egypt at the time of the composition of *Ighāthah*, he states that "because of the fluctuation of the currency, the scarcity of the necessities of life, and malfeasance and poor judgment [on the part of the officials], the situation is continually worsening due to greatly distressed and abominable conditions."[67]

He contends that Egypt's declining conditions are the result of a combination of three main factors. First, the venality of state officials that allowed "the holding of administrative and religious positions . . . and other functions through bribery."[68] Second, the heavy taxation of the peasantry by fief-holders. And third, the widespread circulation of the copper *fulūs* coins following the cessation of silver mintage in Egypt in about 806/1403. The development of this last argument leads the author to trace a lengthy history of Islamic coinage down to his time. This section served as the basis for a later work on the history of Islamic currency: *Shudhūr al-ʿuqūd fī dhikr al-nuqūd*.

After explaining the impact of the crisis on the different social classes, al-Maqrīzī puts forth his own proposals for redressing the situation. His solution is to reintroduce silver coinage and to base the currency on gold and silver only. The rest of the book is devoted to illustrating the merits of his suggested monetary reform.

## A DISCUSSION OF AL-MAQRĪZĪ'S VIEWS

Al-Maqrīzī believes that the state has relinquished its duty to safeguard the public interest because of its corrupt and venal practices. During the Circassian period, it became customary for the sultan to impose the payment of a significant amount of money (*ḍamān*, guarantee) on an individual as a condition for appointment. Although this began as a means to raise quickly needed cash for the treasury, it developed into outright bribery and led to the appointment of officials who are occasionally described in contemporary sources as unqualified, less qualified, or greedy. Even the ranks of the judiciary were not immune from such practices, which reached scandalous proportions in 806/1403–4 when the Shafiʿite chief judge of Cairo (the highest judicial authority in the sultanate) obtained his position after paying a sum of money.[69] It is a fact that during the Circassian period there was an increase in the confiscation of individual wealth and the appropriation of funds belonging to religious endowments (*waqf*) or to the bureau of escheats. Furthermore, contemporary sources frequently mention the imposition of forced sales or forced purchases of commodities on merchants. Occasionally, the sultan borrowed large sums of money from the wealthy Kārimī merchants who specialized in the lucrative pepper trade.[70] These measures were taken because of decreasing revenues and mounting expenditures. Al-Maqrīzī takes a moralizing attitude toward these measures, attributing them to the injustice, greed, and corruption of the government, but makes no effort to investigate their economic or monetary motives. He also stresses the luxurious lifestyle and the beginning of the decline of the state. In this respect, al-Maqrīzī is probably influenced by the views of Ibn Khaldūn regarding the decline of dynasties, since it is well known that he attended a number of his lectures.[71]

A number of inauspicious events dominated the year 806/1403–4 in Egypt. Political instability set in when the authority of the ruling sultan, Faraj (801–15/1399–1412), was challenged by a number of influential military commanders led by Yashbak. Although the sultan had initially gained the upper hand against the rebels following a one-day battle in Cairo, the situation remained unsettled. Two years later, the rebellious commanders claimed victory when the sultan, realizing that he lacked the military strength to oppose them, decided to go into hiding. Yashbak and his allies replaced Faraj with his younger brother ʿAbd al-ʿAzīz, as a figurehead behind whom they effectively controlled the state for over two months (15 Rabīʿ I to 4 Jumādā I 808/10 August–29 October 1405), after which Faraj was finally able to regain his throne.[72]

The year 806/1403–4 also began with an official decision to deal with copper coins (*fulūs*) by weight, at the rate of 6 dirhams of account per *raṭl*.[73] Two months later, orders were issued that, henceforth, the dirham of account (dirham *fulūs*) would be the basis of the Mamluk monetary system, thus doing away with the common *kāmilī* silver dirham as the predominant coin in Egypt.[74] Since the calculation of the exchange rate of the gold dinar in terms of dirhams of account appeared in contemporary sources beginning with the year 803/1401, the 806/1403 decision amounted to a recognition of a fait accompli—namely, the scarcity of silver in Egypt and the government's inability to remedy the problem. Consequently, the government decided to abandon the minting of silver coins altogether and to increase the circulation of the copper *fulūs*. These two factors led to the appreciation of gold and silver: while the dirham of account remained constant at the rate of 6 per *raṭl* of copper *fulūs*, the exchange rate of the gold dinar gradually increased from 38 to 150 dirhams of account between 803/1401 and 808/1405, as shown in appendix 2. By the same token, the rate of the *kāmilī* silver dirham climbed from 1¾ dirhams of account at the beginning of 806/July 1403, to 3⅓ in Ṣafar 807/August 1404 and to 5 in Muḥarram 810/June 1407.[75]

Contemporary sources do not give a clear picture of the transition from the silver dirham to the dirham of account. Appendix 2 shows that the quotation of the rate of gold in dirhams of account began in Ramaḍān 803/April–May 1401, three years before the official decision to base the monetary system exclusively on the dirham of account was finally taken. A brief passage in al-Maqrīzī's *Sulūk* indicates that from 795/1392–93 onward, the *kamilī* silver dirham was handled, by tale, at the rate of 24 copper *fulūs*, the same rate that he gives for the dirham of account at the beginning of 806/July 1403, prior to the adoption of the new system during the same year.[76] Therefore, it is possible that the initial purpose of the Circassian administration was to replace the silver dirham with a unit of account of the same value. Later, the disappearance of silver coinage and the overabundance of copper *fulūs* would result in the depreciation of the dirham of account against gold and silver.

The adoption of the new monetary system was the result of several factors: the silver famine in Europe compelled Venice—the main trading partner of the Mamluks—to cease exporting this metal to Egypt and, according to Mamluk sources, to purchase it in Egypt itself.[77] This situation was reflected in the alloy of the silver dirhams that were struck toward the end of the Baḥrī period. In the words of Paul Balog:

> Each succeeding [Baḥrī] government put more copper into an already saturated situation from which silver was rapidly disappearing. This procedure continued until, at the end of the Baḥrī period, practically the only existing currency was the copper *fals*. . . . This state of utter economic chaos was probably one of the causes of the collapse of the Baḥrī dynasty and the advent of the Burjī Sultans.[78]

Mamluk Egypt had no silver mines of its own and its supply of this metal, as well as gold, depended on external sources: West Africa (*Bilād al-Takrūr*) for gold, Europe and Central Asia for silver. Therefore, only through a favorable trade balance could Egypt secure its supply of these precious metals, an aspect already explained by Eliyahu Ashtor.[79] Despite the moralizing views of most fifteenth-century Mamluk historians, including al-Maqrīzī himself, the monetary situation in Egypt was not exclusively the result of official mismanagement. It was also caused, among other factors, by a decreasing supply of silver, be it through Venice or by way of Iran, and a shrinking of the volume of Mamluk exports due to a decline of local industrial production, especially of sugar and textiles.[80] In the case of Iran, a similar shortage of silver and other monetary difficulties were at the origins of an attempt to do away with the existing currency system and replace it with paper money. This attempt, which took place in 693/1294, was abandoned four months later due to the refusal of the population to accept these notes.[81]

The Circassians were faced with mounting expenditures and decreasing revenues throughout most of their rule over Egypt (784–922/1382–1517), especially from the death of Sultan Barqūq (801/1399) onward. The absence of an established banking system, not only in Mamluk Egypt but in the Muslim world, because of the Islamic prohibition against interest, compelled the Circassian administration to devise ways of meeting its expenses through borrowing from the wealthy Kārimī merchants and dipping into other sources: increased taxation, confiscation of the wealth of political opponents, *waqf* funds, and money held by the bureau of escheats. By 832/1429, Sultan Barsbāy (825–41/1422–37) decreed his monopoly of the spice trade, which, from the end of the twelfth century, had been a lucrative trade in the hands of the Kārimī merchants. The intervention of the state never succeeded in redressing the troubled economic and monetary conditions of Circassian Egypt: budgetary deficits, monetary instability, and increased pauperization remained constant features of Circassian Egypt.

The roots of the economic and financial troubles of Circassian Egypt have not been investigated adequately. The frequency of pestilence is a contributing factor to the worsening economic conditions: twenty plagues hit one part of Egypt or another from the Black Death (749/1348) to 808/1406. To date, only the work of Michael

Dols sheds some light on this topic; specialized studies on the economic effects of pestilence in Egypt are still lacking.[82] This task is further complicated by the absence of useful and reliable demographic data from the period.[83] Although modern scholarship has focused mainly on Circassian Egypt, it appears, as noted by Subhi Labib,[84] that the first symptoms of Egypt's economic woes surfaced during the reign of the Baḥrī sultan al-Nāṣir Muḥammad (698–741/1299–1340), especially in the 1330s: sources mention a scarcity of silver, a wider circulation of copper, and empty state coffers.[85] In 740/1340, this sultan devalued the silver dirham versus the gold dinar, from 20:1 to 25:1, and ordered that his lenders accept repayment in gold dinars (although the loans were based on the silver dirham) to increase the worth of his coffers and enable himself to reimburse his creditors at the new rate by paying only 80 percent of the original amount.[86]

Similarly, the 806/1403 decision to base all transactions on the dirham of account, with its ever-decreasing rate, would permit the Circassian state to acquit itself of its obligations with fewer dinars while increasing the value of its coffers, a typical symptom of its inability to meet its expenses due to decreasing revenues, a well-illustrated fact in contemporary sources. Such was also the case—almost two centuries later—for the Ottomans, when Sultan Murād III (982–1003/1574–95) devalued the asper by half to double the state coffers.[87]

The depreciation of the dirham of account was a feature of the entire Circassian period and would contribute to the decrease in state revenues, since the income from the fiefs (*iqṭāʿ*) depended on the rent of cultivated land as well as on market prices of agricultural products.[88] The fact that prices of foodstuffs did not fully compensate for the depreciation of the dirham of account would lead state officials (as large *iqṭāʿ* holders) to devise solutions to make up for lost revenues and to meet their financial obligations and maintain their standard of living. In this respect, the imposition of higher taxes on land and the hoarding of grain with the aim of driving up prices, as well as the frequent and arbitrary confiscations, forced purchases and loans, and other capricious decrees, would be common features of the Circassian period (see section 3 of the translation).

Egypt emerged from the crisis of 806–8/1403–6 with a wider gap between its rich and its poor, between the hoarders of gold and the holders of copper *fulūs*. Some of al-Maqrīzī's statements regarding the general pauperization of the country should not be viewed merely as a product of medieval exaggeration. For example, by the beginning of 809/June 1406, the supervisors of religious institutions did not abide by the stipulations of *waqf* deeds, which generally based all accounts on the silver dirham, and paid the stipends of teachers and students at the rate of one dirham of account per silver dirham, thus reducing the income of the recipients by four-fifths.

A final remark about al-Maqrīzī's attitude toward the new monetary system in Egypt: the reader will realize that the author of *Ighāthah* is adamantly opposed to the reliance on copper as currency. He even shows some ignorance regarding the early existence of copper coins when he treats the history of Islamic coinage. His views in section 4 of this translation reflect strict adherence to the Shāfiʿite position regarding the copper *fulūs*, a fact that he fails to mention. This may explain why al-Maqrīzī, a prominent Shāfiʿite in his time, has composed a separate work dedicated to the indictment of the monetary policy of the Circassians, particularly the widespread circulation of the copper *fulūs*.[90]

*Al-Maqrīzī's*
*Ighāthat al-ummah bi-kashf al-ghummah*

# *Prologue*

In the name of God, the Merciful, the Compassionate.

God's blessing and peace be upon our master Muḥammad, his family, and his companions. Praise be to God, the One who expedites matters according to His wisdom and who, by His power, makes them pursue their course according to His will. He bestowed His favors upon a people, acquainted them with the secrets of His marvelous creation, and caused them to succeed in following His revived legislation.[1] He granted them speech and intellect, inspired them with knowledge and cognizance, supported them in their utterances, and guided them in their actions so that they would be able to explain the causes of the ordeals that befell mankind. He taught them the way of recovery from the severe trials that had afflicted them. But He led others astray so that they heaped mischief upon the earth and gave them free rein until they destroyed with their trespasses the people and the land. He led them gradually in ways they did not perceive, so that they kept wandering blindly in their error and rejoicing in their vanity, debasing God's servants while scorning to worship their Lord.

I praise Him with the praise of a servant who has so appreciated the extent of the divine graces bestowed upon him that he has become incapable of expressing his thanks, who is aware that matters originate with God and return to Him and thus relies upon Him to ease the difficulty they cause.

God's blessing be upon our Prophet Muḥammad, through whom He guided His servants, and through whose law He put an end to tyranny and mischief. God's blessing upon his family, companions, friends, and beloved ones; an endless and boundless blessing.

Since the period of this manifest trial has persisted, during which time many kinds of degrading suffering have befallen mankind, people think that these ordeals are unprecedented and that nothing similar has ever occurred. But they go to extremes when they maintain that these ordeals will never end and never vanish. This is because they are people who do not understand: ignorant of the causes of events, they cling to old ways and despair of God's mercy. Whoever reflects on this occurrence from its beginning to its end and knows its origin and development realizes that what has befallen the population is caused solely by the malfeasance of the leaders and rulers and their negligence with regard to the public interest. [He also realizes that it] is different from past periods of inflation and from bygone disastrous years. But this [conclusion] needs clarification and elucidation and requires explanation and demonstration. Therefore, I have decided to indicate the causes of this catastrophe and the way in which this terrible calamity has persisted in the country and afflicted the people. I shall conclude by stating the means of eradicating this disease and of eliminating this scourge, while glancing at the prices of our time and giving highlights of past periods of inflation and past ordeals, with the hope that God Almighty will guide those to whom He has given the reins of power over the land and the country, to work toward redressing the situation and providing for the welfare of the people. Indeed, whenever the causes are known, it is easy for the knowledgeable person to remedy all conditions, whether significant or insignificant. I seek God's help in facing both difficult and easy matters; indeed, "He tells the truth and He shows the way" [Qur'ān 33:4].

## SECTION ONE

# A Logical Premise

Know—May God support you with His mercy and guide you to comprehend Him—that bygone events, however difficult experiencing them was, are engaging when recounted. Similarly, future conditions are imagined as being better than those of the present, because the tedium of present conditions embellishes the future in the imagination. Hence, the present is always viewed unfairly and its value denied, because [even] the least of its evils is exaggerated. This is due to the fact that the briefest personal experience leaves a more lasting impression than the lengthiest recounting: the experience of the slightest suffering is more troublesome for the soul than the memory of many past afflictions. Take the example of a person who is kept awake all night by fleas; this makes him recall past nights when he has been kept awake by the heat of fever. Undoubtedly, to imagine that fever and to remember those past nights is easier for him at this time than to endure the fleas creeping all over his body. Certainly, this is true of the present situation, although it is viewed from the standpoint of [subjective] perception rather than reality. This is because no one can prove that the creeping and biting of fleas on the body is worse than the heat of fever and that sleeplessness in health is worse than sleeplessness while on the brink of death. Since these two situations are given only as examples, we must defer to those who say that they are unable to endure the events of their times, claiming that these events are unbearable; but we do not subscribe to their extremist view, which claims that present events are by comparison or analogy more difficult than past ones. Suppose a man arose from his bed in Egypt at dawn on a winter's day and came out to his courtyard, where, when he saw rain falling and the ground covered with water, he said: "This is a very cold day." His statement could neither be refuted nor denied, because he uttered it according to what he felt at that moment and in conformity with a common reaction. If, unable to tolerate the cold that penetrated his body, he returned to this bed, covered himself up, and said: "It is colder today than it is in the lands of the Byzantines and the Turks," his statement would be unfounded and he would be considered as frail, as tender, and as heedless as young girls and women. But let us take him from under his covers and show him children walking and playing in those puddles of water. He would realize then that his previous complaint was exaggerated and was not the result of excessive cold at that time, but was rather due to his own impatience and low endurance.

I shall demonstrate—God willing—through the review of past inflationary periods that they were a hundred times worse and more unbearable than the ordeals that presently afflict the people, even though we are still enduring the present ordeal, while only hearing of past ones.

Know also that what is heard from the past will never—and in no way—affect us as deeply as what exists at present, even though past occurrences were significant and present ones are insignificant, because the least that we can experience affects us more deeply than the multitude we hear about: "God granted wisdom to whom He pleased; and he to whom wisdom is granted has received indeed a benefit overflowing; but none will grasp the message but men of understanding" [Qur'ān 2:269]. "But God tells the truth, and He shows the way" [Qur'ān 33:4].

SECTION TWO

# *The [Years of]* Ghalā' *in Egypt*

Know—May God guard your prosperity and protect you—that since the day God created mankind dearth [*ghalā'*] has alternated with plenty [*rakhā'*] in the world of generation and corruption in all regions, countries, and cities. Narrators have recorded and expounded this fact in historical works and I have resolved—God willing—to compose a separate monograph dealing with the ordeals and catastrophes that have afflicted mankind from Adam to the present time, because I have not seen a work treating this question separately. I shall mention here the most significant incidences of dearth [and famines] that have occurred in Egypt alone, but briefly, avoiding prolixity and profusion. I shall state—seeking the help of God, who is indeed the only supporter—[that] Master Ibrāhīm ibn Waṣīf Shāh (d. 599/1203) mentioned in his work *Akhbār Miṣr li-mā qabla al-Islām,*[1] which is a work of great interest and value, that the first famine to occur in Egypt was during the reign of the seventeenth king of Egypt, namely, Afraws son of Manāwash, son of Harjīb, son of Shahlūf,[2] in whose time occurred the Flood of Noah. The cause of this famine was drought and the scarcity of the Nile waters. The animals' wombs became sterile and death became widespread among them because of the decree of God Almighty that the world be destroyed through the Flood.

Another famine occurred during the reign of Farʿān son of Masūr, the nineteenth king of Egypt before the Flood, and it was caused by injustice and chaos, which increased until they became common practice. [As a result,] drought struck the land and the crops were ruined. The Flood came [during which] King Farʿān perished while intoxicated. He was the first to be named Farʿān.[3]

Then a famine occurred during the rule of Atrīb son of Maṣrīm,[4] the thirteenth king of Egypt after the Flood. It was caused by the drying up of the waters of the Nile, which did not flow for one hundred and forty years. The populace ate the beasts until they all vanished. King Atrīb was obliged to walk and then became weakened by hunger. When the situation became critical and the interruption of the Nile had lasted long and death had overcome the population, Atrīb wrote to Lādhū son of Sām son of Noah to inform him of this. Lādhū wrote to his own brother, Arfakhshadh son of Sām, but received no answer. When God sent Hūd, Atrīb wrote to him begging him to pray for an end to the calamity that had befallen Egypt. Hūd answered him: "I will pray for you on such-and-such a day. Wait for the Nile to flow on that day." When that day arrived, Atrīb assembled the men and women who were left in Egypt—and they were only a few; they prayed to the Almighty God and clamored and implored Him to send rain. This was at midday on a Friday, so God caused the Nile to flow in that hour. But there was nothing left with which to sow the land. Then God sent a revelation to Hūd to dispatch [a message] to Atrīb and tell him to go to the foot of the mountain of Egypt and dig in such-and-such a place. Hūd wrote to Atrīb to inform him of this. The latter assembled his people and they dug. They discovered arches made of lead, under which they found grain as if it had just been placed there, still on its stalks and not yet threshed. They spent eight months in transporting the grain. Part of it was sown, while the remainder fed them for approximately five years. Ṣābir son of Maṣrīm[5] informed his brother [Atrīb] that when the descendants of Cain son of Adam multiplied on the face of the earth and possessed it, they became aware that a catastrophe would occur on earth, so they built the arched lead vault and placed grain in it. Thereby Egypt was cultivated and became so fertile that one *irdabb* sold for one *dānaq*, a prosperity that lasted for two hundred years. Then a famine occurred in the reign of the thirty-second king of Egypt after the Flood, who was the second of the Amalekite sovereigns and the third of the Pharaohs, according to ancient Egyptian historians.[6] The name of this king is a matter of dispute: it is said that his name was Nahrāwas; also that his name was al-Rayyān son of al-Walīd son of Darmagh the Amalekite.[7] During this famine, the affairs of Egypt were administered by Joseph, who was mentioned by God in the Holy Qur'ān;[8] he is also mentioned in the Old Testament[9] and received wide mention in the books of bygone peoples and those who succeeded them, so that there is no need to identify him further.

A famine, drought, [and plague][10] struck [the land], during which the crops and the trees perished, grain and fruit were lost, and cattle perished. This [took place] at the time of the sending of Moses to the Pharaoh. This is detailed in the books of the Israelites and other peoples,[11] but none expressed it better than the saying of God: "And We leveled to the ground the great works and fine buildings that Pharaoh and his people erected" [Qur'ān 7:137] and His saying: "We punished the people of Pharaoh with years of drought and shortness of crops; so that they might receive admonition" [Qur'ān 7:130].

Before the mission of the Prophet Muḥammad, all kinds of catastrophes and ordeals befell the inhabited regions of the earth, especially Egypt, which [suffered] from numerous famines, a fact that we have mentioned already.

After God Almighty brought forth Islam, the first famine to occur in Egypt was in 87/705–6, during the governorship in Egypt of ʿAbd Allāh ibn ʿAbd al-Malik ibn Marwān, who was appointed by his father. The populace regarded it as an evil portent, because it was the first famine and the first calamity that the Muslims experienced in Egypt.[12]

A shortage [of grain] occurred during the rule of the Ikhshidid dynasty (323–58/935–69) in the month of Muḥarram of the year 338/ July 949, in the reign of Abū'l-Qāsim Ūnūjūr ibn Ikhshīd (334–49/ 946–61). His subjects rebelled against him and prevented him from performing the evening prayer in the Old Mosque.[13]

A famine occurred in the year 341/952–53, when rats proliferated in the provinces of Egypt and destroyed grain, vines, and other crops.[14] Then the Nile failed to flood, and prices soared in the month of Ramaḍān [341/January-February 953].[15] By 343/954–55, prices were so high that two and a half *waybah*s of wheat were sold for one dinar. Later, wheat disappeared from the markets, and the populace rebelled and broke the pulpit of the mosque in Old Cairo.

Another famine occurred during the rule of the same Ikhshidid dynasty and lasted nine consecutive years. It began in 352/963–64, during the reign of ʿAlī ibn Ikhshīd (349–55/961–66), when the administration of the country was in the hands of Master Abū'l-Misk

Kāfūr, the Ikhshidid.[16] The cause of this famine was that the level of the Nile stopped at fifteen cubits and four fingers.[17] Hence prices increased after having been low. Whatever had cost one dinar came to cost three. Bread became scarce and almost nonexistent and prices rose until every two *waybahs* of wheat were sold for one dinar. The Nile-level was below normal in the year 353/964–65 and reached only fifteen cubits and four fingers,[18] then fluctuated, increasing once and decreasing again until it reached in the middle of the [Coptic] month of Bābah/October 964 approximately thirteen cubits, then increased slightly and decreased rapidly. This heightened the famine: all provinces were in open rebellion, and farms and crops were pillaged. The population of Egypt became riotous because of the prices; so they entered the Old Mosque in Fusṭāṭ on a Friday and thronged around the prayer niche, causing the death of a man and a woman in this crush, as well as the cancellation of the Friday prayer. This famine continued until 354/965, the year during which the Nile-level reached sixteen cubits and a few fingers.[19] In the year 355/965–66, the Nile-level reached fourteen cubits and some fingers, then receded, and its flow diminished.[20] In the year 356/966–67, the Nile-level reached only twelve cubits and a few fingers,[21] [a low level] the like of which had never occurred since the Islamic conquest.[22] At that time, the affairs of Egypt were run by Master Kāfūr the Ikhshidid and conditions worsened because of severe famine.

When Kāfūr died [in 357/968],[23] unrest increased and riots multiplied. Much strife between the soldiery and the commanders resulted in a great loss of human life. Markets were looted and several buildings were burned. The fear of the populace intensified: they lost their wealth and their spirits. Prices became high and it was difficult to find foodstuffs, to the point that one *waybah* of wheat sold for one dinar. The army became divided and large numbers of soldiers joined al-Ḥasan ibn ʿAbd Allāh ibn Ṭughj,[24] who was at the time in al-Ramlah, and an equal number contacted al-Muʿizz li-Dīn Allāh (341–65/953–75), the Fatimid ruler. Rumors about the marching of the Qarāmiṭah against Egypt increased.[25] News of the arrival of an expedition that al-Muʿizz dispatched from the Maghrib became more frequent until it finally arrived in 358/969.[26] The commander Jawhar entered [Egypt] at the head of the troops of al-Imām al-Muʿizz li-Dīn Allāh and founded al-Qāhirah al-Muʿizzīyah [Cairo]. Among the matters he looked into was the question of prices. A number of millers were flogged, then paraded in public. He grouped the grain brokers in one place and issued orders that grain would be sold there exclusively. He also ordered that a single route would be followed to and from this grain market, so that even one *qadaḥ* of wheat would not leave this market except under the supervision of Sulaymān ibn ʿAzzah, the *muḥtasib*.[27] This famine lasted until the year 360/970–71, during which epidemics worsened and diseases spread.[28] Death was so frequent that the people were unable to provide shrouds for all the dead and bury them, so that corpses were thrown into the Nile. When the year 361/971–72 began, prices slackened, the land became fertile, and prosperity ensued.[29]

A period of inflation occurred in the year 387/997–98, during the reign of al-Ḥākim bi-Amr Allāh (386–411/996–1021) and the administration of Abū Muḥammad al-Ḥasan ibn ʿAmmār.[30] It was caused by an insufficient level of the Nile, which reached only sixteen cubits and a few fingers.[31] Prices rose sharply and wheat was in high demand but was unattainable. The populace lived in a heightened state of fear, women were kidnapped in the streets, and the situation deteriorated. The price of bread reached one dirham the four *raṭl*s; then the situation eased when prices dropped.[32]

In the year 395/1004–5, the Nile leveled off to the point that the canal was opened at the end of the month of Misrā (end of August 1005) at fifteen cubits and seven fingers.[33] It later reached sixteen cubits and a few fingers.[34] Prices soared and transactions came to a halt. The dirhams in circulation then were called *muzāyadah* and *qiṭaʿ*. The populace suffered from these coins: the dinar was equivalent to twenty-six of these dirhams, but this ratio increased to one dinar for thirty-four dirhams in the year 397/1006–7, thus leading to soaring prices and increased confusion among the people, who grew reluctant to change their money.[35] As a result, matters came to a halt. Orders were given to take twenty cases of dirhams from the public treasury and distribute them among the money changers. Public notice was given that any transaction involving the *qiṭaʿ* and *muzāyadah* dirhams was forbidden and that any holdings of these dirhams should be taken to the mint within three days. This measure was oppressive to the people because it caused them a financial loss. In fact, the new dirhams were exchanged for four *qiṭaʿ* and *muzāyadah* ones.[36] Orders were issued that bread be sold at the rate of twelve *raṭl*s for one dirham of the new ones and that the dinar would equal eighteen [of the same] dirhams.[37] A number of millers and bakers were flogged and paraded in public because of the rush of the populace to buy bread, which was sold unbaked only.[38] The Nile did not reach its normal level and crested at thirteen cubits and a few fingers, causing prices to soar.[39] Orders were issued to Masʿūd al-Ṣaqlabī, *mutawallī al-sitr*,[40] to look into the question of prices. He assembled the granary owners, the millers, and the bakers, seized the grain that existed in Sāḥil al-Ghallah,[41] and ordered that it be sold only to the millers. He priced wheat at one dinar minus one *qīrāṭ* per *tallīs*, barley at one dinar the ten *waybah*s, and wood at one dinar the ten *ḥamlah*s. He also regulated the prices of all other grain and commodities and flogged a group of people and paraded them in public. The populace calmed down when bread became available but later they rushed to buy it so that it became unavailable by late evening. Therefore, Masʿūd al-Ṣaqlabī ordered wheat to be sold exclusively to the millers and he strictly enforced this order. Several granaries were searched and the wheat found in them was distributed among the millers at the official price. Still, conditions worsened: the price of one *ḥamlah* of flour reached one and a half dinars and that of bread one dirham for six *raṭl*s. The level of the Nile ceased to increase and the populace prayed for rain twice. Prices soared and one *ḥamlah* of flour was sold at six dinars. The canal was opened when the Nile-level was only at fifteen cubits. Consequently, conditions worsened: one *tallīs* of wheat reached four dinars; one *waybah* of rice sold for one dinar; one *raṭl* of mutton for one dirham; ten *raṭl*s of onions for one dirham; eight *ūqīyah*s of cheese[42] for one dirham; eight *ūqīyah*s of cooking oil for one dirham; and one *raṭl* of lamp oil for one dirham.[43]

In the year 398/1007–8, the level of the Nile increased to fourteen cubits and a few fingers,[44] [a fact] that caused misery to the populace. This situation continued unchanged until 399/1008–9, the year when the canal was opened on the fifteenth of Tūt [12 September 1008],[45] while the level of the Nile was fifteen cubits. The waters receded on the nineteenth of Tūt [16 September 1008] and further diminished. Conditions became unbearable and the people became oppressed by hunger.[46] They gathered at Bayn al-Qaṣrayn,[47] imploring al-Ḥākim bi-Amr Allāh to look after their welfare and requesting him not to neglect their affairs. He mounted his donkey and rode about through Bāb al-Baḥr.[48] He then stopped and said: "I shall go to the Rāshidah Mosque.[49] I swear by God that when I return, if my donkey can set foot in a single place devoid of grain, I will cut off the head of whoever possesses any grain whatsoever. I will burn his house and confiscate his wealth." Then he left [for the mosque] and tarried until late in the afternoon. Every inhabitant of Old and New Cairo who possessed any amount of grain rushed to bring it from his house or domicile and to deposit it in the streets. The fee for a donkey reached one dinar for a single trip. The people were overjoyed and gratified. Al-Ḥākim ordered that the quantity needed for daily consumption be provided by the grain merchants, granting them a respite to comply and the choice either to sell grain at the official price, which would include a profit margin in their favor, or to refuse to do so. If they chose the second alternative, he would seal the quantities they were holding and would not permit them to sell any portion of it until the new crops would be available. They therefore answered his call and obeyed his order. Prices decreased and harm was averted and "With God rests the end of all affairs" [Qur'ān 22:41].

A dearth of grain occurred during the reign of al-Mustanṣir (427–87/1036–94) and the vizirate of al-Nāṣir li-Dīn Allāh Abū Muḥammad al-Ḥasan ibn ʿAlī ibn ʿAbd al-Raḥmān al-Yāzūrī.[50] It was caused by the failure of the Nile to reach its plenitude in the year 444/1052–53,[51] while the royal grain silos were empty, and led to heightened privation. The cause of the emptiness of the silos was the following: this vizir was accorded the functions of judge[52] during the vizirate of Abū'l-Barakāt.[53] He used to go to the mosque in Old Cairo every Saturday and Tuesday and sit, following the tradition of his predecessors, in the extension of the mosque to hold his court, then return to Cairo after the afternoon prayer.

There was in every market of Old Cairo a master[54] who supervised the affairs of every craft. During periods of privation, bread would be tasteless whenever it became cold because of its high degree of impurity. The master of the bakers had a shop where he sold bread, and next to it was another shop that belonged to a wretch[55] who was selling bread at the current price of one dirham and an eighth per four *raṭl*s. The wretch noticed that his bread was getting almost stale and feared that it would remain unsold, so he announced it at four *raṭl*s for one dirham to attract customers. People thronged around him until all the bread was sold out because of his indulgence, while the bread of the master was left unsold. The latter grew resentful and referred this incident to two agents of the *ḥisbah*, who fined the wretch ten dirhams. When the chief judge Abū Muḥammad al-Yāzūrī was on his way to the mosque, the wretch appealed to him. The judge then summoned the *muḥtasib* and rebuked him for the action taken against the man. The *muḥtasib* stated that it was customary to use masters in the markets to oversee the members of each craft and that their word had been always accepted. Since the master of the bakers in such-and-such a market had presented himself and asked for two agents of the *ḥisbah*, this led them to believe that his disapproval justified such a measure. The chief judge then summoned the baker and rebuked him for his action and ordered his dismissal from the position of master and gave the wretch thirty gold *rubāʿis*. The wretch was overcome with joy. He returned to his shop and when the dough was baked he announced it at five *raṭl*s for one dirham. Customers preferred him, so that other bakers, fearing that their bread would get stale, decided to sell it at the same price. He therefore announced that his bread would be sold at the rate of six *raṭl*s for one dirham, and necessity led the other bakers to imitate him. When he noticed that they were following suit, he decided to defy and irritate the former master by reducing the price of bread and increasing the quantity of bread to be sold for one dirham by one *raṭl* at a time. Other bakers followed suit, because they feared that their bread would remain unsold, until bread was sold at ten *raṭl*s for one dirham. News of this spread throughout the whole city so that the populace heard of it and rushed to him. By the time the chief judge left the mosque, bread was being sold in the entire city at ten *raṭl*s for one dirham.

Every year, the sultan[56] bought one hundred thousand dinars' worth of grain for his own commercial dealings. When al-Yāzūrī returned to Cairo where his house was located, he had an audience with the sultan and informed him of God's gracious grant that day in bringing down prices and of the profuse prayers of the populace for the sultan. [He added] that God had caused this and had decreased prices through His goodwill toward His servants and subjects. This had occurred without a determined cause or agent but because of God's benevolence and as a result of a strange coincidence. [This judge also informed the sultan that] the royal commerce in grain would be injurious to the Muslims and that grain prices might fall from the price that the sultan had paid to purchase it, thus making it impossible to sell that grain, which would then spoil in the silos and become a [total] loss. [Al-Yāzūrī then advised the sultan] to engage in commerce that would not burden the populace and would be many times more profitable than that of grain, with no risk of spoilage or decreasing prices: such as commerce in wood, soap, iron, lead, honey, and the like. The sultan followed al-Yāzūrī's advice. This situation continued and prosperity lasted for two years.

The Nile failed to reach its plenitude in the fifth year of al-Yāzūrī's administration, in the year 447/1055–56.[57] At that time the [royal] grain silos contained no more than what was necessary for the rations[58] of the palace staff and for the meals of the sultan and his retinue only. The vizir Abū Muḥammad was very preoccupied, and [wheat] prices soared to eight dinars for one *tallīs*.[59] The situation became unbearable for the people and bread became scarce. Thereupon, he took adequate measures that barely allowed the populace to remain alive. [He realized] that the merchants were taking advantage of the financial strain on their suppliers [i.e., the peasants], who had to meet the payment of taxes to the administration and were being pressed to meet this obligation. The grain merchants started to buy the crops before they had reached maturity, at a price that would guarantee them a profit. They then presented themselves to the [relevant] bureau and paid to the *jahbadh*[60] the taxes owed by the peasants. This would then be recorded in the register[61] of the *jahbadh*, together with the value of the next crop and the amount paid by the merchant on behalf of the peasants. Whenever the crops reached the threshing floor, the merchants would transport them to their storehouses. The vizir Abū Muḥammad al-Yāzūrī forbade such dealings and wrote to all the provincial governors to review the registers of the *jahbadh*s and to list the amounts paid by the merchants on behalf of the peasants, as well as the price at which the crop had been purchased. He [further instructed them] to give the merchants a refund equivalent to the amount they had paid to the administration [on behalf of the peasants], with a profit of one-eighth of that amount to mollify the merchants. [The governors were also told that] they should affix their seals to the storehouses and record the quantities of grain stored in them. When the vizir received word that this [had been carried out], he provided boats and transported the grain from the provinces to the royal silos in Old Cairo. He set the price of one *tallīs* [of wheat] at three dinars, whereas it had previously been eight dinars. He delivered to the bakers the quantities they used to purchase in order to supply the markets. He also consigned the quantities needed to supply the two cities of Cairo and Old Cairo. This amounted to one thousand *tallīses* to be provided daily: seven hundred for Old Cairo and three hundred for Cairo. Al-Yāzūrī performed his task superbly for twenty months until the harvest of the crops two years later, which relieved the populace and ended inflation. People did not suffer in the least, thanks to his good administration.[62]

After the vizir Abū Muḥammad [al-Yāzūrī] was killed,[63] the state enjoyed neither righteousness nor stability. The affairs of the state were in disarray, and no praiseworthy or efficient vizir was appointed. The office of vizir became highly discredited: no sooner would a vizir take office than he would become the target of gossip and the butt of false accusations and would resign his office after only a short time. The people mixed with the sultan and drew close to him by presenting him with an increased number of written notes. The sultan never rebuked anyone for the content of a note. Hence, every unworthy person presented himself to the sultan, and several scoundrels won his good graces. Such persons grew in number until their notes were given precedence over those of high-ranking officials and dignitaries. They wrote notes about every subject, to the point that the sultan was receiving eight hundred of them daily. He became confused and the situation deteriorated. Discord prevailed among his subjects, and the vizirs were too weak to carry out their tasks because of their short tenure. The vizir, from the time the robe of honor was bestowed upon him to the time he left office, was constantly on guard against those who would slander him to the sultan. Then these rogues would stand up against the vizir, and it would be useless for him to defend himself.[64] [This led to] the ruin of the provinces and to a decrease in state revenues. The rogues took control of most of the revenues and laid their hands on the revenue-generating sources. As a result, the revenues of Lower Egypt came to represent only a minimal fraction of what they previously were. Prior to these years of civil strife, these amounted to six hundred thousand dinars, collected twice a year: on the first of Rajab and on the first of Muḥarram. While revenues decreased sharply, expenditures increased greatly. Adversaries agreed to unite against the sultan: they continued to claim their pay, and he would give it to them in full. They constantly stood at his door and prevented him [from leaving his own quarters]. They acted boldly toward the vizirs, whom they treated disdainfully and made the targets of their arrows. In fact, the periods between the dismissal of vizirs and the appointment of others were longer than their tenure in office. These rogues exceeded proper bounds and were emboldened to the point that they went beyond claiming their dues [and resorted] to confiscations. They depleted the wealth of the caliph, emptied his coffers, and compelled him to sell his belongings. These were bought by the populace at a just price, but when these rogues laid their hands on an item, they would take it at a price ten times cheaper than its real value, and no one dared to ask them to pay more. Later, their boldness increased to the point that they proceeded to assess the value of the items offered for sale. Whenever the assessors arrived, they would be frightened by these rogues. Consequently, they would assess items valued at one thousand [dirhams] at only one hundred or less. Al-Mustanṣir and the public treasurer were aware of this; however, they were unable to exact what was due from these rogues. The situation of the state deteriorated and authority vanished. When these rogues realized that nothing was left for them to take, they divided the provinces among themselves and plunged them into a state of utter confusion. They took over these provinces as if they had conquered them by force.[65] This lasted for five or six years, then the Nile failed to reach its plenitude and the ensuing rise in prices was so high that it dispersed their coalition, severed their friendship, and disunited them. God sowed enmity and hatred among them and they killed each other until He destroyed most of them and effaced their traces: "Now such were their houses, in utter ruin, because they practiced wrongdoing" [Qur'ān 27:52].

During the reign of [the same] al-Mustanṣir occurred the famine that had an atrocious effect and left a horrid memory. It lasted seven years[66] and was caused by the weakness of the sultan's authority, the deterioration of the affairs of state, the usurpation of power by the military commanders, the continuous strife among the Bedouins, the failure of the Nile to reach its plenitude, and the absence of cultivation of the lands that had been irrigated. This began in 457/1064–65. It resulted in rising prices and increased famine, and was followed by an epidemic.[67] The lands remained uncultivated and fear prevailed. Land and sea routes became unsafe, and travel became impossible without a large escort; otherwise, one would be exposed to danger. Famine spread because of want of victuals, to the point that a loaf of bread was sold as if it were a novelty at an auction in Zuqāq al-Qanādīl,[68] in Old Cairo, for fifteen dinars.[69] One *irdabb* of wheat was sold at eighty dinars.[70] So many dogs and cats were consumed that dogs became scarce, and a dog that was destined for a meal was sold at five dinars. Conditions worsened to the degree that people ate each other. People were constantly on their guard. Groups of people sat in the upper stories of their houses, holding cords and ropes at the end of which they attached hooks. When someone passed by, they would cast at him and quickly snatch him away and cut up his flesh and eat it.[71] Ultimately, al-Mustanṣir was compelled to sell everything in his palace, including precious objects, clothes, furniture, weapons, and the like. He was reduced to sitting on a mat, his administrative apparatus collapsed, and his dignity was lost.[72] The women of the palaces came out—their hair undone and screaming: "Hunger! Hunger!"—wanting to take the road to Iraq, but they would fall at al-Muṣallā[73] and die of starvation.[74] Al-Mustanṣir was in such need that he sold the ornaments that decorated the tombs of his ancestors. One day the vizir arrived to meet with him, riding a female mule. The populace ate it, so he hanged a number of them. Ultimately, al-Mustanṣir was unable to secure his own food. There was a woman, named Sharīfah bint Ṣāḥib al-Sabīl,[75] who used to send him a bowl full of crumbled bread daily, [a gesture] that was among her many pious and charitable deeds during this famine. In fact, she spent all her wealth, which was boundless, on pious deeds. Al-Mustanṣir had no nourishment except what she used to send him: once during the day and once at night.[76]

Among the strange occurrences was that a lady who belonged to a wealthy family took a one-thousand-dinar necklace of hers and offered it to several [merchants] to barter in exchange for flour. Each of them refused and rid himself of her, until finally someone felt compassion for her and sold her one *tallīs* of flour in Old Cairo. This woman lived in Cairo, and when she received the flour, she gave some of it to those who were guarding it against the looters on the road. When she reached Bāb Zuwaylah, she took it from the guards and walked a short distance away. The populace rushed upon her and snatched the flour. In the rush she succeeded in grabbing a handful of flour. This was her entire share, which she later kneaded and baked. Then she took the loaf of bread and reached one of the gates of the palace. She stood on an elevated place and held the loaf high, so that people could see it, and shouted as loud as she could: "Inhabitants of Cairo! Pray for our lord al-Mustanṣir, through whose reign God rendered the people fortunate and repeatedly bestowed upon them the blessings of the excellence of his administration to the point that this loaf of bread cost me one thousand dinars!"[77] When al-Mustanṣir was informed of this, he felt annoyed, offended, and moved. He therefore summoned the governor, threatened and menaced him, and swore in front of him by God that if bread did not appear in the markets and prices did not decrease, he would cut off his head and confiscate his wealth. The governor departed and brought out of prison a group of persons who had been condemned to death and dressed them in wide cloaks, round turbans, and floating scarfs. He then assembled the grain merchants and the bakers and held a grand council. He ordered that one of this group be brought forward, and the [condemned person] entered magnificently dressed. When he stood in front of the governor, the latter addressed him: "Woe unto you! It did not suffice you that you betrayed the sultan and stole the money of the state, that you caused the ruin of the provinces and destroyed the crops, thus leading to the deterioration of the state and the ruin of the population?! Cut off his head!" His order was executed on the spot and the dead person was left lying in front of him. Then the vizir ordered that another of them be brought, and said to him: "How did you dare violate the decree forbidding the hoarding of grain and continue to act against this law so that others followed in your footsteps, thus causing the ruin of the population?! Cut off his head!" This order was carried out on the spot. He then ordered that a third person be brought in.

The assembly of merchants, millers, and bakers stood up and said: "O Commander! Enough of this! We will bring out the grain and turn the mills in order to supply the market with bread. We will lower the prices for the population and sell bread at one dirham a *raṭl*."

The governor answered: "The population will not be content with this."

They answered: "Two *raṭl*s."

The governor agreed to this [price] after they begged him. They fulfilled their promise, while God provided His creatures with relief and swelled the Nile. This ended the strife: people cultivated the land and prosperity followed. Hardship was lifted and distress eased. The story of these [years of] famine is well known and the relevant information that is provided here is sufficient: "It is God that gave you want or plenty, and to Him shall be your return" [Qur'ān 2:245].

A grain shortage occurred during the reign of Caliph al-Āmir bi-Aḥkām Allāh (495–524/1101–30)[78] and the vizirate of al-Afḍal [Abū'l-Qāsim Shāhanshāh],[79] when the price of wheat reached one hundred and thirty dinars for every one hundred *irdabb*s. The caliph entrusted the commander Abū ʿAbd Allāh ibn Fātik, later surnamed al-Ma'mūn al-Baṭā'iḥī,[80] with the situation. He ordered the grain storehouses sealed and summoned the owners to give them the choice of having their warehouses remain sealed until the coming of the new crop or selling wheat at thirty dinars for every hundred *irdabb*s, in which case he would lift his previous order. He released the storages of those who agreed to sell at this price, while he kept the storehouses of those who refused sealed. He made an estimate of the daily needs of the population for grain and assessed the quantities of grain that were stored by the merchants who had agreed to sell at the official rate. The additional quantity that was needed was drawn from the state silos and sold to the millers according to the official price. The situation remained unchanged until the harvest of the new crop. Prices then fell, thus compelling the merchants who kept their grain in the [sealed] storehouses to sell for fear of worms. They sold it at an insignificant price and regretted missing the opportunity to sell at the previous price.

A horrible famine and a devastating drought occurred in the reign of al-Ḥāfiẓ li-Dīn Allāh (525–44/1131–49) and the vizirate of al-Afḍal ibn Walakhshī.[81] However, this famine did not last long.[82] The above-mentioned al-Afḍal rode to the Old Mosque in Old Cairo and summoned all those who had any connection with the grain business. He punished a number of those who hoarded grain or sold it at a high price. He required them to satisfy the daily needs [of the population] and supervised the implementation of this ordinance in person. So severe was he in his punishment that no one dared to oppose him. The situation remained so until God blessed the population with prosperity, and the affliction that had befallen them was lifted. "Verily, my Lord understood best the mysteries of all that He planned to. For verily He is full of knowledge and wisdom" [Qur'ān 12:100].

Grain prices increased during the rule of al-Fā'iz (549–55/1154–60)[83] and the vizirate of al-Ṣāliḥ Ṭalā'iʿ ibn Ruzzīk,[84] when one *irdabb* [of wheat] reached five dinars because of the failure of the Nile to reach its plenitude. There was an unlimited amount of grain in the royal silos, from which he released large quantities and distributed them among the millers. He lowered prices, forbade hoarding, and ordered that available quantities be sold. He also was very generous toward a number of afflicted and poor persons. Sayf al-Dīn al-Ḥusayn,[85] together with a number of commanders and high officials of the palace, was also generous in relieving the populace. This situation did not last long: God sent relief and prosperity spread.[86]

A famine occurred under the Ayyubid dynasty, during the rule of al-ʿĀdil Abū Bakr ibn Ayyūb (596–615/1200–1218) in the year 596/1200.[87] It was caused by the interrupted increase of the Nile-level, which fell short of normal and reached only twelve cubits and a few fingers.[88] Hunger compelled flocks of people to leave their villages and move to Cairo. When spring came, winds blew and an epidemic and destruction followed. Foodstuffs disappeared to the point that adults were compelled to eat small children: a father would eat his own son roasted and cooked, and a woman would eat her own child. In fact, a number of people were punished for practicing anthropophagy. This practice spread and defied all legal authorities. It was common to find under the garments of a man or a woman a youngster's shoulder, a thigh, or a piece of flesh. Sometimes a person would enter his neighbor's home and find a pot on the fire. Waiting for it to be ready, he would find that it contained the flesh of a child. This practice was predominant among wealthy families. The flesh of children was available surreptitiously in the markets and streets from both men and women, and in less than two months, thirty women were condemned to drowning because of this. The situation worsened to the point that the nourishment of many people consisted of human flesh, to which they became accustomed. The prohibition against anthropophagy was relaxed because of the unavailability of foodstuffs, including all types of grain, vegetables, and everything else that the earth produced. At the end of spring [597/1201][89] during the month of Barmūdah [end of April 1201], the riverbed of the Nile had dried up and no water flowed between Old Cairo and the Nilometer, as well as between Old Cairo and Giza. The water became altered in taste and odor. Later, the water level started to increase gradually until the sixteenth of Misrā/9 August 1201, when it increased by one finger, then leveled off for a few days, before it increased sharply by a maximum of one cubit a day until it reached fifteen cubits and sixteen fingers,[90] then receded abruptly. The country did not profit, however, because of this abrupt fall. Death decimated the villagers to the point that in a village of five hundred inhabitants only two or three survived. Dikes were not maintained, and no public works were carried out because of the lack of oxen. So many were lost that one head of cattle was sold for seventy dinars, while an emaciated [ox sold] for sixty. The streets of Old Cairo and Cairo and the trails of all the villages of the provinces became filled with the stench of the many corpses. The quantity of grain that was sown, although insignificant, was eaten by worms. It was impossible to remedy [this situation] because of the lack of grain reserves and of oxen. People continued to consume the flesh of children, while chicken disappeared altogether. Ovens were fired with wood from the houses, and a number of respectable persons used to go out at night, collect firewood from the vacant houses, and sell it in the morning. In all the alleys of Cairo and Old Cairo, only a few inhabited houses were to be seen. A man in the countryside of Lower and Upper Egypt would die holding a plow. When a second man replaced him, the same fate befell him. For three consecutive years, the Nile rose only insignificantly,[91] so that the [price of one] *irdabb* of wheat reached eight dinars. Al-ʿĀdil [Abū Bakr ibn Ayyūb] released a quantity of grain to the poor. He also divided the latter among the wealthy [to be fed], assembled twelve thousand of them in the place where camels were fenced, which was adjacent to the palace, and fed them generously. The commanders and the affluent and wealthy people acted in a similar manner. It would happen that—among these poor people—some would fall dead when their stomachs suddenly became full after a long period of privation. Hence a large number of them were buried every day. Indeed, within a short period of time, the sultan, al-ʿĀdil, provided for the burial of approximately two hundred twenty thousand persons. People used to fall in the streets from starvation. Not a day passed without a number of people being eaten. Crafts came to a halt and [economic] conditions came to a standstill. Both foodstuffs and people perished, thus leading to this saying: "[This was] a predatory year that devoured the necessities of life."[92]

When God succored His creatures through the flooding of the Nile, no one was left to plow or sow. The military, along with their grooms and servants, set out to carry out this task themselves.

However, most of the land remained uncultivated because of the lack of peasants. Animals vanished to the point that a pullet was sold at two and a half dinars, but the silos became filled with grain and bread was available and sold at one dirham and a half the *raṭl*. Many wealthy people claimed that this famine was similar to the one that had occurred during the years of Joseph. [These people] desired to buy the wealth of the population of Egypt by hoarding grain. Therefore they held it and refused to sell it. But when prosperity returned, all their grain rotted, became worthless, and was thrown away. Calamity befell many of those who had enriched themselves through [the hoarding of] grain. Subsequently, some met horrifying deaths, while others lost their wealth. "For your Lord is on a watchtower" [Qur'ān 89:14]. He is indeed "the Accomplisher of what He planned" [Qur'ān 85:16].

Drought and famine occurred under the rule of the Turkish dynasty during the reign of al-ʿĀdil Kitbughā (694–96/1295–97) in the year 696/1296–97,[93] when no rain fell in the region of Barqah. There drought struck, springs dried up, and famine befell the inhabitants because of the lack of foodstuffs. About thirty thousand souls left with their families and their livestock and took the road to Egypt. Most of them perished from hunger and thirst, and a very small number of them arrived, in utter fatigue. In Syria the rains of early spring came so late that the sowing season was missed. The people prayed for rain three times, but their prayers were not answered. Then the populace assembled and went out to pray for rain; they shouted and implored God Almighty. He then sent them succor and rain, and they returned to the city under a heavy downpour. In Egypt the Nile ceased to increase and prices started to rise. In Jerusalem and along the littoral of Palestine rain was late, the sowing season was missed, wells dried up, and the spring that was located in Sulwān near Jerusalem ran dry.

In 694/1294–95, the Nile-level reached sixteen cubits and seventeen fingers but quickly receded thereafter.[94] The canal of Abū'l-Munajjā was opened three days before its usual time, for fear that the waters might recede further. One *irdabb* of wheat reached one hundred dirhams; that of barley sixty; that of beans fifty; while meat reached three dirhams per *raṭl*. Grain was brought from the [royal] silos and distributed among the bakeries. Those persons who were entitled to rations[95] were given six rations in two months. The allotment for the royal services[96] and the rations for those who were entitled to receive them amounted to six hundred and fifty *irdabb*s of wheat and barley per day. The *ḥawā'ij khānah*[97] was allocated twenty thousand *raṭl*s of meat per day. Disturbances occurred in the conduct of the affairs of the state because of the lack of revenues and the increase in expenditures. The confiscation of the wealth of the governors and administrators increased, while forced purchases of goods were imposed upon the merchants at exorbitantly high prices.

The year 695/1295–96 began with the people distressed because of high prices and diminishing income. However, they placed their hopes on the coming crop, which was almost due. When the crop became ripe, a wind coming from the direction of Barqah[98] blew like a storm and darkened the horizon, carrying a yellow dust that covered the crops in the area. The crops, which were not extensive at that time, withered and completely failed. This wind and dust spread to the provinces of al-Buḥayrah, al-Gharbīyah, and al-Sharqīyah[99], and reached Upper Egypt. The crops withered: the summer crops, such as rice, sesame, colocasia, and sugarcane, as well as other irrigated cultures, all failed. Consequently, prices soared. This wind was followed by diseases and high fevers that afflicted the entire population, thus causing the prices of sugar, honey, and other products needed by the sick to soar. Fruit disappeared, a pullet was sold for thirty dirhams, a watermelon for forty, one *raṭl* of watermelon for one dirham.[100] The price of one *irdabb* of wheat reached one hundred and ninety [dirhams],[101] that of barley one hundred and twenty,[102] while that of beans and lentils reached one hundred and ten.[103] Drought struck the area of Jerusalem, the littoral of Palestine, and the cities of Syria, as far as Aleppo. [There, the price of] one *ghirārah* of wheat reached two hundred and twenty dirhams, while that of barley was half that price. One *raṭl* of meat reached ten dirhams, while that of fruit [was] four times as many. More than twenty thousand *ghirārah*s [of grain] that were stored in Karak, Shawbak, and [along] the Palestinian littoral were sent to the cities, [although] they had been kept originally as provisions and destined to supply military expeditions. Drought also struck Mecca, where the price of one *irdabb* of wheat reached nine hundred dirhams and that of barley seven hundred. This caused its inhabitants to emigrate and only a few remained in the city. The villages of the Hijaz became depopulated. In Yemen foodstuffs vanished and epidemics heightened. Its inhabitants sold their children to buy food. They also fled to Ḥaly Banī Ya'qūb,[104] where they joined those who emigrated from Mecca, thus overcrowding the area. All except a small group died of hunger. Drought also struck the eastern regions, where animals perished, pastures were desolated, and not a drop of rain fell.

Conditions worsened in Egypt, where people from the outlying areas flocked and where famine became unbearable; bread was looted from the [bakeries'] ovens and from the shops. It even happened that when one carried dough to a [bakery's] oven, the mob would snatch it away, and there would be no bread left to bake. Hence, bread would not be taken out of an oven unless a number of men, armed with sticks, were present to protect it from the looters. Nevertheless, there were those who would throw themselves on the bread to grab some, not minding the blows that their heads or bodies might receive because of the severe hunger that afflicted them. When this situation exceeded the limits [of endurance], the sultan ordered that the poor and needy be assembled and distributed among the commanders: he allocated one hundred of them to every commander of one hundred; fifty to every commander of fifty; and so on until every commander of ten received ten. Among the commanders, some fed their quota in a communal repast. Some gave them each a loaf of bread; some distributed biscuits; while others handed out flat bread. This alleviated the hunger of the populace. Epidemics intensified throughout the countryside and in the villages, and disease spread in Cairo and Old Cairo. The number of deaths multiplied, and medicines were so much in demand for the sick that a druggist located at the beginning of the Daylam quarter in Cairo sold thirty-two thousand dirhams [of medicines] in one month. A shop known as al-Sharīf 'Aṭūf, in Sūq al-Suyūfiyīn, made a similar sale. This was also the case of a store in al-Wazīrīyah and another outside Bāb Zuwaylah. Being in great demand, physicians became highly paid, and their revenues increased. The daily income of a physician was one hundred dirhams. Later, people were unable to cope with the large number of deaths. The number of [the deceased] whose names were recorded in the official registers exceeded three thousand souls a day. As for those found dead in the streets, they were countless and filled the earth. Wells and trenches were dug to bury them en masse. The streets, quarters, and markets became filled with the stench of corpses. Anthropophagy was widespread, especially the eating of youngsters. Thus, it was common to find a piece of human flesh next to a corpse's head or to apprehend a person and find on him a shoulder, a thigh, or another limb of a child. Villages became depopulated to the point that the village that previously consisted of one hundred inhabitants now had approximately twenty left. Most of the inhabitants of such villages were found dead in bean fields, for when they found beans they did not stop eating them until they died. Guards were unable to repel these people because of their large numbers.[105]

Despite these conditions, the grain crop was many times more abundant than expected. Amīr Fakhr al-Dīn Alṭunbughā al-Misāḥī had among his cultivated lands one hundred *faddān*s of beans. He prevented no one from eating them on the spot but permitted no one to carry any away. When it was threshing time, he became dissatisfied with the person whom he had entrusted with the cultivation [of his land], so he went in person to supervise the threshing of those one hundred *faddān*s. Noticing a huge heap of pods from the beans that the poor had consumed while still green, he walked around it and examined it but did not find a single bean in it. He then ordered that it be threshed after the crop, so that he could make use of [the resulting] fodder. Thereby, he obtained seven hundred and sixty *irdabb*s of beans. This was viewed as a blessing for his charity and a gain for his pious deeds: "God gives manifold increase to whom He pleases, and God cares for all and He knows" [Qur'ān 2:261].

The profits of the merchants and vendors augmented and their gains increased. The gain of a vendor was one hundred to two hundred dirhams per day, while that of an itinerant vendor was thirty. Craftsmen made similar profits, with which they were content for the duration of this calamity. A large number of those who profited from [speculation in] grain during this dearth such as the commanders, soldiers, and others became afflicted either in their bodies by an epidemic or in their finances by utter ruin, so that they enjoyed no benefit. Some of these had in their possession six hundred *irdabb*s of wheat that they sold for one hundred and fifty [dirhams] per *irdabb*, and higher. When the price [of wheat] increased beyond the one they had sold at, they regretted having already marketed it, but regret was of no avail. When they received the money for [their] grain, they spent it on improving and decorating houses, going to extremes in making them strong and of high quality. Once these works were completed and the owners thought they were able to keep up [their houses], the command of God came to pass, and fire consumed all of them, thus rendering them useless.

Strife broke out between the sultan and the commanders, and the authority of the vizir Fakhr al-Dīn ibn al-Khalīlī[106] was undermined. The injustice of the sultan's retinue and mamluks increased with frequent instances of their tyranny. Their greed in taking bribes and protection money increased, their coercion of the commanders and their aberrant behavior heightened. People speculated in the *fulūs* as soon as they were minted. Subsequently it was announced that one *raṭl* of *fulūs* would be fixed at two dirhams and the weight of the *fals* would be one dirham. This was the first time in the history of Egypt that *fulūs* were measured by weight.[107]

The injustice of the vizir—namely, Fakhr al-Dīn ibn al-Khalīlī, the boon companion of the sultan—was unbearable, because the affairs of state came to a standstill as a result of mounting expenditures. He allocated the revenues of the bureau of escheats to pay for lunches and dinners and seized money bequeathed, whether it was left to a son or anyone else. Whenever a son would claim the inheritance of his father or a legal heir would claim his share of the inheritance, the vizir would require him to prove his kinship or his right to inherit. Neither one could do so without prolonged troubles and hardships. Once this authentication was accomplished, the vizir would refer the claimant to the bureau of escheats. When another person would die leaving property in the same manner, the vizir would act toward the heirs in the same fashion, so that they would be unable to present their claims and would renounce them.

The situation of the merchants worsened because of the forced purchases to which they were subjected, which were made at high prices and [for large] amounts. Confiscations of the property of the governors and the wealthy also increased. Injustice toward the population of the provinces became unbearable when levies for the royal reserves of grain were taken from the fields. The populations of Damascus, Nāblus, Baʿlabakk, al-Biqāʿ, and other places were also afflicted. These were days of extreme hardship because of famine, the spread of diseases and death, and the prevailing injustice.

At the end of this famine, a miraculous event—which was very peculiar and unheard of—occurred: a peasant of Jubbat ʿAssāl, a village in the vicinity of Damascus in Syria, took his ox to a watering place where a number of farmers had brought their animals for the same purpose. He let the ox drink, and when sated, the ox spoke intelligibly to the people at the watering place: "Praise and thanks be to God! God Almighty threatened this nation with seven years of drought, but the Prophet Muḥammad interceded on the nation's behalf." When the Prophet ordered the ox to convey this [information], it [the ox] said to him: "O Messenger of God, what sign would lend me credence among people?"

The Prophet answered: "That you would die [immediately] after conveying the message." After finishing its speech, the ox ascended to an elevated place, whence it fell to its death. Word about the ox spread throughout the village, and people rushed from all directions and took its hair and bones as charms. Whenever they used these in incense for a sick person, he would recover. A report about this was notarized by the judge of that locality; it was presented to the sultan and read by the commanders. News of this occurrence spread far and wide among the people.

Subsequently, prices decreased and God brought relief. "And in the creation of yourselves and the fact that animals are scattered through the earth, are signs for those of assured faith. And in the alternation of night and day, and the fact that God sends down sustenance from the sky, and revives therewith the earth after its death, and in the change of the winds, are signs for those that are wise" [Qur'ān 45:4–5].

At the beginning of the month of Rajab 736/February 1336, a shortage of grain occurred in Egypt during the reign of al-Malik al-Nāṣir Muḥammad ibn Qalāwūn (709–41/1309–40). Wheat was scarce and the price of one *irdabb* reached seventy dirhams, while that of beans reached fifty. Bread was one dirham for five *raṭl*s and was almost unavailable. Wheat disappeared from the markets. Groups of people crowded around every baker's shop, even though bread became as dark as dregs. At each shop, the governor assigned four of his agents, armed with clubs, to drive away the people, so that bread would not be looted. The populace appealed to the sultan earnestly and called for his help. The sultan gathered the commanders and said to them: "Commanders, one month upon you; the second upon me; and the third upon God!" Thereupon, the commanders opened the silos and sold wheat at thirty dirhams per *irdabb*. This relieved the populace. In the month of Shaᶜbān [736]/15 March–12 April 1336, the sultan released his reserves and sold wheat at twenty-five dirhams an *irdabb*. Then came the new crops of beans and barley, of which the populace ate until the month of Ramaḍān [736]/13 April–12 May 1336, when the new crop of wheat became available and prices decreased.[108]

A famine occurred during the reign of al-Ashraf Shaʿbān (764–78/1363–76).[109] It was caused by the failure of the Nile to reach its plenitude in the year 776/1374: indeed, it did not attain sixteen cubits.[110] The canal was opened, [causing] the water level to drop and prices to increase. Thus, the price of an *irdabb* of wheat reached one hundred and fifty dirhams, while that of barley reached one hundred. The price of bread reached one dirham for every *raṭl* and a half. Footstuffs became scarce and were rarely available. So many people died of hunger that they filled the streets. This was followed by an epidemic that caused further deaths.[111] During this time, the price of a pullet reached one hundred dirhams and higher, while that of a watermelon reached one hundred and fifty. A beggar would ask for bread just to smell it, then he would cry out and die. The sultan gave orders to collect the poor, whom he distributed among the commanders and the wealthy merchants. This famine lasted approximately two years; then God sent succor to mankind and caused the Nile to flow, quenching the land's thirst. Prosperity returned after desperation had prevailed and many had thought that hardship would endure and relief was unlikely. This was an episode to which we ourselves were eyewitnesses, and an ordeal that we endured.[112] Indeed, "He is the One that sends down rain even after men have given up all hope, and scatters His mercy far and wide. And He is the Protector, worthy of all praise" [Qur'ān 42:28].

*SECTION THREE*

# *The Causes of Our Ordeals*

Know—May God protect and guide you, and not deprive you of His bounty and divine providence—that from reports that have reached us from all countries of the world, from antiquity to modern times, and according to [our] knowledge of the conditions of existence and the nature of civilization, as well as that of the history of mankind, the periods of dearth [*ghalā'*] that have befallen mankind since the Creation have been caused largely by natural catastrophes sent by God. Such is the case of the failure of the Nile to reach its plenitude in Egypt; the droughts in Syria, Iraq, the Hijaz, and elsewhere; or a disaster that strikes the grain crops: such as a hot wind that burns them, strong winds that wither them, locusts that would devour them, and the like. This is the Almighty's customary treatment of His creatures: whenever they disobey Him and violate His divine law, He calls down a calamity upon them as a punishment for their actions.[1]

As for this [recent] ordeal that has befallen Egypt, it differs from the aforementioned disasters and may be explained by the fact that in the year 796/1393–94, the Nile failed to reach its plenitude; hence most of the land remained unirrigated and uncultivated.[2] Consequently, [grain] prices rose so [sharply] that the price of an *irdabb* of wheat reached seventy dirhams.[3] Then God aided His creatures by raising the waters of the Nile to the extent that they flooded the whole land [in 797/1394–95].[4] Subsequently, people needed large quantities of seed, but they had only minimal amounts of grain on hand, because most of the land had been left uncultivated in 796/

1393–94, as mentioned already. As a result, prices increased so greatly that the price of one *irdabb* of wheat reached around two hundred dirhams and that of barley one hundred and five. This is characteristic of Egypt since ancient times: whenever the Nile delays in flooding, prices continue to increase for two years. Thus, following the harvest of the crops of 798/1395–96, prices decreased until they returned to their preinflationary level or thereabout.[5]

This continued until the death of al-Ẓāhir Barqūq in the middle of Shawwāl 801/20 June 1399.[6] On that date, in Cairo, one *irdabb* of wheat sold for less than thirty dirhams.[7] The next day its price reached forty dirhams.[8] Prices continued to rise until one *irdabb* [of wheat] sold for more than seventy dirhams in the year 802/1399–1400.[9] Wheat prices remained at this level until the Nile failed to reach its plenitude in 806/1403–4.[10] This led to a calamity: prices soared so high that the price of one *irdabb* of wheat exceeded four hundred dirhams [of account].[11] Prices of other commodities, such as foodstuffs, drink, and clothing, followed a similar trend, thus causing an increase unheard of in recent times in the wages of such persons as construction workers, laborers, craftsmen, and artisans.[12] Finally, succor came from Almighty God in the year 807/1404–5: the level of the Nile rose greatly, and the entire land benefited from this; thus, the people were in need of seed. At that time, abundant quantities of grain were under the control of high officials and other influential persons. This [grain shortage] was due to two factors; first, the state monopoly kept foodstuffs out of the reach of the people unless they agreed to pay the prices set by the officials;[13] second, the increase in grain [prices] in the year 806/1403–4, which was unparalleled in living memory. Because of these factors, as well as others that will be mentioned later, the situation became critical; conditions became perilous, disaster was widespread and calamity universal, to the degree that more than one-half of the population of the land [of Egypt] died of hunger and cold. Death was so prevalent that even the animals perished in the years 806/1403–4 and 807/1404–5.[14] They became so scarce that their prices reached levels that we are embarrassed to mention.[15]

We are presently at the beginning of the year 808/1405–6,[16] and because of the fluctuation of the currency,[17] the scarcity of the necessities of life, and malfeasance and poor judgment [on the part of the officials], the situation is continually worsening due to greatly distressed and abominable conditions.

Three causes, and only three, contributed to this situation: the first cause, the source of this decay, is the holding of administrative and religious positions such as the vizirate, judgeships, provincial governorships, the *ḥisbah*, and other functions through bribery, to the point that it has become impossible for anyone to secure any of these positions without paying large amounts of money. Consequently, every ignorant, corrupt, unjust, and oppressive person has reached a highly regarded and important position that he never expected to attain. [This was possible] through connections with a courtier and a pledge of money to the sultan in return for the desired position.[18] The nomination and investiture take place so rapidly that the new appointee does not have on hand even a small fraction of the amount promised. His only recourse is to go into debt to secure the equivalent of half the amount pledged.[19] Taking into consideration his needs for distinctive attire, horses, servants, and the like, his debts continue to multiply, and his creditors harass him. Naturally then, he connives and heedlessly seeks to acquire wealth, not caring if this brings about the ruination of a number of souls, the spilling of blood, and the enslaving of free women. He is also compelled to impose taxes on his retinue and aides and to demand immediate payment from them. Consequently, they turn to the possessions of the subjects and neither abstain nor refrain from exerting themselves to seize these possessions. While the wretched [official] is engaged in collecting money to pay back his creditors, he is importuned by the commanders and courtiers of the sultan. In the case of a provincial official, a dignitary [may] pay a visit. This will require [him] to stage a costly banquet and to make sumptuous offerings of slaves, horses, or other appropriate gifts. Unexpectedly, he hears that someone else, who has pledged a larger sum of money, has replaced him. Since he is still in debt, his furniture, animals, and other belongings are confiscated. He is in a pitiful condition, having already lost his belongings as we have mentioned, and he will be severely punished. He has no recourse other than to pledge an additional sum in order to keep the same position or to be appointed to another one.

When the rural population was burdened with a multitude of taxes and a variety of injustices, their situation became precarious, so they scattered and deserted their land. Consequently, tax receipts and revenues decreased because of diminishing agriculture, depopulation, and emigration. This was the result of the cruelty of the officials toward these people and [later] toward those who remained of them.

As previously mentioned, this was the situation during the reign of al-Ẓāhir Barqūq until the grain shortage of the year 796/1393–94, which was described above. The damage that it inflicted upon the populace was minimal. This was due to two factors: first, the foodstuffs that the population had stored sustained them through this shortage; second, al-Ẓāhir Barqūq's charitable deeds were so numerous, and his piety so steadfast, that—to my knowledge—no one died of hunger during the grain shortage of 797–98/1394–96.[20]

Appointment to office through bribery was common policy until the death of al-Ẓāhir Barqūq. The demise of this sultan was followed by strife among the state dignitaries, which led to feuding and warring, circumstances which I described in a separate monograph.[21] This troubled period was marked by rebellion among the rural population[22] and by the spread of swindlers and brigands. Roads became unsafe and travel within the country was impossible except at great risk. Meanwhile, the state dignitaries persisted in their ignorance, neglected the welfare of [God's] servants, and were preoccupied with pleasures, so that they proved true God's words of chastisement: "When We decide to destroy a population, We send a definite order to those among them who are given the good things of this life and yet transgress, so that the Word is proved true against them: then We destroy them utterly" [Qur'ān 17:16].

The second cause is the high cost of land: a number of persons were promoted to the service of the commanders, whose friendship they were seeking through money that they collected as taxes, to the point that they became their masters. Then they desired further to curry favor with them [i.e., the commanders], and no means was closer to their hearts than money. They reached to the lands that were within the fiefs [*iqṭāʿāt*] of the commanders, summoned the peasants who were renting them, and increased the rent. As a result, the revenues of their clients among the commanders grew, and they adopted this [method] as a means through which they granted their graces to them and a favor that they counted against them whenever they wished to do so. They made this increase an annual practice so that nowadays [the rent of] one *faddān* is ten times what it was before these events.[23] Of course, when the rent of one *faddān* of land multiplied to the degree that we have mentioned, and the price of one *irdabb* of wheat needed for seed reached the level previously mentioned, the expenses for plowing, sowing, harvesting, and the like increased; the outrages of the governors and their subordinates became greater and their oppression of the peasants intensified; the levies for the upkeep of dikes and similar works became more frequent; the grain crop obtained in these conditions required greater expenses and increased costs that were beyond the reach of the peasants. In addition, since the start of these injustices, the land has ceased to be bountiful and has not yielded its customary crop. Of course, loss is rejected by everyone and no one loses willingly. Because most of the grain was in the possession of the influential officials of the state and the military commanders, whose desire for pleasures had increased and whose greed for securing the comforts of life had become great, prices remained high and there was almost no hope that they would come down. These [factors] caused the ruin of most of the villages and the majority of the lands remained uncultivated. Grain and other products of the earth diminished, since most of the peasants had died or become vagrants in the countryside because of hardships over the years and the loss of their animals. [This shortage was due] to the inability of the landowners to sow their lands because of the high price of seed and the decreased numbers of peasants. For the aforementioned reasons the country was on the verge of ruin and destruction. "Such was the practice approved of God among those who lived aforetime: no change would you find in the practice approved of God" [Qur'ān 33:62].

SECTION FOUR

# [Currency]

## [ISLAMIC CURRENCY]

The third cause [of this situation] is the circulation of the *fulūs*. Know—May God grant you toward every good an easy path, and on every grace a sign and a guide—that it has always been God's custom toward His creatures and His continuous wont from the Creation to the occurrence of these events and the perpetration of the crimes that we have mentioned, in all corners of the earth and among every nation, that the currency that has been used to determine prices of goods and costs of labor consists only of gold and silver. [This is true of] the Persians, Byzantines, Israelites, Greeks, Ancient Egyptians, even the Nabataens and the Tubbaʿ who were the princelings of Yemen, the native Arabs and the Arabized. This continued following the rise of Islam among the various dynasties, which took it upon themselves to advocate its mission and to adhere to its law, including the Umayyads in Syria and in Spain, the Abbasids in the East, the ʿAlawīs [or ʿAlīds] in Tabaristan, the Maghrib, and the lands of Egypt, Syria, and Yemen. [This was also the case with] the Turkish dynasty of the Saljuqs, the state of Daylam, the Mongols in the Orient, and the Kurdish dynasty in Egypt, Syria, and Diyār Bakr, then under the Turkish rulers of Egypt. According to all reports, either valid or invalid, no nation or group of people is ever known to have paid for goods or remunerated for works in ancient or recent times in a currency other than that of gold and silver. In fact, it is said that the first to mint the dinar and the dirham was Adam, who said that life is not enjoyable without these two currencies. This was related by al-Ḥāfiẓ ibn ʿAsākir (d. 571/1176) in his *Tārīkh Dimashq*.[1]

I shall narrate to you some reports in this regard to illustrate the veracity of what I have pointed out. I say—seeking the help of God my Lord, indeed He is the only Protector—know—may God increase your knowledge and grant you intelligence and comprehension—that the dirham was, and still is, the currency of mankind at all times, so that it is said that the first to mint dinars and dirhams and make jewelry out of gold and silver was Fāligh son of Ghābir son of Shālikh son of Arfakhshad son of Sām son of Noah, since whose time people have [always] used currency. The latest dirhams [of these ancient times] were of two types: the black of full weight[2] and the old *ṭabarī*s.[3] These were the currencies of widest use. There were also dirhams called *jawrafī*s.

The currency that was in circulation among the Arabs in pre-Islamic times consisted of gold and silver only. From other countries, the Arabs received gold dinars, among which were the imperial[4] dinars from the Byzantine empire, and silver dirhams of two types: black of full weight and old *ṭabarī*s. The respective weights of the dinar and the dirham in pre-Islamic times were double their weight in Islamic times.[5] The *mithqāl* was called either a dirham or a dinar. In pre-Islamic times neither was used as a currency by the inhabitants of Mecca, who adopted in their transactions the *mithqāl*, a weight for the dirhams and the dinars. They also used for buying and selling weights that they had adopted among themselves. These were the *raṭl*, equivalent to twelve *ūqīyah*s, and the *ūqīyah*, equivalent to forty dirhams. Thus, the *raṭl* [of Mecca] would be equivalent to four hundred and eighty dirhams. Today in Egypt the *raṭl* is equivalent to twelve *ūqīyah*s, and one *ūqīyah* is equivalent to twelve dirhams. Thus, one [Egyptian] *raṭl* equals one hundred and forty-four dirhams. One *raṭl* of Damascus is now equivalent to twelve *ūqīyah*s, and one *ūqīyah* is fifty dirhams. Thus, one *raṭl* is six hundred dirhams.

[In pre-Islamic Mecca] one *nish* (originally *niṣf* [meaning half], of which the *ṣ* has been transformed into a *sh* and thus pronounced *nish*), which was one-half of one *ūqīyah*, was equivalent to twenty dirhams, and one *nawāt* was five dirhams. The dirhams were of two sorts: the *ṭabarī*s, each weighing eight *dānaq*s, although it was also said four; the *baghlī*s, each weighing four *dānaq*s, although it was also said [that they weighed] eight. The weight of the *jawrafī* dirham was four and a half *dānaqs*, and that of the *dānaq* was eight and two-fifths average unshelled *ḥabbahs* [i.e., grains] of barley, of which the extremities had been cut. The *baghlī* dirham was also called "of full weight"[6] and weighed the same as the dinar: this was the weight of the dirhams of Persia. As for the *jawāz* dirhams, each ten of them weighed three less than the *baghlīs*, so that every seven *baghlīs* would weigh ten *jawāz* dirhams. The dinar was called *dīnār* because of its weight, but it was [also] a coin. The weight of every ten dirhams was six *mithqāls*. The weight of one *mithqāl* was twenty-two *qīrāṭs* minus one *ḥabbah*, and it also weighed seventy-two *ḥabbahs* of the [size] already mentioned.

It is said that [the weight of] the *mithqāl* has not varied since it was established, neither in pre-Islamic nor in Islamic times. It is also said that the one who invented weight in ancient times began by inventing the *mithqāl* and made it [equivalent to the weight of] sixty *ḥabbahs*, each *ḥabbah* being the weight of one hundred grains of wild mustard seeds of average size. He made a weight equivalent to one hundred grains of mustard, then he made a second weight equivalent to the first weight plus [another] one hundred grains [of mustard], then a third weight, until [he made] a weight equivalent to five weights [i.e., five hundred grains of mustard]. This [last] weight became the equivalent of one-twelfth of a *mithqāl*. He then doubled it for a weight of [one-sixth, then] one-third of a *mithqāl*, then he composed [another multiple]: one-half of a *mithqāl*, then one, five, ten *mithqāls*, and [other] multiples. Accordingly, the weight of one *mithqāl* would be six thousand grains [of mustard]. The balance-type scales were used for weighing.[7]

When God sent forth His prophet Muḥammad, [the Prophet] confirmed all these [weights] used by the inhabitants of Mecca and said: "The weight is that of Mecca," and according to another version [he said]: "The weight is that of Medina."[8] The Messenger of God prescribed the *zakāt* on money accordingly: for every five *ūqīyahs* of pure and unadulterated silver he imposed [a *zakāt* of] five dirhams, i.e., the equivalent of one *nawāt*, and for every twenty dinars he imposed half a dinar.[9] This [system] was adopted without the slightest alteration by Abū Bakr (11–13/632–34) during his tenure as caliph, following [the death of] the Messenger of God. When ʿUmar ibn al-Khaṭṭāb (13–23/634–44) became caliph, he kept the currencies as they were and did not alter them until the year 18/639–40, during the sixth year of his caliphate,[10] when deputations came to him, among which one arrived from Baṣrah and included [among its members] al-Aḥnaf ibn Qays.[11] The latter spoke to ʿUmar about matters that concerned the inhabitants of Baṣrah. ʿUmar dispatched Maʿqil ibn Yasār to Baṣrah, where he dug the Maʿqil river canal for the inhabitants,[12] established the *jarīb*, and imposed two Sasanian[13] dirhams a month.

ʿUmar [ibn al-Khaṭṭāb] issued dirhams after the Sasanian fashion and of the same shape but added on some of them "Praise be to God,"[14] on others "The Messenger of God,"[15] on others "There is no God but He alone,"[16] and "ʿUmar" on others. The effigy [represented on the coin] was that of the [Sasanian] king, not that of ʿUmar. This caliph also set the weight of every ten dirhams at six *mithqāls*.[17] When ʿUthmān [ibn ʿAffān] (23–35/644–56) was invested with the caliphate, he issued dirhams on which was engraved "God is Great."[18]

When Muʿāwiyah ibn Abī Sufyān (41–60/661–80) [the first Umayyad caliph] held the reins of power, he placed Baṣrah and Kūfah under the authority of Ziyād ibn Abīh.[19] The latter said to Muʿāwiyah: "O Commander of the Faithful, the pious servant [of God] and Commander of the Faithful ʿUmar ibn al-Khaṭṭāb reduced the [weight of the] dirham and increased the [volume of the] *qafīz*, which became the basis of the tax levied for the stipends of the army and upon which depended the subsistence of [their] offspring. He did all this in a spirit of generosity toward his subjects. If you establish a [weight] standard that will be less than that [of the dirham struck by ʿUmar], it will ease the conditions of the population further and increase your reputation for pious conduct." Therefore, Muʿāwiyah struck black dirhams, each weighing slightly less than six *dānaqs*, i.e., fifteen *qīrāṭs* minus one or two *ḥabbahs*.[20] Ziyād [ibn Abīh] struck dirhams accordingly. He ordered that they would be handled as if ten weighed seven *mithqāls* and engraved on them ["In the name of God, my Lord."][21] These were used as if they had the weight of dirhams. Muʿāwiyah also struck dinars embossed with his effigy girt with a sword.[22] A dinar of low quality fell into the hands of an old soldier. He brought it to Muʿāwiyah, threw it in front of him, and said: "O Muʿāwiyah, your coinage is the worst we have ever seen!" Muʿāwiyah answered him: "I shall deprive you of your pay and I shall clothe you with a camel's blanket."

When ʿAbd Allāh ibn al-Zubayr (d. 73/692)[23] assumed power in Mecca, he struck round dirhams. Indeed, he was the first to strike round dirhams. Previously, dirhams had been crude, without impression, and clipped. ʿAbd Allāh made them round and engraved on one side "Muḥammad is the Messenger of God"[24] and on the other "God commands equity and justice."[25] His brother Muṣʿab ibn al-Zubayr (d. 72/691)[26] struck dirhams in Iraq and set [the weight] of every ten of them at seven *mithqāl*s and used them to pay the soldiery.[27] When al-Ḥajjāj ibn Yūsuf al-Thaqafī (d. 95/714) arrived in Iraq [to administer it] on behalf of ʿAbd al-Malik ibn Marwān (65–86/685–705), he said: "We must not retain anything that has been initiated by the hypocrite," and changed [the currency].

When ʿAbd al-Malik ibn Marwān consolidated his power following the execution of ʿAbd Allāh and Muṣʿab, the two sons of al-Zubayr ibn al-ʿAwwām, he inquired about the currency, weights, and measures and struck dinars and dirhams in the year 76/695–96. The cause of this was as follows: he used to begin his letters to the Byzantines with the heading: "Say: He is God the One,"[28] along with mention of the name of the Prophet and the date. The king of the Byzantines wrote him, saying: "You have made such-and-such innovations. Renounce them! Otherwise we will engrave offensive inscriptions about your prophet on our dinars." ʿAbd al-Malik was troubled by this response. He spoke to Khālid ibn Yazīd ibn Muʿāwiyah, who advised him to do away with Byzantine dinars, prohibit their use, and strike for the people dirhams and dinars on which there would be mention of God. Thus, ʿAbd al-Malik struck the dinar and the dirham:[29] he set the weight of the dinar at twenty-two Syrian *qīrāṭ*s minus one *ḥabbah*, and that of the dirham at exactly fifteen *qīrāṭ*s, one *qīrāṭ* being equal to four *ḥabbah*s, and one *dānaq* at two and a half *qīrāṭ*s. He wrote to al-Ḥajjāj in Iraq ordering him to mint them there. Al-Ḥajjāj struck the dirhams and engraved on them: "Say: He is God the One,"[30] and forbade anyone else to mint coins. When, therefore, a Jew by the name of Sumayr minted dirhams, al-Ḥajjāj placed him under arrest with the intention of putting him to death. Sumayr said to him: "The alloy of my dirhams is superior to yours, so why do you wish to put me to death?" However, al-Ḥajjāj still resolved on putting him to death. Thereupon, Sumayr devised standard weights[31] for the people in the hope of being set free, but al-Ḥajjāj did not do so. Previously, people had no knowledge of standard weights, but weighed one dirham against another. Thus, after Sumayr devised standard weights, some people renounced the former practice. These dirhams reached Medina of the Messenger of God where a group of the Companions still lived. They objected only to the engraving, because it included an effigy.[32] In fact, Saʿīd ibn al-Musayyib[33] used them in buying and selling and found nothing defective about them.

ʿAbd al-Malik ibn Marwān struck gold [dinars] according to the Syrian *mithqāl*. These were called the *mayyālah* dinars, greater by two dinars per hundred. It was also reported that the motive behind ʿAbd al-Malik's [decision to] strike dinars and dirhams was that Khālid ibn Yazīd ibn Muʿāwiyah ibn Abī Sufyān said to him, "O Commander of the Faithful, the scholars of the Old Testament mention that they find in their books that the caliph who will live longest is the one who will glorify God on the dirham." ʿAbd al-Malik resolved to do so and thus founded the Islamic currency. The one who minted dirhams at that time was a Jew by the name of Sumayr. Accordingly, dirhams were ascribed to him and became known as *sumayrī* dirhams. ʿAbd al-Malik sent the die of the dirhams to al-Ḥajjāj in Iraq. From there, al-Ḥajjāj sent it to the provinces so that dirhams would be struck accordingly. He also sent orders to [the officials] of the garrison cities that they should inform him every month of the amounts of money they had collected to enable him to keep a full record. He also ordered them to mint Islamic dirhams in the provinces and to send them to him periodically. He imposed [the payment of] one dirham out of one hundred [to cover the price of] firewood and the minter's fee. On one side of the dirham he engraved "Say: He is God the One"[34] and on the other "There is no other god but God."[35] He also put a marginal inscription around both sides. On one side it was "[Bismillāh.] This dirham was minted in the city of . . ."[36] and on the other "Muḥammad is the Messenger of God, Who had sent him with guidance and religion of truth, to proclaim it over all religion, even though the pagans may detest it."[37]

Trustworthy persons have reported that ʿAbd al-Malik [ibn Marwān] was compelled to take this measure after considering [these facts]: since time immemorial, dirhams have been either black and of full weight or old *ṭabarīs*. Hence, when ʿAbd al-Malik looked into the affairs of the Islamic community, he said that these dirhams would last forever and that, according to the rules of *zakāt*, five dirhams should be taken out of every two hundred [dirhams] or every five *ūqīyahs*. He feared that if he decided that all dirhams would be made similar to the large black ones, the amount of *zakāt* on two hundred of them would be minimal. If he made the dirhams similar to the *ṭabarīs* (always with the implication that whenever they reached two hundred *zakāt* should be paid on them), this would be harmful and excessive for the person with money. Consequently, ʿAbd al-Malik adopted a middle position that guaranteed the implementation of the *zakāt* without decreasing it or harming the population and that was in accordance with the practice of the Messenger of God.

Prior to the reign of ʿAbd al-Malik, and until the time he took the above-mentioned decisions, Muslims used to pay half the *zakāt* in large dirhams and the other half in small ones. When people met with ʿAbd al-Malik to discuss his decision concerning the coinage, he took a full-weight dirham, weighed it, and found that it weighed eight *dānaq*s. He then [weighed] a small dirham and found that it weighed four *dānaq*s. He subsequently combined them, increasing the weight of the small dirham and decreasing that of the large, thus making two dirhams of equal weight, each weighing exactly six *dānaq*s. He also looked into the *mithqāl*, the weight of which had remained constant and stable since time immemorial: every ten dirhams, each weighing six *dānaq*s, being equivalent to exactly seven *mithqāl*s.[38] He confirmed this [ratio] and adopted it with no change.

The dirhams struck by ʿAbd al-Malik had three merits: first, they [conformed to the rule] that the weight of seven *mithqāl*s equaled that of ten dirhams. Second, ʿAbd al-Malik made the weight uniform: the dirham came to weigh six *dānaq*s instead of having large and small dirhams. Third, these [dirhams] were in conformity with the practice of the Messenger of God with regard to the obligation of [paying] *zakāt* without loss or excess. Thus, the Prophet's tradition was followed and the Islamic community agreed on [the new dirham].

The weight of this unanimously accepted legal dirham was set, as already mentioned, at seven *mithqāl*s the ten, and the weight of one dirham was fifty and two-fifths *ḥabbah*s of barley with the specifications already described. It was also called the dirham of measures[39] since the legal *raṭl* is a multiple of it, while the *mudd* is a multiple of the *raṭl* and the *ṣāʿ* is a multiple of the *mudd*. In fact, the weight of ten silver dirhams was established at seven *mithqāl*s of gold because gold is heavier than silver. Indeed, it seems as if one experimented with one *ḥabbah* of silver and another of gold, weighed both of them, and observed that gold was heavier than silver by three-sevenths of one dirham. Hence, the weight of ten dirhams is seven *mithqāl*s, because if one adds three-sevenths of one dirham to the [weight of] the same dirham, it will equal one *mithqāl*. If one subtracts from one *mithqāl* three-tenths of its weight, it will equal the weight of one dirham. Every ten *mithqāls* weigh fourteen and two-sevenths dirhams. It is also said that the person who established weights set the dirham at sixty *ḥabbahs* and the weight of every ten dirhams at seven *mithqāls*. Accordingly, the weight of one *ḥabbah* is seventy grains of mustard. Based on this, multiples of the dirham up to one thousand were formed [by using the same method we] mentioned above in relation to the *mithqāl*.

Al-Ḥajjāj struck white dirhams and engraved on them "Say: He is God the One."[40] To this the Qur'ān readers said, "May God fight him! What evil has he afflicted the people with? [This coin] is now handled by impure [persons] and menstruating women!" Before then, the legend on the dirhams was engraved in Old Persian. Some of the Qur'ān readers abhorred touching the [new] dirhams whenever they were in a state of impurity. Accordingly, these [dirhams] came to be known as *al-makrūhah* [the reprobate ones], an expression that came to stigmatize and identify them.

Mālik [ibn Anas] (d. 179/795)[41] was asked about changing the legend on the dinars and the dirhams, because it contained excerpts from the Qur'ān. He answered: "Many people were [following the religious prescriptions] when coins were first struck during the reign of ʿAbd al-Malik ibn Marwān. No one then disapproved of them and I have not seen any scholar who disavowed them. Though it has reached me that Ibn Sīrīn (d. 110/730)[42] abhorred using these [coins] in buying and selling, people continued to use them and I have not seen anyone who has prohibited them here [i.e., Medina]."

ʿAbd al-Malik [ibn Marwān] was told: "These white dirhams contain excerpts from the Qur'ān and are handled by Jews, Christians, impure [persons], and menstruating women. It will be advisable for you to erase [the inscription]."

He answered: "Do you wish [other] nations to allege against us that we have erased our [belief in the] unity of God and the name of our Prophet?" When ʿAbd al-Malik ibn Marwān died [in 85/705], the situation remained unchanged. He was succeeded by his son al-Walīd (86–96/705–15), then by Sulaymān ibn ʿAbd al-Malik (96/715–17), then by ʿUmar ibn ʿAbd al-ʿAzīz (99–101/717-20).

During the reign of Yazīd ibn ʿAbd al-Malik (101–5/720–24), the *hubayrī* [dirhams] were struck in Iraq by ʿUmar ibn Hubayrah,[43] at a standard weight of six *dānaqs*. He was the first to [enforce] strictly the weight standard of the dirhams; he also refined silver more than any of his predecessors. When Hishām ibn ʿAbd al-Malik (105–25/724–43), who was fond of money, became caliph, he ordered Khālid ibn ʿAbd Allāh al-Qasrī[44] in the year 106/725–26 to change the standard to the weight of seven [*dānaqs*] and to close the mints in all cities except Wāsiṭ [in Iraq], where dirhams began to be minted with enlarged dies. Khālid was stricter than his predecessors with regard to the refining of silver. Dirhams were minted according to Khālid's die until his dismissal in 120/737–38.[45] He was succeeded by Yūsuf ibn ʿUmar al-Thaqafī,[46] who was so strict that when one day he inspected the weight and found that one dirham was missing one *ḥabbah*, he gave every worker [in the mint] a thousand lashes. Since there were one hundred workers, one hundred thousand lashes were given because of one [missing] *ḥabbah*.[47]

Yūsuf ibn ʿUmar al-Thaqafī reduced the size of the coin and set its weight at [six *dānaqs*].[48] He minted the dirhams solely at Wāsiṭ until the assassination of al-Walīd ibn Yazīd in the year 126/744. When Marwān ibn Muḥammad al-Ḥimār (127–32/744–50), the last caliph of the Umayyad dynasty, ascended the throne, he struck dirhams at the mint of Ḥarrān, in the Jazīrah area, until he was killed. Of the coinage of the Umayyad dynasty, the *hubayrī*, *khālidī*, and *yūsufī* dirhams were finest.[49]

Then the Abbasid dynasty came to power. Al-Saffāḥ (132–36/749–54) struck dirhams in al-Anbār,[50] making them of the same shape and form as the dinar, and inscribed the words "Abbasid coinage" on them.[51] He also reduced [their weight] by one *ḥabbah*, then by two. When Abū Jaʿfar al-Manṣūr (136–58/754–75) rose to power, he reduced them by three *ḥabbahs*. These dirhams were called "three-fourths of one *qīrāṭ*," because the *qīrāṭ* equaled four *ḥabbahs* and the dirhams were [reduced] by three-fourths of one *qīrāṭ*. Then the *hāshimī* dirhams were put in circulation; [their weight] was set according to the *mithqāl* of Baṣrah after having been based on the *mayyālah mithqāls* of full weight. During the reign of al-Manṣūr, the *hāshimī* dirhams kept the [legal] proportion to the *mithqāl*, while the older ones remained short three-fourths of a *qīrāṭ*.[52] This lasted until the year 158/775 when al-Mahdī (158–69/775–85) issued new coins that were round and had points.[53] As for Mūsā al-Hādī ibn al-Mahdī (169–70/785–86), no coinage of his is known.[54] The situation remained unchanged until the month of Rajab of the year 178/October 794, when the decrease in the weight of the dirhams reached one *qīrāṭ* minus one-fourth of one *ḥabbah*.

When Hārūn al-Rashīd (170–93/786–809) entrusted Jaʿfar ibn Yaḥyā ibn Khālid al-Barmakī (d. 187/802) with the [supervision of] the mint, the latter struck his name on the dinars and the dirhams[55] [that were minted at] Madīnat al-Salām [i.e., Baghdad, the City of Peace] and at al-Muḥammadīyah, which was in the region of Rayy [in Iran].[56] He also struck dinars weighing one hundred [and one] *mithqāls* each, which he used to distribute among the people during the [feasts of] Nawrūz and Mihrajān.[57] These bore the [following] verses:

> A gold [coin] purer than the royal mint's
> bearing the name of Jaʿfar
> exceeding one hundred by one
> a pauper who obtains it becomes wealthy.[58]

The Abbasids also had "dinars of the purse"; these were double the weight of those in circulation. On each of these dinars was engraved: "The mint of al-Ḥasanī, for the purse of the Commander of the Faithful."[59] These dinars were bestowed by the Commander of the Faithful upon singers and the like. [The word] "al-Ḥasanī" referred to the Ḥasanī Palace, which is still located in the city of Baghdad and which was built by al-Ḥasan ibn Sahl.[60]

The decrease in the weight of the dirhams became one *qīrāṭ* minus one *ḥabbah*, and this continued unchanged until the month of Ramaḍān of the year 184/800–801, when [the decrease] became four *qīrāṭ*s and one and a half *ḥabbah*s. Consequently, these dirhams became accepted only in bulk or at the market price of their [silver] content and were later withdrawn from circulation.

When [Hārūn] al-Rashīd put Jaʿfar ibn Yaḥyā [al-Barmakī] to death [in 187/802] and entrusted al-Faḍl ibn al-Rabīʿ (d. 208/824)[61] with the vizirate, he appointed al-Sindī ibn Shāhaq to [supervise] the mint. The latter minted dirhams that kept the legal proportion to the weight of the dinar. Indeed, the uninterrupted tradition is that dirhams must always be proportionate with the dinar. Al-Sindī's coinage was of excellent quality, for he was extremely strict with regard to the refining of gold and silver.[62]

In the month of Rajab 191/May–June 807, the [weight of the] *hāshimī* dinars decreased by half a *ḥabbah*, although they kept their market value as if they still weighed one *mithqāl* each. Later, the weight of the dinar returned to one *mithqāl*. This continued until the reign of al-Amīn Muḥammad ibn Hārūn al-Rashīd (193–98/809–13), who entrusted al-ʿAbbās ibn al-Faḍl ibn al-Rabīʿ with the [supervision of the] mint. The latter engraved in large characters: "My Lord is Allāh"[63] on the top line of the coins, and "al-ʿAbbās ibn al-Faḍl" on the bottom line.[64] When al-Amīn was killed and people rallied round ʿAbd Allāh al-Ma'mūn (198–218/813–33), the latter was unable to find anyone capable of making a die, so coins were engraved on a lathe in the same manner in which seals were engraved.

At the beginning of the Islamic era, people used scales for weighing. When ʿAbd Allāh ibn ʿĀmir[65] was appointed governor of Baṣrah in the year 29/649–50, he added an indicator to the scales. Indeed, he was the first to introduce this indicator [among the Muslims].

During the reign of al-Ma'mūn and until his death, the coinage situation remained generally unchanged.[66] Al-Ma'mūn was succeeded by Abū Isḥāq al-Muʿtaṣim (218–27/833–42), al-Wāthiq (227–32/842–47), and al-Mutawakkil (232–47/847–61), successively. The latter [reigned] until his assassination by the Turks,[67] who came to hold power jointly with the Abbasids. The state became expert in luxury, and the light of divine guidance faded. Precepts of the divine law and religious prescriptions changed when the Turks innovated and invented ways that God did not allow, among which was the adulteration of dirhams.[68] It is said that the first to have debased dirhams and minted them adulterated and of mediocre alloy was ʿUbayd Allāh ibn Ziyād, when he escaped from Baṣrah in the year 64/683–84.[69] [Later,] the dirhams of mediocre alloy spread in the cities in the heyday of the non-Arab dynasties.[70] This created confusion in Iraq, where the monetary situation was unsettled. I hope that God may grant me success in giving details of this, God willing.

## [EGYPTIAN CURRENCY SINCE THE MUSLIM CONQUEST]

In Egypt the currency used to pay for goods and labor has consisted mainly of gold. This was the case under the dynasties of both pre-Islamic and Islamic times. The validity of such an assertion is proven by the fact that the amount of taxes in Egypt, in both ancient and recent times, has been [based] on gold, as you will read in detail—God willing—since I intend to compose a separate monograph that will cover the state of taxes in Egypt in general from the time [this country] became inhabited, and from the beginning of its history until the present time.[71]

In order to prove the validity of [my] premises, it will suffice to quote the words of Abū Hurayrah (d. ca. 58/678),[72] who said: "The Messenger of God said: 'May [God] protect the dirham and *qafīz* of Iraq, the *mudd* and dinar of Syria, and the *irdabb* and dinar of Egypt.' "[73] This saying was recorded by Muslim (d. 261/875)[74] and by Abū Dāwūd [al-Sijistānī] (d. 275/889).[75] Indeed, the Prophet mentioned the measure and the currency of every country, indicating that gold was the currency of Egypt. This saying of the Prophet is proof of the validity of the measure taken by ʿUmar ibn al-Khaṭṭāb when he dispatched ʿUthmān ibn Ḥanīf to Iraq upon its conquest in the year 16/637. The latter imposed on the population of the Sawād [in Iraq] ten dirhams for every *jarīb* of vine, eight dirhams for every *jarīb* of palm-trees, six dirhams for every *jarīb* of sugarcane and fruit trees, four dirhams for every *jarīb* of wheat and two dirhams for every *jarīb* of barley. He wrote to ʿUmar to inform him of these measures, and ʿUmar approved them.[76]

When Egypt was conquered, precisely in the year 20/641, ʿAmr ibn al-ʿĀṣ imposed two dinars on every Copt in the country. These taxes amounted to twelve million dinars the first year, [although] it was also said that sixteen million dinars were collected. The poll tax was imposed on every non-Muslim male who was settled in Egypt and cultivated the land; this amounted to four dinars [per person] annually, in addition to the land tax. That was approved by ʿUmar ibn al-Khaṭṭāb.[77] As for the inhabitants of the Sawād [in Iraq], they were accorded the status of *ahl al-dhimmah*[78] by ʿUmar [ibn al-Khaṭṭāb], who imposed forty dirhams on every adult male among them. This tax amounted to a total of one hundred and eighty-seven million dirhams, [although] it was also said [that it amounted to] one hundred million sixty thousand dirhams.[79] The land tax in the Sawād is still paid in dirhams. If it were not for fear of prolixity, I would enumerate [detailed] accounts that would fill an entire volume and prove that the currency of Egypt has always been based on gold alone. "But over all endowed with knowledge is One, the All-Knowing" [Qur'ān 12:76].

As for silver, it was used in Egypt in [making] jewelry and vessels.

A small quantity of it was sometimes minted for transactions related to daily household needs. The first mention I have come across of [silver] dirhams in Egypt was during the reign of al-Ḥākim bi-Amr Allāh (386–411/996–1021), one of the Fatimid caliphs. Amīr al-Mukhtār ʿIzz al-Mulk Muḥammad ibn ʿUbayd Allāh ibn Aḥmad al-Musabbiḥī (d. 420/1029) wrote in his *al-Tārīkh al-kabīr*:[80]

> In the month of Rabīʿ I (he means the year 397) the quantities of dirhams called *qiṭaʿ* and *muzāyadah* that were in circulation increased. As a result, they were exchanged at the rate of thirty-four dirhams for one dinar. Prices soared, and the affairs of the people became unsettled. Consequently, these dirhams were withdrawn and twenty cases full of new dirhams were brought from the treasury and distributed among the money changers. A decree proclaiming the withdrawal [of the old dirhams] and prohibiting their use in transactions was issued, and anyone who possessed any quantity of them was allowed three days to bring them to the mint. The populace became disturbed and the *qiṭaʿ* and *muzāyadah* dirhams reached the rate of four for one new dirham. It was also decided that the rate of the new dirham would be eighteen for one dinar. Thereupon it was recorded in historical chronicles that silver was minted as a currency in Egypt, and that these [coins] were known among the [different] dirhams as *al-muswaddah*. They were the currency used by the inhabitants of Old Cairo, Cairo, and Alexandria and became known as the currency of Egypt. When I sojourned in Alexandria [I saw that] its inhabitants used this currency only, which they called *wariq*. The caliphs and kings of Egypt adopted different views as to the rate of the dirham, a difference that has not been settled yet.

By "*muswaddah* dirhams" is meant those composed of copper mixed with a small quantity of silver. They were an accepted currency until the Ayyubids became the masters of Egypt and Syria during the reign of Muḥammad al-Kāmil ibn al-ʿĀdil (615–35/1218–38). In Dhū'l-Qaʿdah 622/November 1225, al-Kāmil ordered the mintage of round dirhams and decreed that transactions with the old Egyptian dirhams, known as *wariq* to the Egyptians, were prohibited. Hence people avoided the *wariq* dirhams and refrained from using them; indeed, "the subjects follow the religion of the ruler." The *kāmilī* dirhams, which people still used in my lifetime, consisted of two-thirds silver and one-third copper.[81] [This alloy was obtained by] adding [the weight of] fifty dirhams of copper to one hundred [dirhams] of silver.

The dirhams were so widespread during the reign of the last Ayyubids and during the rule of their Turkish slaves [i.e., the Mamluks] in Egypt that their available quantities far surpassed those of the gold [dinars]. These dirhams became [the currency] with which valuable goods were sold and evaluated, in relation to which prices of goods and costs of labor were generally [calculated], and in which land taxes, rent, and the like were paid. [The weight of] one of these dirhams was eighteen *kharrūbahs*; the *kharrūbah* was equivalent to three *qamḥahs* and the *mithqāl* to twenty-four *kharrūbahs*. Weight standards vary in Egypt and Syria: one hundred Syrian *mithqāls* weigh one and one-fourth *mithqāl* less in Egypt, and this proportion is also true for the dirhams.

[The use of copper] *fulūs* [was adopted] because [of the existence] of goods of insignificant value, which were sold at less than one dirham or at a fraction of it, so people in ancient and recent times needed [a medium of exchange] other than gold and silver, with a value proportional to these goods. However, according to what is known of the history of mankind, this [medium of exchange] has never been called a currency since time immemorial, not even for one hour of a day. It has never been given the status of currency next to gold and silver. Mankind adopted different practices and views with regard to the medium of exchange for these insignificant goods. In Egypt, Syria, Arab and Persian Iraq, Persia, and Byzantium, in early and recent times, the kings of these areas, because of their haughtiness and vehemence, their desire to further their power, their blind ambition and megalomania, adopted copper and minted a small quantity of it in small pieces for the purchase of insignificant goods. These pieces of copper were called *fulūs* by the Arabs. Of these *fulūs*, only a small quantity was ever in circulation, and they were never accorded the status of either of the two currencies. The reason behind their mintage for the first time in Egypt during the reign of [Sultan] al-Kāmil was the following: a woman stopped the *khaṭīb* [preacher] of the mosque of Old Cairo, who then was Abū'l-Ṭāhir al-Maḥallī, and asked him for a legal opinion: "Is it legally permitted to drink water?"

He answered: "O slave of God, what forbids the drinking of water?"

She said: "The sultan has struck these dirhams [i.e., the *kāmilī* dirhams], and I buy a waterskin for half a dirham. I hand the water carrier one dirham, and he gives me back half a dirham in *wariq*. Therefore, it is as if I bought water and half a dirham from him for one dirham."

Abū'l-Ṭāhir disapproved of this. He met the sultan and discussed this matter with him. Hence [the sultan] ordered the minting of *fulūs*.[82]

In Baghdad, the prosperity of which exceeded that of all other cities, bread was used for purchasing most goods. This is supported by what I learned from the letter sent by al-Shaykh al-Ra'īs Abū'l-Qāsim ibn Abī Zayd to one of his brothers, giving him an account of the countries that he visited and of their conditions, following his departure from Egypt and his sojourn in Baghdad sometime after the year 400/1010. He said after a long preamble:

> As for bread, its dough is left exposed at the front of the store and swarms of flies flock to it. It is then baked in ovens filled with smoke. These [flat] loaves are then [taken out] extremely dry [and crisp]. People use them as a medium of exchange in the markets, as if they were dirhams, and consider them a conventional currency. They even have established rules according to which they do not accept those with broken edges or those that are moldy, the same way they do not accept dirhams of mediocre alloy or adulterated dinars. They use the loaves in purchasing most of their food and perfume, and in paying the [fee for the] public bath. This same [bread] is accepted by wine merchants, tavern owners, cloth merchants, and perfumers. A [flat] loaf made out of semolina has an exchange value set higher than that of the other [loaves]. Because of such care and precaution, sixty loaves are sold for one *qīrāṭ*.

I have copied from a manuscript of the work of the *ḥāfiẓ* of the Maghrib, Muḥammad ibn Saʿīd (d. 685/1286), entitled *Janā' al-naḥl wa ḥayā' al-maḥl*[83] and written by his own hand, the following excerpt:

> One of these merchants (he was referring to one of the merchants that he met in Baghdad during his sojourn there) showed me a note written in the script of Cathay. He mentioned that it was made of mulberry leaves and was pliable and soft. If someone in Khanbaliq in China needed five dirhams, he could present this note instead.

The king [of Khanbaliq] imprints his seal on these notes and receives the equivalent [in gold or silver].

A reliable person informed me that he saw the inhabitants of a number of cities in Upper Egypt use *kūdah* [i.e., seashells], called *wadaʿ* in the rest of Egypt, for buying and selling insignificant goods, the same way people in Egypt use *fulūs* nowadays. A trustworthy man informed me that in some regions of India a large number of edibles are purchased with gallnuts and dates. I myself saw the people of Alexandria pay for vegetables, citrus fruit, salad greens, and the like with pieces of bread. These were used [even] for buying bread. This [practice] continued until about 770/1368–69. I have also seen very recently people in the countryside of Egypt purchase many necessities and edibles, using chickens, bran, or flax of inferior quality as means of exchange. All these people have adopted the above-mentioned means to purchase only goods of insignificant value, and no one has used these means of exchange as currency worth hoarding or enabling one to purchase anything of value.

The mintage of *fulūs* continued under al-Kāmil's successors. Accordingly, large quantities of *fulūs* were issued. These came into circulation together with other copper coins that were not officially sanctioned, a fact that caused confusion among the population. Therefore, it fell upon the governors to remedy the situation.

In the beginning, forty-eight [copper] *fulūs* equaled a *kāmilī* dirham. The *fals* was equivalent to four *qiṭaʿ*, each of which was used at the same rate as the *fals* and bought the same type of goods.[84] This gave tremendous relief to the needy people. This situation remained unchanged until after the year 759/1357–58, when one of the provincial officials seduced those holding the reins of power into the love of profit. He secured the mintage of the *fulūs* for himself, in exchange for a sum of money that he agreed to pay. He set the weight of the *fals* at one *mithqāl* and established the rate of the dirham at twenty-four *fulūs*.[85] This measure oppressed the people, upon whom it had a devastating effect. In fact it caused them a great loss: what is now bought for one dirham used to be bought for half a dirham. [Gradually,] people became accustomed to it, since they are "creatures of habit." Despite this, the *fulūs* were not used to purchase anything valuable, but only for daily household expenses, and for [buying] needed vegetables, salad greens, and the like.

When al-ʿĀdil Kitbughā became sultan (694–96/1295–97), the injustices of the vizir Fakhr al-Dīn ʿUmar ibn ʿAbd al-ʿAzīz al-Khalīlī became more frequent, and the members of the sultan's entourage and his mamluks oppressed the population. Because all were greedy in [accumulating] wealth and receiving bribes and protection money, new *fulūs* were minted. These were so light that people avoided them. Hence it was proclaimed in 695/1295–96 that they would be valued by weight and that one *fals* would be the weight of one dirham [of minted copper]. Then it was announced that the exchange rate of one *raṭl* of *fulūs* would be two [silver] dirhams. This was the first time in Egypt that [the value of] the *fulūs* was determined by weight and not by tale.[86]

During the reign of al-Ẓāhir Barqūq (784–801/1382–99), the Ustādār Maḥmud ibn ʿAlī was entrusted with the supervision of the royal treasury. He was greedy for profits and for accumulating wealth. Among his evil deeds was a large increase in the quantities of *fulūs*: he dispatched [his men] to Europe to import copper and secured the mint for himself in exchange for a sum of money. Under his administration *fulūs* were minted at the Cairo mint. He also opened a mint in Alexandria for the purpose of striking *fulūs*. Extremely large quantities of *fulūs* came into the hands of the people and they circulated so widely that they became the dominant currency in the country.[87] [Silver] dirhams then became scarce for two reasons: first, because they ceased altogether to be minted; second, the quantities that were in the possession of the people were melted down to make jewelry because the commanders of the sultan and their retinues had become masters of the art of luxury and prided themselves on wearing sumptuous clothing and magnificent apparel. Despite this, gold was still to be found in circulation, though formerly it had been in the possession of a few people. This was because of the large quantities [of gold dinars] that al-Ẓāhir Barqūq used to bestow upon the commanders of state and the dignitaries, or [gave] to cover the expenses of wars and expeditions, or [distributed] during periods of grain shortages and high prices. Consequently, when al-Ẓāhir [Barqūq] died, there were three currencies: first, [copper] *fulūs*, which had the widest circulation; second, gold [dinars], which were found in lesser proportions than the *fulūs*. As for silver, it became so scarce and unavailable that it ceased to be a currency.[88] Prior [to this], one gold dinar was equivalent to as many as thirty [silver] dirhams. Then the quantity of gold [dinars] that was in the hands of the people increased to the point that even the poorest subjects possessed [these coins]. The circulation of the *fulūs* became extremely widespread and increased greatly, so that all goods and labor costs were calculated mostly in *fulūs*.

One *mithqāl* of gold [i.e., one dinar] was equivalent to one hundred and fifty dirhams [of account]; one silver dirham was equivalent to five dirhams [of account]. One dirham [of account] corresponded to [a weight of] twenty-four [dirhams of copper]. [Therefore, one *raṭl* of *fulūs* was valued at six dirhams of account.][89] In Alexandria one *mithqāl* of gold was equivalent to three hundred dirhams [of account]. This caused a catastrophe that rendered money useless and foodstuffs scarce; at the same time, necessary goods became unavailable because of the variety of currencies. It is feared that if this should continue, the population of this country will be in an unbearable situation: "When God desires evil for a people, there can be no turning back, apart from Him they have no protector" [Qur'ān 13:11].

*SECTION FIVE*

# *A Description of the Population*

Know—May God guard you with His sleepless eye and His fearsome might—that the population of Egypt is divided on the whole into seven categories. This first category embraces those who hold the reins of power. The second [is formed of] the rich merchants and the wealthy who lead a life of affluence. The third [encompasses] the retailers, who are merchants of average means, as are the cloth merchants. This also includes the small shopkeepers. The fourth category embraces the peasants, those who cultivate and plow the land. These are the inhabitants of the villages and of the countryside. The fifth category is made up of those who receive a stipend (*al-fuqarā'*)[1] and includes most legists, students of theology, and most of the *ajnād al-ḥalqah*[2] and the like. The sixth category [corresponds to] the artisans and the salaried persons who possess a skill. The seventh category [consists of] the needy and the paupers; and these are the beggars who live off the [charities of] others.

As for [members of the] first category, those who hold the reins of power, their situation during these ordeals is as they wished it to be. To those who lack any sense of observation and have no knowledge of the conditions of existence, [we say] that the members of this category receive more than they did before these ordeals. This is clear when we consider their revenues from land taxes: for instance, a parcel that was taxed 20,000 [silver] dirhams before these events is now taxed 100,000 dirhams [of account].[3] It is incorrect to assume that they are wealthier than before, for their wealth has decreased if compared with the wealth of their peers [who lived] before [these ordeals]. This becomes clear when [we realize] that anyone who possessed 20,000 dirhams in the past was able to spend whatever he desired or chose, then save whatever amount God permitted, because these were [silver] dirhams and were equivalent to 1,000 *mithqāls* of gold or an approximate amount [at the rate of 20 silver dirhams per *mithqāl*].[4] As for now, he receives 100,000 dirhams [of account], valued at 666 *mithqāls* of gold [at the rate of 5 dirhams of account per silver dirham and of 150 dirhams of account per *mithqāl*],[5] that he spends on his daily needs for meat, vegetables, spices, oil, and the like, as well as on the essential clothing for himself and his family, and on his needs for horses, armor, and the like. Before these ordeals, he used to purchase all these items for [only] 10,000 silver dirhams or a similar amount.[6] If all people, high and low, were affected—although not in an equal fashion—by the difference between current prices and those that had existed before these ordeals, we would have mentioned it. We must touch briefly upon this matter [later on], God willing. If those holding the reins of power were sincere and inspired with rectitude, they would have realized that they were reaping no benefit at all, neither from the increase of the land [taxes] nor from the increase in the rate of gold that is the origin of this distress and the cause of these ordeals. On the contrary, they are incurring a loss. This situation is the result of deceit on the part of their subordinates who have been seeking to obtain whatever they wish. "But the plotting of evil will hem in only the authors thereof" [Qur'ān 35:43].

In the second category, that of the rich merchants and the wealthy who lead a life of affluence, the merchant, for instance, who makes a profit of 3,000 dirhams [of account] from [the sale of] his goods receives it in [copper] *fulūs* or in the amount of 20 *mithqāls* of gold [at the rate of 150 dirhams of account per *mithqāl*],[7] which he spends on necessities, such as food and clothing for himself and his family. If he thought about it, he would realize, for example, that when he used to make a profit of 1,000 [silver] dirhams for selling the same goods, [that sum] would have met his expenses more closely than the [current] 3,000 dirhams [of account].[8] Out of ignorance this miserable person claims that he is making a [higher] profit, while in fact he is losing. He will soon discover the truth and see that expenses have devoured his money and that the variety of currencies has wasted it. [Only] then will he realize that his view is erroneous and that his assumption is false. "And those whom God leads astray, no one can guide" [Qur'ān 13:33].

The [members of the] third category, i.e., the cloth merchants and the small shopkeepers, are living off whatever profit they can make during these ordeals. They content themselves only with larger profits, even though a few hours later in the same day they will spend the amount they have gained on necessities. Indeed, they will be lucky if they do not have to go into debt for the rest of their needs. They will content themselves with what they can afford, according to the old saying:

> I shall be content to bear the brunt of my whims
> and to dispose of them without debt or profit.

As for [the members of] the fourth category, those who cultivate and plow the land, most of them have perished as a result of the calamities of the years that we have mentioned and the successive ordeals caused by the lack of irrigation of the lands. However, a number of them have become wealthy, namely, those persons whose lands were irrigated during the years of drought. From cultivating them, they gained large sums of money with which they have been able to support themselves [during] these times. Some of them have accumulated extensive wealth and enjoyed a life of great affluence. They exceeded their goals and surpassed their expectations: "It is God who gave you want or plenty, and to him shall be your return" [Qur'ān 2:245].

In the fifth category are the majority of legists and students of theology, legal witnesses, most of *ajnād al-ḥalqah*, and those of similar situation who receive a landed property or a stipend from the sultan or from another source: these are either dead or wishing death because of the calamity that has befallen them. For example, if one of them receives 100 dirhams [of account], he gets them in *fulūs* equivalent to two-thirds of one *mithqāl* [of gold] [at the rate of 150 dirhams of account per *mithqāl*]. He will also have to spend all this money on items that were formerly worth only 20 silver dirhams.[9] Hence they all have become afflicted by poverty and privation, and their situation has worsened. "Whatever misfortune happens to you, is because of the things your hands have wrought, and for many of them He grants forgiveness" [Qur'ān 42:30].

The sixth category includes those who possess a skill, salaried persons, porters, servants, stablemen, weavers, masons, unskilled construction workers, and the like. Their wages have increased manyfold. Of this category, only a few have remained, since most have died. Thus, one finds them only after a long search and with great difficulty. "With God rests the end and decision of all affairs" [Qur'ān 22:41].

The seventh category comprises the needy and the poor. Most of them have perished of hunger and cold, so that only a minimal fraction of them remains: "He cannot be questioned for His acts, but they will be questioned for theirs" [Qur'ān 21:23].

*SECTION SIX*

# *Current Prices and Present Ordeals*

Know—May God grant you eternal happiness and felicity—that the currency that has become commonly accepted in Egypt is the *fulūs*. They are used in exchange for all sorts of edibles, all types of drinks, and other common goods. They are accepted for payment of land taxes, the tithe on the profits of merchants, and other imposts due the sultan. They are used to estimate labor costs for all works, whether significant or insignificant. Indeed, the people of Egypt have no currency other than the *fulūs*, with which their wealth is measured. Each *qinṭār* of *fulūs*—a weight equivalent to 100 Egyptian *raṭl*s—corresponds to 600 dirhams [of account].[1] Therefore, one [Egyptian] *raṭl* [of copper *fulūs*, a weight of 144 dirhams, corresponds to 6 dirhams [of account]. One dirham [of account] of these is equivalent to a weight of 2 *ūqīyah*s [of copper *fulūs*], that is, a weight of 24 dirhams.[2] This is an innovation and a calamity of recent origin. It has no root among any community that believes in a revealed religion, nor [does it have] any legal foundation for its implementation. Therefore, its innovator cannot claim that he is imitating the practice of any bygone people, nor can he draw upon the utterance of any human being. He can only cite the resultant disappearance of the joy of life and the vanishing of its gaiety; the ruination of wealth and the annihilation of its embellishments; the reduction of the entire population to privation and the prevalence of poverty and humiliation: "That God might accomplish a matter already enacted" [Qur'ān 8:42].

As far as prices and exchange rates are concerned, one *mithqāl* of gold reached 150 dirhams [of account] in Cairo and its quarters, while in Alexandria the same *mithqāl* reached 300. Coined silver was equivalent, by weight, to 5 dirhams [of account] per dirham.[3]

The price of one *irdabb* of wheat reached 450 dirhams [of account], plus the following charges: 10 for brokerage; 7 for transportation; 3 for sifting; 30 for grinding, all of which add up to 50 dirhams [of account]. For one *irdabb* of wheat, one collects only 5 *waybahs* of pure grain; thus he incurs a loss of one-sixth of the initial volume. Hence, one *irdabb* of refined wheat costs 600 dirhams [of account].[4] The price of one *irdabb* of barley or beans reached over 300 dirhams [of account], of chickpeas 500 and of peas 800. One head of cattle sold for 100 *mithqāls* of gold—the equivalent of 15,000 dirhams [of account].[5] One *raṭl* of raw beef sold for 7 dirhams [of account] and that of mutton for 15.[6] A chicken sold for 100 dirhams [of account], i.e., 20 silver dirhams,[7] while the price of a goose ranged from 200 dirhams [of account] [i.e., 40 silver dirhams] to 50 silver dirhams [i.e., 250 dirhams of account].[8] One sheep sold for more than 2,000 dirhams [of account], and one camel for 7,000. One *qadaḥ* of pumpkin seeds [sold] for 120 dirhams [of account]; one *qadaḥ* of rice for 15; one *irdabb* of carrot seeds for 500; one *qadaḥ* of radish seeds for 150; one *qadaḥ* of turnip seeds for 300; one *qinṭār* of sesame oil for 1,200 dirhams [of account], excluding additional charges. A watermelon in season sold for 20 dirhams [of account], while one *raṭl* of grapes in season sold for 4 dirhams [of account]; one *qinṭār* of gourds sold for 100 dirhams [of account]; one *raṭl* of sugar for up to 70 dirhams [of account]; one *qinṭār* of olive oil for 550 dirhams [of account]. A cotton garment sold for 1,500 dirhams [of account]; one cubit of unbleached linen cloth for slightly over 10 dirhams [of account]; one chicken egg for half a dirham [of account]; one lemon for 3 dirhams [of account] and one *raṭl* of uncarded linen for 20 dirhams [of account].

In Alexandria and Tarūjah one *qadaḥ* of wheat reached 40 dirhams of account and that of barley 30. One *raṭl* of bread reached 10 dirhams of account; one *raṭl* of mutton 60; a medium-size chicken slightly over 50 dirhams [of account]; one chicken egg 2 dirhams [of account]; and one *ūqīyah* of oil 4 dirhams [of account].

In Cairo one *qadaḥ* of purslane seeds reached 60 to 70 dirhams [of account]; one *raṭl* of pears over 50 dirhams [of account]; one *qinṭār* of willow leaves 30,000 dirhams [of account]; one *qinṭār* of woodwaxen 15,000 dirhams [of account]; one water-lily 1 dirham [of account];

one cucumber 1½ dirhams [of account] and one pullet 37 dirhams [of account]. Two cotton cloaks that were already washed and were part of an inheritance were sold for 2,240 dirhams [of account].[9] Prices of other goods were equally high.

Anyone who considers these prices in light of the rate of gold and silver will realize that they have increased only slightly,[10] but if he considers them in relation to the abundance of the *fulūs* that has afflicted the people, he will find this is a frightening abomination that is too odious to mention. This is the cause of the deteriorating situation and worsening conditions. It has led the population to privation and extinction and has left the country on the verge of ruin and naught: "God does whatsoever He desires" [Qur'ān 2:253].

*SECTION SEVEN*

# *The Means to Eradicate This Disease*

Since the causes of these ordeals have been explained already, it remains—for those whose minds God has cleared and removed the veil of error from their sight—to know the ways to eradicate these calamities that have befallen the people, so that their situation would return to what it was previously. We shall say [in this context]: Know—May God guide you to your own righteousness and inspire you to follow the straight paths of your fellow humans—that the currencies that are legally, logically, and customarily acceptable are only those of gold and silver, and that any other [metal] is unsuitable as a currency. By the same token, the situation of the people cannot be sound unless they are obliged to follow the natural and legal course in this regard [i.e., the currency], namely, that they should deal exclusively with gold and silver for pricing goods and estimating labor costs. This is an easy matter for those for whom God has smoothed the way: the price of 100 dirhams of pure and unadulterated silver is 6 *mithqāls*[1] of gold, to which is added ¼ dinar at current prices to be paid to the mint as a fee to cover the price of copper [used in the alloy], the taxes due the sultan, the cost of firewood, the wages of workers, and the like. Once minted, [a weight of 100 dirhams of pure silver] becomes 150 silver dirhams in coins at a cost of 6¼ *mithqāls*[2] of gold, as has been mentioned above. Hence the exchange rate for one *mithqāl* of minted gold is 24 silver dirhams in coins.[3] The same *mithqāl* of gold is equivalent nowadays in minted copper, called *fulūs*, to 23⅓ *raṭls*, [each *raṭl* is worth 6 dirhams of account, and] each *mithqāl* is calculated by the [present] administration to be the equivalent of 140 dirhams of account: this is the exchange rate of the dinar in dirhams of account at this time.[4]

Whenever God guides the person who is entrusted with the destiny of His subjects to the right path, he should respect the gold-silver ratio when striking silver currency. This will lead to an end to this general decay and to a return of prices and costs of labor to the level that existed prior to these ordeals, God willing. As already mentioned, it is clear that one *mithqāl* of gold will be exchanged for 24 silver dirham coins, and that 24 silver dirhams are exchanged for 23⅓ *raṭls* of *fulūs*, and each silver dirham is equivalent to [a weight of] 140 dirhams in copper coins,[5] which will be spent for purchasing insignificant goods and for [daily] household expenses. This will greatly benefit the population and [cause] prices to drop. Shortly thereafter, people will rush to the mint and bring forth such large quantities of [hoarded] silver that it will surpass the capacity of the mint. Consequently, the situation will improve, conditions will ease, wealth will be abundant, and prosperity will increase infinitely. "God knows and you know not" [Qur'ān 2:216].

## *SECTION EIGHT*

# *The Merits of This Proposal*

Know—May God embellish you with virtues, and protect you from the disgraces of vices—that whoever is governed by tradition, enslaved by custom, imprisoned by his own frivolity to the point that he knows only what he is familiar with does not aspire to the knowledge of what is hidden from him and does not conceive of anything beyond his perception. He will say: "It is futile for you to tire your mind, prolong your effort, contradict your own opinion, and surpass the achievements of others, when, despite extended effort, it is a foregone conclusion that gold [dinars] and [copper] *fulūs* will keep the same ratio with no change whatsoever, and without the least increase or decrease in their respective values."

We shall answer: "God speaks the truth when He says: 'Are those equal—those who know and those who know not?' " [Qur'ān 39:9]. It is beyond doubt that our above-mentioned [proposal] contains two great advantages: first, with regard to prices and goods, the conditions of the populace will return to what they were before these ordeals. Second, the gold [dinars] and the [copper] *fulūs* that are now in the hands of the people and constitute the most common currencies nowadays will retain their value without any increase or decrease. In addition, this will allow a return to the conditions of prosperity and low prices that prevailed prior to those ordeals.

I swear by my life that anyone gifted with a minimal share of judgment and cognizance can neither ignore the value of these two great advantages nor deny the soundness of these two great benefits, unless he intends to betray his pledge to God and his loyalty toward

Him, with regard to the protection of the welfare of [His] servants by causing mischief and destroying the people: "God guides not the guile of the treacherous" [Qur'ān 12:52]. I say, seeking God's help, He is indeed the [only] Helper:

> I did not miss the support of your tongue
> since I lack the support of your hand.

Know—May God guide you to lend your ear to the truth and inspire you to advise His creatures—that it has been proved through the preceding [arguments] that the decaying [economic] conditions are the result of malfeasance rather than the increase in prices. If God would guide those whom He has entrusted with the welfare of His servants to reinstate gold as the exclusive basis for transactions as it was previously—to link the value of goods and of all [types of] work either to the dinar or to minted silver that would later be adopted as currency and thereby reinstate the silver dirham as [the unit] for measuring the price of goods and the cost of labor—this would lead to the succor of the community, the amelioration of the [general] situation, and the checking of the decay that heralds destruction.

It is clear that if currency regained its previous status, anyone who received money, whether from land tax, rent from a property, a salary from the sultan, income from a religious endowment, or wages, would receive it in gold or in silver, according to whatever the officials deemed appropriate, and would spend it on his needs for food, drink, clothing, and other necessities. Despite the unstable [economic] conditions through which we are now living, if [my proposal] were put into practice, anyone who received any money in these two currencies would not feel cheated at all. This is because prices based on the [silver] dirham and the [gold] dinar would be—with few exceptions—hardly different from those with which we were familiar before these ordeals. Increases in the prices of those few exceptions would be caused by either of the following: first, the poor judgment and ignorance of the officials vested with the supervision of [economic] matters; this is the likeliest [cause]. Second, a disaster that strikes a natural product and causes its scarcity: such was the case with beef following the sweeping death that hit cattle in 808/1405,[1] and, to a lesser degree, the case of sugar following the reduced planting of sugarcane and the [subsequently] diminished quantities that were refined in the years 807/1404–5 and 808/1405–6.[2]

Nevertheless, had there been officials who were bestowed with [divine] guidance and inspired with reason, the situation would have been different from that of the present ordeals. The money that anyone now receives from land tax or any other source consists instead of [copper] *fulūs*, which are, as already mentioned, weighed by the *raṭl*, while gold, silver, and all goods such as foodstuffs, clothing, and the like have become luxuries. Land taxes are also calculated in dirhams of account. Hence it is said: "Each dinar is [worth] such-and-such [a number of] dirhams of account, and each silver dirham is [equivalent to] such-and-such [a number of] dirhams of account. [Prices of] clothing and all other goods, as well as all taxes in the country, are [calculated] in such-and-such [a number of] dirhams of account. Of necessity any sentient being, even he whose ignorance reduces him to stupidity, knows that money comes mainly from land taxes, the value of goods sold or work performed, charity, and donations. This money must be spent on necessities and other human needs, either in an economical manner or with extravagance and waste. If one obtains a certain amount of these *fulūs* [i.e., dirhams of account] and spends it to meet a personal need, he will realize that he has been outrageously cheated.

If 60,000 dirhams of account reach the sultan's treasury, the official responsible for that bureau will receive the money in the form of 100 *qinṭārs* of [copper] *fulūs* [at the rate of 6 dirhams of account per *raṭl*],[3] or a proportional amount of gold. But if this sum of money is channeled to the vizirate and the vizir decides to purchase with these 60,000 dirhams of account—equivalent to [the weight of] 100 *qinṭārs* of [copper] *fulūs* [coins] or of a proportional amount of gold—the state meat rations that are needed, he can buy 66⅔ *qinṭārs*[4] of meat at 900 dirhams the *qinṭār*.[5] Prior to the present ordeals, 60,000 [silver] dirhams were sufficient to purchase 1,500 *qinṭārs* of meat, at 40 [silver] dirhams the *qinṭār*.[6] Indeed, the exorbitant difference between the first [price] and the second is a despicable crime!

If one considers all the state revenues and expenditures, then looks into the wealth of the commanders, and then further to the state officials of lower ranks, such as the vizirs, judges, chief secretaries, wealthy merchants, and other dignitaries, one finds, for instance, a middle-class person with a monthly income of 300 dirhams (calculated on the basis of 10 dirhams per day). If, prior to the present ordeals, he wanted to provide for his family's needs, he could buy, for example, with these 10 [silver] dirhams 3 *raṭl*s of mutton for 2 [silver] dirhams,[7] the necessary seasonings for 2 [silver] dirhams, and for 4 [silver] dirhams he [could] purchase food for his children, family, and servants, if any. Today he receives 10 dirhams of account, a weight of 20 ūqīyahs [of copper *fulūs*].[8] If he wishes to buy 3 *raṭl*s of meat, he will pay 27 dirhams of account.[9] He will also spend 10 dirhams of account for the necessary seasonings and other ingredients to prepare an average meal. Hence a meal for his children and family will cost him no less than 37 dirhams of account. How then can a person whose income is 10 [dirhams of account] spend 37 for one meal? This does not include his needs for oil, water, rent, animal fodder, clothing, and other necessities, the list of which is too long to mention, and about which it will suffice to state that they are commonly known to everyone. This is indeed the cause of the end of wealth in Egypt and the ruination of its [economic] conditions. Accordingly, prosperity has declined and poverty and need have conquered the population. "Yet, had your Lord willed, they would never have done it" [Qur'ān 6:112].

Had God guided those whom He entrusted with the welfare of [His] servants to restore the currency to what it was formerly, anyone who would receive these 10 dirhams would receive them in silver and would know that—even at current prices—they would be sufficient [not only] to meet his needs but even to exceed them. In fact, the meal that we have estimated at 37 dirhams of account would now cost 6 1/6 silver dirhams. This is calculated according to the rate that 6 dirhams of account, a weight of 12 *ūqīyahs* [i.e., one *raṭl*], are worth one silver dirham.[10] Therefore, the population has not been afflicted by inflation, but by malfeasance on the part of the rulers, so that God eliminated the wealth of the people and afflicted them with poverty and humiliation, as a punishment "Because of the meed that the hands of men have earned, that God may give them a taste of some of their deeds: in order that they may turn back from Evil" [Qur'ān 30:41].

These two examples are sufficient for those from whose hearts God has eliminated greed and guided them to succor the people and make the country flourish: "With God is the decision, in the past and in the future" [Qur'ān 30:4].

## COLOPHON

The author—May God have mercy upon him—said: "It was possible for me to compose and revise this treatise in a single night of the month of Muḥarram in the year 808/July 1405. God guides whom He wishes. Praise be to God alone, and Peace be upon the Prophet, after whom no other prophet will come."

## APPENDIX ONE

# *Measures, Weights, and Currency*

### MEASURES OF CAPACITY

| | |
|---|---|
| *Baṭṭah* or *Buṭṭah* | = 1½ *waybahs* = ¼ *irdabb* = 24 *qadaḥs*. *Furāt*, 9:428.<br>1 *baṭṭah* of flour weighs 50 *raṭls*. *Sulūk*, 3:818, 1134; *Nuzhat*, 2:180. |
| *Ghirārah* | Sack. Equals 1½ *irdabbs*. Ibn Mammātī, *Qawānīn*, p. 365.<br>In Damascus = 3 *irdabbs* of Cairo. 1 *ghirārah* of Damascus = 2 *ghirārahs* of Cairo. *Sulūk*, 3:1121. |
| *Ḥamlah* or *Ḥiml* | Load. Equivalent to 2 *tallīses* = 6 *baṭṭahs* = 1½ *irdabbs* = 9 *waybahs*. *Sulūk*, 3:826.<br>1 *ḥamlah* of flour weighs 300 *raṭls*. *Sulūk*, 3:826, 982; Ibn Mammātī, *Qawānīn*, p. 365. |
| *Irdabb* | = 96 *qadaḥs* = 6 *waybahs* = 4 *baṭṭahs* = ⅔ *ḥamlah* = 24 *rubʿs*. *Ṣubḥ*, 3:445. |
| *Mudd* | = ¼ *ṣāʿ* = 1/96 *irdabb*. De Sacy, *Poids*, p. 160.<br>In Damascus = 4 *qadaḥs*. *Sulūk*, 3:1048.<br>1 *mudd* of grain weighs 1⅓ *raṭls*. de Sacy, *Poids*, pp. 159–60, 162–63, 167.<br>In nineteenth-century Egypt = 1.04279 liters. Mahmoud Bey in Sauvaire, *JA*, 8th series, 8 (1886): 148–49.<br>It seems that the *mudd* is equivalent to the *qadaḥ*; see *ṣāʿ*. |
| *Qadaḥ* | Cup. Equals 1/96 *irdabb* = 1/16 *waybah*. *Ṣubḥ*, 3:445. |
| *Qafīz* | = 9 *ṣāʿs* = 36 *mudds*. Sauvaire, *JA*, 8th series, 7 (1886): 125. |
| *Quffah* | Basket. 1 *quffah* of *fulūs* weighs 115 *raṭls*. *Sulūk*, 3:1098. |

| | |
|---|---|
| | 1 *quffah* of *fulūs* weighs between 112 and 120 *raṭls*. *Sulūk*, 3:1132. |
| *Ṣāʿ* | = 4 *mudds* = 1/24 *irdabb*. De Sacy, *Poids*, p. 160; Sauvaire, *JA*, 8th series, 7 (1886): 140. |
| | Therefore, the *ṣāʿ* is equivalent to 4 *qadaḥs*. |
| *Tallīs* or *Tillīs* | = 1/2 *ḥamlah* = 3 *baṭṭahs* = 3/4 *irdabb*. |
| | One *tallīs* of flour weighs 150 *raṭls*. Ibn Mammātī, *Qawānīn*, p. 365. |

## MEASURES OF LENGTH

| | |
|---|---|
| *Dhirāʿ* | Cubit. Equals 24 *iṣbaʿ*s. *Sulūk*, 3:1115; *Furāt*, 9:412 |
| | Average *dhirāʿ* of the Nilometer = 0.541 meters. |
| | Common *dhirāʿ* = 0.462 meters. |
| | For a listing of other types of cubits, see Popper, *Systematic Notes*, 2:34–36. |
| *Iṣbaʿ* | Finger. Equals 1/24 *dhirāʿ* [cubit]. *Furāt*, 9:412; *Sulūk*, 3:1115. |
| | Average *iṣbaʿ* of the Nilometer = 0.0225 meters. |
| | Common *iṣbaʿ* = 0.01925 meters. |

## MEASURES OF AREA

| | |
|---|---|
| *Faddān* | Common measure of land in Egypt to the present. = 400 sq *qaṣabahs* of land = 20 × 20 *qaṣabahs* = 14,400 sq cubits = 1.35 acres. Sauvaire, *JA*, 8th series, 8 (1886): 519; Popper, *Systematic Notes*, 2:37. |
| *Jarīb* | A measure of Iraq. Equals 60 × 60 cubits = 3,600 sq cubits = 10 × 10 *qaṣabahs* = approximately 1/4 Egyptian *faddān* or 1/3 acre. Al-Māwardī, in Sauvaire, *JA*, 8th series, 8 (1886): 486. |

## MEASURES OF WEIGHT

| | |
|---|---|
| *Dānaq* or *Dāniq* | = 1/6 legal dirham. *Ighāthah*, pp. 50, 56–57. |
| | One legal *dānaq* = 8 2/5 *ḥabbah*. *Ighāthah*, pp. 56–57; *Nuqūd*, p. 5. |

| | |
|---|---|
| | It is generally considered to weigh 10 *ḥabbahs*. G. C. Miles, "Dirham," *EI*[2], 2:319–20. |
| Dirham [Legal dirham] | = 6 *dānaqs* = 50.4 *ḥabbahs*. *Ighāthah*, p. 56. |
| | = 50 to 60 *ḥabbahs*. G. C. Miles, "Dirham," *EI*[2], 2:319–20. |
| | = 7/10 *mithqāl*: legal standard weight used as the basis for coinage. *Ighāthah*, p. 56. |
| | = 2.975 g. Ph. Grierson, "The Monetary Reforms of ʿAbd al-Malik: Their Metrological Basis and Their Financial Repercussions," *JESHO* 3 (1960): 254. |
| [Dirham weight] | Estimated at 3.0898 g by the French Commission of 1845, an estimate accepted by Sauvaire. Sauvaire, *JA*, 8th series, 4 (1884): 317. |
| | Commonly accepted as weighing 3.186 g. Edward Zambaur, "Dirham," *EI*, 1:978–79. |
| *Ḥabbah* | Grain. Average-sized, unshelled grain of barley, of which the extremities are cut. *Ighāthah*, p. 50. |
| | Equivalent to the weight of 100 grains of mustard seeds (*khardal*). *Ighāthah*, p. 50. |
| | = 1/48 to 1/72 *mithqāl*, but generally accepted as 1/60 *mithqāl* = 1/10 *dānaq*. Edward Zambaur, "Ḥabba," *EI*[2], 3:10–11. |
| *Khardal* | Mustard. 100 mustard seeds = 1 *ḥabbah*. *Ighāthah*, p. 50. |
| *Kharrūbah* | Carob seed. In Ayyubid times = 1/18 dirham. 3 *qamḥahs* = 1/24 *mithqāl*. *Ighāthah*, p. 66; Sauvaire, *JA*, 8th series, 3 (1884): 420. |
| *Mithqāl* | Legal weight of the dinar. See Dinar. |
| *Nawāt* | In pre-Islamic times = 5 dirhams = 1/8 *ūqīyah* of the time. *Ighāthah*, p. 49; *Nuqūd*, p. 4. |
| *Nish* | In pre-Islamic times = 1/2 *ūqīyah* = 20 dirhams of the time. *Nuqūd*, p. 4; de Sacy, *Poids*, p. 158. |
| *Qamḥah* | One grain of wheat. Equals 1/48 dirham (in Cairo). Sauvaire, *JA*, 8th series, 3 (1884): 429, note 2. |
| | = 1/3 *kharrūbah* (in Ayyubid times). *Ighāthah*, p. 66. |

*Qinṭār* — Quintal. Equals 100 *raṭls* = 1,200 *ūqīyahs* in Cairo. *Ṣubḥ*, 3:445; *Sulūk*, 3:1112; *Ighāthah*, p. 76.

*Qīrāṭ* — Carat. Equivalent to 1/24 of a measure. A weight proportional to that of the legal dirham to calculate the weight of coins. See Dinar. Edward Zambaur, "Ḳirāṭ," *EI*, 2:1023–24.

*Raṭl, Riṭl*, or *Ruṭl* — Pound. In pre-Islamic times = 12 *ūqīyahs* = 480 dirhams of the time. *Ighāthah*, p. 49.

In Cairo = 12 *ūqīyahs* = 144 dirhams. *Ighāthah*, pp. 49, 76; *Ṣubḥ*, 3:445.

1 *raṭl* of pepper = 128 dirhams. de Sacy, *Poids*, p. 163.

In Damascus = 12 *ūqīyahs* = 600 dirhams. *Ighāthah*, p. 49.

*Ūqīyah* — Ounce. In pre-Islamic times = 40 dirhams of the time. *Ighāthah*, p. 49.

In Cairo = 12 dirhams. *Ighāthah*, p. 49; *Ṣubḥ*, 3:445.

In Damascus = 50 dirhams. *Ighāthah*, p. 49.

## CURRENCY

Dinar or *Mithqāl* — The *mithqāl* is the legal weight of the gold dinar. The weight of the *mithqāl* is 10/7 of that of the legal dirham.

One dinar = 20 *qīrāṭs*. One dinar = 4.25 g. *Ighāthah*, p. 48; Ph. Grierson, "The Monetary Reforms of ʿAbd al-Malik"; G. C. Miles, "Dirham," $EI^2$, 2:319–20.

Silver Dirham — The legal weight of the silver dirham is 7/10 that of the dinar and is equal to 14 *qīrāṭs*. This weight is 2.975 g. This legal weight is referred to in Arabic as *dirham al-kayl*, the dirham of measurements. Same sources as above, plus de Sacy, *Poids*, pp. 148–49, 162–63; John Walker, *Arab-Sassanian Coins*, pp. cxlvii–cxlviii.

Dirham of Account — Arabic: *dirham fulūs*. A unit of account, which was used to calculate the respective value of existing coins and into which they were converted. This unit was introduced following the collapse of the gold-silver monetary system of the Mamluks due to the scarcity of silver. References to this money of account began to appear in 1401, although the official decision to adopt it as the basis of the monetary system was taken almost three years later, in 1403. Until 824/1421, the *raṭl* of *fulūs* remained constant at 6 dirhams of account. *Ighāthah*, pp. 76, 80–81; Popper, *Systematic Notes*, 2:61, refers to it as "trade dirham."

*Fulūs* — Singular: *fals*. These were copper coins used primarily as small change. During the rule of the Ayyubid al-Kāmil (615–35/1218–38), 1 *kāmilī* silver dirham equaled 48 *fulūs* coins. According to al-Maqrīzī, *fulūs* weighing 1 dirham each were used by weight for the first time in 695/1295–6 during the rule of Kitbughā (694–96/1295–97) at the rate of 2 silver dirhams per *raṭl* of *fulūs*. Between 650/1252 and 695/1295–96, 1 copper *fals* weighed 1 *mithqāl*, and 24 were exchanged for 1 silver dirham.

A dramatic increase in the circulation of *fulūs* took place during the reign of Barqūq (784–801/1382–99) when the Ustādār Maḥmūd ibn ʿAlī was in charge of the mint of Alexandria. The scarcity of silver led to the wide circulation of *fulūs*, a typical monetary feature of the rule of the Circassian Mamluks. The dirham of account became a theoretical unit that allowed the conversion of gold and silver coins into dirhams of *fulūs* and vice versa. The weight of the *fals* coin varied and seems to have decreased in the years 1403 to 1406 to between ⅕ and ¼ dirham weight (*Sulūk*, 3:1132; *Ighāthah*, p. 77). W. Popper (*Systematic Notes*, 2:61) is in error when he states that the *fals* weighs 4 dirhams. This error is due to his mistake in translating *naqd* as "coins" when al-Maqrīzī meant "value," referring to the "dirhams of account." *Ighāthah*, p. 76–77, 80–81; *Nuqūd*, pp. 39–41; *Sulūk*, 3:1132; *Ṣubḥ*, 3:443; Popper, *Systematic Notes*, 2:60–61.

*Sikkah* — Originally, this meant the die with which dinars and dirhams were minted. It became synonymous with "coinage." Abū'l-Ḥasan ʿAlī ibn Yūsuf al-Ḥakīm, *al-Dawḥah al-mushtabikah fī ḍawābiṭ dār al-sikkah*, ed. Ḥusayn Mu'nis (Madrid: Maʿhad al-dirāsāt al-islāmīyah, 1960), p. 40; Ibn Khaldūn, *The Muqaddimah*, tr. Franz Rosenthal, 2:54; al-Māwardī, *al-Aḥkām al-sulṭānīyah*, p. 155.

## Types of dinars mentioned in the text

*Mayyāl* — *Mayyālah* (tilting) dinars were issued by the Umayyad caliph ʿAbd al-Malik ibn Marwān (65–86/685–705) and weighed slightly more than the legal weight of 1 *mithqāl*: 100 *mayyālah* dinars = 102 *mithqāl*s. *Ighāthah*, p. 54; de Sacy, *Poids*, p. 21.

*Qayṣarī* or *Hiraqlī* — Translated here as "imperial dinars," but literally means Caesarean or Heraclean. In *Ighāthah*, p. 48, al-Maqrīzī mentions *al-danānīr al-qayṣarīyah* (the Caesarean dinars), while in de Sacy, *Poids*, p. 155, he mentions *al-danānīr al-hiraqlah* (the Heraclean dinars), probably a reference to the Byzantine emperor Heraclius (610–41). He probably meant the Byzantine gold *solidus*.

## Types of dirhams mentioned in the text

*Abyaḍ* — *Al-darāhim al-bīḍ* (white dirhams). These were the dirhams whose content in silver was equivalent or superior to ⅔, but they do not form a separate type. This was the case, according to al-Maqrīzī, of the dirhams issued by al-Ḥajjāj, the governor of Iraq under the Umayyad caliph ʿAbd al-Malik ibn Marwān. *Ighāthah*, p. 57; de Sacy, *Monnoies*, p. 25; Sauvaire, *JA*, 7th series, 15 (1880): 270–71.

*Baghlī* — Dirhams of "full weight" from Persia. Although al-Maqrīzī is uncertain as to their weight when he states that they weighed either 4 or 8 *dānaq*s, it seems that their weight was the latter. *Nuqūd*, p. 3 (weight: 1 *mithqāl*); *Ighāthah*, p. 49 (either 4 or 8 *dānaq*s); de Sacy, *Poids*, p. 146 (before the reform of ʿAbd al-Malik, their weight was double that of the dirham); Walker, *Arab-Sassanian Coins*, p. cxlviii.

*Hāshimī* — A term applied to Abbasid coinage in general.

*Hubayrī* — Issued by ʿUmar ibn Hubayrah, governor of Iraq during the rule of Yazīd ibn ʿAbd al-Malik (101–5/720–24). According to al-Maqrīzī, they weighed 6 *dānaqs*. *Ighāthah*, p. 58; *Nuqūd*, p. 16.

*Jawāz* — A general term applied to dirhams meeting the legal weight of 7⁄10 *mithqāl*. *Ighāthah*, p. 50; *Nuqūd*, p. 3.

*Jawrafī* — Also mentioned as *jawraqī* in other works by al-Maqrīzī. These dirhams are supposed to be of Persian origin but are impossible to identify. Al-Maqrīzī states that they weighed 4½ *dānaqs*. *Ighāthah*, p. 50.

*Kāmilī* — Issued by the Ayyubid al-Kāmil (615–35/1218–38), with a silver content of ⅓. For some unknown reasons, *kāmilī* was used to refer to silver coinage down to al-Maqrīzī's time. *Ighāthah*, pp. 65–66; Sauvaire, *JA*, 7th series, 19 (1882): 29–32; Balog, "History of the Dirhem," seems unaware of the two meanings of *kāmilī*. See also Michael L. Bates, "Crusader Coinage with Arabic Inscriptions," p. 433, note 36.

*Khālidī* — Struck at Wāsiṭ in 106/725–26 by Khālid ibn ʿAbd Allāh al-Qasrī during the rule of Hishām ibn ʿAbd al-Malik (105–25/724–43). They weighed 7 *dānaqs* and were of finest quality. *Ighāthah*, p. 58.

*Makrūh* — *Al-darāhim al-makrūhah* (the reprobate dirhams), struck by al-Ḥajjāj. So called because a number of Qur'ān readers objected to the Qur'ānic verse inscribed on them and abhorred touching them. *Ighāthah*, p. 57.

*Muswadd* — *Al-darāhim al-muswaddah* (the blackish dirhams) do not correspond to any specific coin but refer to dirhams containing ⅓ silver or less. Some dirhams of the Mamluk period, which belong to this category, were analyzed by Balog and contain 27 to 30 percent silver. *Ṣubḥ*, 3:443; Sauvaire, *JA*, 7th series, 15 (1880): 275–76; Balog, *Coinage of the Mamluk Sultans*, p. 40.

*Sumayrī* — According to al-Maqrīzī, the *sumayrī* dirhams were the first dirhams issued by the Umayyad caliph ʿAbd al-Malik ibn Marwān and minted by a Jew by the name of Sumayr. *Ighāthah*, pp. 54–56; Walker, *Arab-Sassanian Coins*, p. cxlix.

*Ṭabarī* — According to al-Maqrīzī, the *ṭabarī* dirhams were of Persian-Sasanian origin and minted in Tabaristan. They weighed either 8 or 4 *dānaq*s, but the latter weight seems more probable. Numismatic evidence shows that this is erroneous, since the *ṭabarī* half-dirham was issued by the Ispahbad of Tabaristan in the eighth century. Michael Bates, "Arab-Sasanian Coins"; *Ighāthah*, p. 49; *Nuqūd*, pp. 4–5; Walker, *Arab-Sassanian Coins*, p. cxlviii.

*Wāfī* — The *wāfī* dirhams (dirhams of full weight) do not constitute a separate type of coins but are those meeting or exceeding the legal weight of the dirham. *Nuqūd*, p. 3; Sauvaire, *JA*, 7th series, 19 (1882): 66–67.

*Wariq* — Dirhams of low silver content. This is also a generic term for silver. Ibn Mammātī, *Qawānīn*, pp. 310–11.

## *Miscellaneous*

*Mubahraj* — *Mubahrajah, maghshūshah, zughl*, and *zuyūf* are adjectives used to denote adulterated or "bad" dirhams. Sauvaire, *JA*, 7th series, 15 (1880): 455–57; 19 (1882): 60–61.

*Muzāyadah* — Same as *qiṭa*ᶜ.

*Nuqrah* — This originally meant "ingot" but came to be synonymous with silver. Sauvaire, *JA*, 7th series, 19 (1882): 61–64.

*Qiṭa*ᶜ — These were fractions of the dirham obtained by clipping. Sauvaire, *JA*, 7th series, 19 (1882): 61–64.

## APPENDIX TWO

# Exchange Rates

| Date | Currency | Exchange Rate | Source |
|---|---|---|---|
| 786/1384–85 | 1 dinar | 20 dirhams | *Inbā'*, 1:295 |
| 787/1385–86 | 1 dinar | 20 dirh. | Ibid., p. 302 |
| 788/1386 | 1 dinar | 20 dirh. | Ibid., p. 322 |
| | 1 dinar | 24 dirh. | *Sulūk*, 3:550 |
| Dhū'l-Q 788/ Nov.–Dec. 1386 | 1 dinar | 23¼ dirh. | Ibid., p. 553; *Nuzhat*, 1:143[a] |
| 789/1387–88 | 1 dinar | 25 dirh. | *Inbā'*, 1:337 |
| 790/1388 | 1 dinar | 25 dirh. | Ibid., pp. 353–54 |
| 796/1393–94 | 1 dinar | 25 dirh. | *Inbā'*, 1:475 |
| 9 Rab II 796/ 11 Feb. 1394 | 1 dinar | 26½ dirh. | *Sulūk*, 3:807 |
| 798/1395–96 | 1 dinar | 25 dirh. | *Inbā'*, 1:510 |
| Muḥ 801/ Sept.–Oct. 1398 | 1 dinar | 31 dirh. | *Sulūk*, p. 916 |
| 1 Ram 801/ 7 May 1399 | 1 dinar | 32 dirh. | *Nuzhat*, 1:488 |
| 11 Shaw 801/ 16 June 1399 | 1 dinar | 30 dirh. | *Inbā'*, 2:51 |
| | 1 ducat | 24 dirh. | Ibid. |
| | 1 dinar | 36 dirh. | Ibid.[b] |
| | 1 ducat | 30 dirh. | Ibid.; *Nuzhat*, 1:493[b] |
| 801/1398–99 | 1 dinar | 31–33 dirh. | *Inbā'*, 2:37 |

Note: Compare this table with Eliyahu Ashtor, *Les métaux précieux*, p. 49. In the exchange rate column the symbol – following the amount indicates "and/or less."

[a]This rate was given for a forced purchase of wheat.

[b]New official rate.

| Date | Currency | Exchange Rate | Source |
|---|---|---|---|
| Second half of 801/ Mar.–Sept. 1399 | 1 dinar | 25 dirh. | Ibid., p. 52[c] |
| | 1 ducat | 20 dirh. | Ibid. |
| 15 Shaw 801/ 20 June 1399 | 1 dinar | 23 dirh. | *Sulūk*, 3:964[d] |
| 16 Shaw 801/ 21 June 1399 | 1 dinar | 30 dirh. | Ibid.[e] |
| 8 Dhū'l-Q 801/ 12 July 1399 | 1 dinar | 30 dirh. | Ibid., p. 967; *Inbā'*, 2:52 |
| | 1 ducat | 28 dirh. | Ibid.; *Sulūk*, 3:967 |
| 14 Dhū'l-Q 801/ 18 July 1399 | 1 dinar | 30 dirh. | Ibid., p. 968 |
| | 1 ducat | 28 dirh. | Ibid. |
| Muḥ 802/ Sept.–Oct. 1399 | 1 dinar | 30 dirh. | Ibid., p. 977 |
| | 1 ducat | 25 dirh. | Ibid. |
| Muḥ 803/ Aug.–Sept. 1400 | 1 dinar | 30 dirh. | Ibid., p. 1027. |
| | 1 ducat | 29 dirh. | Ibid. |
| Ram 803/ Apr.–May 1401 | 1 ducat | 39 dirhams of account | *Sulūk*, 3:1059[f] |
| | 1 ducat | 38 dirh. a. | Ibid. |
| | 1 ducat | 35 dirh. a. | Ibid. |
| | 1 dinar | 38 – dirh. a. | Ibid. |
| End 803/ Mid-1401 | 1 dinar | 40 dirh. a. | Ibid., p. 1070 |
| | 1 ducat | 37 dirh. a. | Ibid. |
| 1 Muḥ 804/ 11 Aug. 1401 | 1 dinar | 36 dirh. a. | Ibid., p. 1076 |
| | 1 ducat | 34 dirh. a. | Ibid. |
| Muḥ 805/ Aug. 1402 | 1 dinar | 50 dirh. a. | Ibid., p. 1091 |
| | 1 ducat | 47 dirh. a | Ibid. |

[c]The rate decreased due to the abundance of gold, caused by the distribution of stipends among the soldiers in gold dinars.
[d]Rate at Sultan Barqūq's death.
[e]Rate on the day after Sultan Barqūq's death.
[f]Official rate.

| Date | Currency | Exchange Rate | Source |
|---|---|---|---|
| 3 Jum II 805/ 29 Dec. 1402 | 1 dinar | 65 dirh. a. | Ibid., p. 1098; *Nuzhat*, 2:158 |
| | 1 ducat | 60 dirh. a. | Ibid.; *Sulūk*, 3:1098 |
| Shaw 805/ Apr.–May. 1403 | 1 dinar | 60 dirh. a. | Ibid., p. 1104; *Inbā'*, 2:233[g] |
| | 1 ducat | 45 dirh. a. | Ibid.; *Sulūk*, 3:1104[g] |
| Beg. Muḥ 806/ 21 July 1403 | 1 dinar | 60 dirh. a. | Ibid., p. 1111 |
| | 1 ducat | 45 dirh. a. | Ibid. |
| Beg. Ṣaf 806/ Aug. 1403 | 1 dinar | 64 dirh. a. | Ibid., p. 1115; *Nuzhat*, 2:178 |
| | 1 ducat | 50+ dirh. a. | Ibid.; *Sulūk*, 3:1115 |
| Rab I 806/ Sept.–Oct. 1403 | 1 dinar | 70 dirh. a. | Ibid., p. 1116 |
| | 1 ducat | 60 dirh. a. | Ibid. |
| 19 Rab II 806/ 5 Nov. 1403 | 1 dinar | 72 dirh. a. | *Nuzhat*, 2:182 |
| Jum I 806/ Nov.–Dec. 1403 | 1 dinar | 73 dirh. a. | Ibid., p. 183 |
| | 1 ducat | 57 dirh. a. | Ibid. |
| Raj 806/ Jan.–Feb. 1404 | 1 dinar | 80 dirh. a. | *Inbā'*, 2:261 |
| Ram 806/ Mar.–Apr. 1404 | 1 dinar | 90 dirh. a. | *Sulūk*, 3:1122 |
| | 1 ducat | 70 dirh. a. | Ibid. |
| 4 Shaw 806/ 15 Apr. 1404 | 1 dinar | 100 dirh. a. | Ibid., p. 1123 |
| | 1 ducat | 75 dirh. a. | Ibid. |
| Muḥ 807/ Jul.–Aug. 1404 | 1 dinar | 90 dirh. a | Ibid., p. 1130 |
| | 1 ducat | 70 dirh. a. | Ibid. |

[g]Official rate.

| Date | Currency | Exchange Rate | Source |
|---|---|---|---|
| Beg. Ṣaf 807/ Aug. 1404 | 1 dinar | 110 dirh. a. | Ibid.; *Nuzhat*, 2:195 |
| | 1 dinar | 200 dirh. a. (in Alexandria) | Ibid.; *Sulūk*, 3:1130 |
| | 1 ducat | 70 dirh. a. | *Nuzhat*, 2:195 |
| 15 Jum I 807/ 19 Nov. 1404 | 1 dinar | 100 dirh. a. | Ibid., p. 1134 |
| | 1 ducat | 80 dirh. a. | Ibid. |
| Ram 807/ Mar. 1405 | 1 ducat | 70–80 dirh. a. | Ibid., p. 1153 |
| 10 Dhū'l-Ḥ 807/ 9 June 1405 | 1 dinar | 80 dirh. a. | Ibid., p. 1160; *Inbā'*, 2:297 |
| | 1 ducat | 60 dirh. a. | Ibid.; *Sulūk*, 3:1160 |
| Muḥ 808/ June–July 1405 | 1 dinar | 140 dirh. a. | Ibid., p. 1170 |
| | 1 ducat | 120 dirh. a. | Ibid. |
| 20 Ṣaf 808/ 23 Aug. 1405 | 1 dinar | 125 dirh. a. | *Inbā'*, 2:318 |
| Ṣaf-Rab I 808/ Aug.–Sept. 1405 | 1 dinar | 120 dirh. a. | *Nuzhat*, 2:209 |
| | 1 ducat | 100 dirh. a. | Ibid. |
| Mid-Rab I 808/ Sept. 1405 | 1 dinar | 150 dirh. a. | *Sulūk*, 4:3 |
| | 1 ducat | 130 dirh. a. | Ibid. |
| 27 Rab I 808/ 22 Sept. 1405 | 1 dinar | 140 dirh. a. | Ibid.[h] |
| | 1 dinar | 120 dirh. a. | Ibid. |

[h]The cause of the decreasing rate was the scarcity of copper *fulūs*. The populace preferred to sell them to the coppersmiths to be melted. One *raṭl* of copper *fulūs* was valued at 6 dirhams of account, while the market price was 20 dirhams of account.

*APPENDIX THREE*

# *Wheat Prices*

(PRICE PER *IRDABB*)

| Date | Price | Source |
|---|---|---|
| Muḥ 784/ Mar.–Apr. 1382 | 105 dirhams | *Sulūk*, 3:466 |
| 784/1382 | 100 dirh. | *Inbā'*, 1:253 |
| End Muḥ 784/ mid–Apr. 1382 | 40 dirh. | *Sulūk*, 3:466 |
| 784/1382 | 40 dirh. | *Inbā'*, 1:253[a] |
| 785/1383 | 8–15 dirh. | Ibid., p. 279; *Sulūk*, 3:509 |
| 785/1383 | 8–10 dirh. | *Nuzhat*, 1:83 |
| 787/1385 | 30 dirh. | *Sulūk*, 3:538; *Nuzhat*, 1:123 |
| Dhū'l-Ḥ 787/ Jan. 1386 | 50 dirh. | *Sulūk*, 3:538; *Nuzhat*, 1:123; *Inbā'*, 1:303[b] |
| Dhū'l-Q 788/ Nov.–Dec. 1386 | 23¼ dirh. | *Sulūk*, 3:553; *Inbā'*, 1:318[c] |
| 790/1388 | 8 dirh. | Ibid., p. 353 |
| 6 Dhū'l-Q 796/ 2 Sept. 1394 | 40 dirh. | *Sulūk*, 3:818[d] |
| End 796/ Sept.–Oct. 1394 | 40 dirh. | *Inbā'*, 1:476; *Nuzhat*, 1:391[d] |

Note: Compare this table with Eliyahu Ashtor, *Histoire des prix et des salaires*, pp. 287–88.
[a]New crop.
[b]Low level of the Nile.
[c]Price quoted for the forced purchases imposed on the merchants.
[d]Increase caused by the low level of the Nile and the anticipation of a diminished crop.

| Date | Price | Source |
|---|---|---|
| 796/1394 | 80 dirh. | *Inbā'*, 1:476 |
| 12 Ṣaf 797/ 7 Dec. 1394 | 70 dirh. | *Nuzhat*, 1:399; *Sulūk*, 3:826 |
| 6 Rab I 797/ 30 Dec. 1394 | 66 dirh. | *Nuzhat*, 1:403 |
| Rab II 797/ Jan.–Feb. 1395 | 70 dirh. | *Inbā'*, 1:486 |
| Rab II 797/ Jan.–Feb. 1395 | 66 dirh. | *Sulūk*, 3:831; *Furāt*, 9:401; *Inbā'*, 1:486 |
| End Shaw 797/ mid–Aug. 1395 | 80 dirh. | *Nuzhat*, 1:414[e] |
| 27 Dhū'l-Q 797/ 13 Sept. 1395 | 80 dirh. | *Sulūk*, 3:842[e] |
| 797/1394–95 | 80 dirh. | *Inbā'*, 1:487; *Furāt*, 9:416 |
| 2 Muḥ 798/ 17 Oct. 1395 | 60 dirh. | *Inbā'*, 1:507; *Furāt*, 9:427; *Sulūk*, 3:849; *Nuzhat*, 1:421 |
| 9 Muḥ 798/ 24 Oct. 1395 | 100 dirh. | *Sulūk*, 3:849 |
| Muḥ 798/ Oct.–Nov. 1395 | 110 dirh. | *Inbā'*, 1:507 |
| End Rab I 798/ mid–Jan. 1396 | 175 dirh. | *Sulūk*, 3:856[f] |
| 7 Jum I 798/ 17 Feb. 1396 | 175 dirh. | *Nuzhat*, 1:427[f] |
| 798/1396 | 170 dirh. | *Inbā'*, 1:170 |
| Jum I 798/ Feb.–Mar. 1396 | ca. 165 dirh. | *Sulūk*, 3:856 |
| Jum I 798/ Feb.–Mar. 1396 | 130 dirh. | Ibid; *Nuzhat*; 1:427[g] |

[e]High level of the Nile and need for seed.
[f]Wheat shortage.
[g]Imported wheat.

| Date | Price | Source |
|---|---|---|
| Mid-Jum II 798/ beg. Apr. 1396 | 50 dirh. | *Sulūk*, 3:859; *Inbā'*, 1:508; *Nuzhat*, 1:429[h] |
| 26 Jum II 798/ 6 Apr. 1396 | 120 dirh. | *Sulūk*, 3:860; *Inbā'*, 1:508[i] |
| Beg. Muḥ 799/ Oct. 1396 | 50–60 dirh. | *Nuzhat*, 1:439 |
| 9 Rab I 799/ 11 Dec. 1396 | ca. 28 dirh. | *Sulūk*, 3:872; *Furāt*, 9:457 |
| Mid-Rab I 799/ mid-Dec. 1396 | 30 dirh. | *Nuzhat*, 1:446 |
| 799/1396–97 | 36 dirh. | *Sulūk*, 3:872; *Furāt*, 9:457 |
| 15 Shaw 801/ 20 June 1399 | 25 − dirh. | *Sulūk*, 3:982[j] |
| 16 Shaw 801/ 21 June 1399 | 40 dirh. | Ibid.[k] |
| Muḥ 802/ Sept.–Oct. 1399 | 40 dirh. | Ibid., p. 977 |
| Mid-Muḥ 802/ mid-Sept. 1399 | 60 dirh. | Ibid., p. 982[l] |
| Rab I 802/ Nov. 1399 | 70 Dirh. | Ibid., p. 993[m] |
| Rab I 802/ Nov. 1399 | 50 dirh. | Ibid.[n] |
| 12 Shaᶜb 802/ 8 Apr. 1400 | 75 dirh. | Ibid., p. 1013 |
| Muḥ 803/ Aug.–Sept. 1400 | 50 − dirh. | Ibid., p. 1027 |

[h]More imported wheat on the market.
[i]Wheat became scarce. Merchants refused to sell because of low prices.
[j]Date of Sultan Barqūq's death.
[k]Day following Sultan Barqūq's death.
[l]The level of the Nile was receding.
[m]Civil strife in Cairo.
[n]Great fluctuation of prices.

| Date | Price | Source |
|---|---|---|
| 1 Muḥ 804/ 11 Nov. 1401 | 50− dirh. | Ibid., p. 1076 |
| Muḥ 805/ Aug. 1402 | 60 dirhams of account | Ibid., p. 1091 |
| Raj 805/ Jan.–Feb. 1403 | 70 dirh. a. | Ibid., p. 1100; *Inbā'*, 2:235[o] |
| Dhū'l-Ḥ 805/ June–July 1403 | 95 dirh. a. | *Sulūk*, 3:1107 |
| 1 Muḥ 806/ 21 July 1403 | 100 dirh. a. | Ibid., p. 1111 |
| Ṣaf 806/ Aug.–Sept. 1403 | 130− dirh. a. | Ibid., p. 1115[p] |
| Rab I 806/ Sept.–Oct. 1403 | 180 dirh. a. | Ibid., p. 1116[p] |
| 2 Rab I 806/ 19 Sept. 1403 | 220 dirh. a. | *Nuzhat*, 2:181[p] |
| 20 Rab I 806/ 7 Oct. 1403 | 240 dirh. a. | Ibid.[p] |
| 20 Rab I 806/ 7 Oct. 1403 | 250 dirh. a. | *Sulūk*, 3:1116[p] |
| Jum II 806/ Dec.–Jan. 1403–4 | 260 dirh. a. | Ibid.[p] |
| Jum II 806/ Dec.–Jan. 1403–4 | 270 dirh. a. | *Nuzhat*, 2:184[p] |
| Beg. Raj 806/ mid-Jan. 1404 | 300 dirh. a. | Ibid.[p] |
| Raj 806/ Jan.–Feb. 1404 | 320 dirh. a. | *Sulūk*, 3:1120[p] |
| Raj 806/ Jan.–Feb. 1404 | 400 dirh. a. | *Inbā'*, 2:261[p] |
| End Raj 806/ mid-Feb. 1404 | 400 dirh. a. | *Nuzhat*, 2:186[p] |

[o]Prices increased as a result of the official decision to decrease the volume of the basket (*quffah*) of *fulūs*, while keeping its price constant.
[p]Low level of the Nile and epidemics.

| Date | Price | Source |
|---|---|---|
| Sha<sup></sup>ᶜb 806/ Feb.–Mar. 1404 | 400 dirh. a. | *Sulūk*, 3:1122[p] |
| 806/1404 | 300 dirh. a. | *Inbāʾ*, 2:268[p] |
| 806/1404 | 250 dirh. a. | Ibid.; *Sulūk*, 3:1126[q] |
| Muḥ 807/ July–Aug. 1404 | 250 dirh. a. | Ibid., p. 1130 |
| 807/1404 | 400 dirh. a. | Ibid., p. 1134 |
| Ṣaf 807/ Aug.–Sept. 1404 | 220 dirh. a. | Ibid., p. 1133[r] |
| 807/1404 | 200 dirh. a. | Ibid., p. 1155 |
| 807/1404 | 100–150 dirh. a. | Ibid. |
| Muḥ 808/ June–July 1405 | 170 dirh. a. | Ibid., p. 1170 |
| Rab I 808/ Aug.–Sept. 1405 | 220 dirh. a. | Ibid., 4:3 |
| Rab I 808/ Aug.–Sept. 1405 | 180 dirh. a. | Ibid., p. 5 |
| Dhū'l-Ḥ 808/ May–June 1405 | 130 dirh. a. | Ibid., p. 19 |
| Dhū'l-Ḥ 808/ May–June 1405 | 120 dirh. a. | Ibid., p. 22 |

[q]New crop.
[r]Al-Maqrīzī mentions that wheat sold previously at 400 dirhams of account.

## APPENDIX FOUR

# *Barley Prices*

(PRICE PER *IRDABB*)

| Date | Price | Source |
|---|---|---|
| End Muḥ 784/ Mid-Apr. 1382 | 50 dirhams | *Sulūk*, 3:466[a] |
| End Muḥ 784/ Mid-Apr. 1382 | 22 dirh. | Ibid. |
| 785/1383 | 6–8 dirh. | Ibid., p. 509; *Inbā*, 1:279; *Nuzhat*, 1:88 |
| 787/1385 | 20 dirh. | *Sulūk*, 3:538; *Nuzhat*, 1:123[b] |
| 6 Dhū'l-Q 796/ 2 Sept. 1394 | 20 dirh. | *Sulūk*, 3:818[c] |
| Dhū'l-Ḥ 796/ Oct. 1394 | 20 dirh. | *Furāt*, 9:387; *Nuzhat*, 1:391 |
| 12 Ṣaf 797/ 7 Dec. 1394 | 40 dirh. | *Sulūk*, 3:826; *Nuzhat*, 1:399 |
| 16 Rab II 797/ 8 Feb 1395 | 33 dirh. | *Sulūk*, 3:831; *Furāt*, 9:401; *Nuzhat*, 1:403 |
| End Shaw 797/ mid–Aug. 1395 | 54 dirh. | Ibid., 1:414; *Sulūk*, 3:842[d] |
| End 797/ Oct. 1395 | 50 dirh. | *Furāt*, 9:416; *Inbā'*, 1:487 |

Note: Compare this table with Ashtor, *Histoire des prix et des salaires*, pp. 295–96.
[a]New crop.
[b]Low level of the Nile.
[c]The Nile-level receded quickly.
[d]The Nile-level was high and created great demand for seed.

| Date | Price | Source |
|---|---|---|
| Beg. 798/ Oct.–Nov. 1395 | 50 dirh. | *Furāt*, 9:428 |
| Mid-Jum II 798/ Mar. 1396 | 30 dirh. | *Sulūk*, 3:859 |
| Jum II 798/ Mar. 1396 | 30 dirh. | *Nuzhat*, 1:429[e] |
| 25 Jum II 798/ 5 Apr. 1396 | 48 dirh. | *Sulūk*, 3:860[f] |
| 25–26 Jum II 798/ 5–6 Apr. 1396 | 60 dirh. | Ibid. |
| Beg. Muḥ 799/ Oct. 1396 | 30 dirh. | *Nuzhat*, 1:439 |
| Mid-Rab I 799/ Mid–Dec. 1396 | 25 dirh. | Ibid., p. 446 |
| 15 Shaw 801/ 20 June 1399 | 15 dirh. | *Sulūk*, 3:982[g] |
| Muḥ 802/ Sept. 1399 | 25 dirh. | Ibid., p. 977 |
| Mid-Muḥ 802/ mid–Sept. 1399 | 35 dirh. | Ibid., p. 982 |
| Rab II–Jum I 802/ Dec.–Jan. 1399–1400 | Prices were decreasing | *Inbā'*, 2:93[h] |
| Muḥ 803/ Aug.–Sept. 1400 | 30 – dirh. | *Sulūk*, 3:1027 |
| 1 Muḥ 804/ 11 Aug. 1401 | 25 – dirhams of account | Ibid., p. 1076 |
| Muḥ 805/ Aug. 1402 | 40 dirh. a. | Ibid., p. 1091 |
| Raj 805/ Jan.–Feb. 1403 | 70 dirh. a. | Ibid., p. 1100[i] |

[e]Import of barley.
[f]This was the official price. The previous price was 60 dirhams.
[g]This corresponded with Sultan Barqūq's death.
[h]The previous price was 25 dirhams.
[i]Prices increased as a result of the official decision to decrease the volume of the basket (*quffah*) of *fulūs*, while keeping its price constant.

| Date | Price | Source |
|---|---|---|
| Raj 805/ Jan.–Feb. 1403 | 70+ dirh. a. | *Inbā'*, 2:235 |
| Dhū'l-Ḥ 805/ June–July 1403 | 60+ dirh. a. | *Sulūk*, 3:1107 |
| 1 Muḥ 806/ 21 July 1403 | 60–70 dirh. a. | Ibid., p. 1111 |
| Rab I 806/ Sept.–Oct. 1403 | 100 dirh. a. | Ibid., p. 1116[j] |
| 6 Rab I 806/ 23 Sept. 1403 | 110 dirh. a. | *Nuzhat*, 2:180[j] |
| 11 Rab I 806/ 28 Sept. 1403 | 130 dirh. a. | Ibid., p. 181[j] |
| 20 Rab I 806/ 7 Oct. 1403 | 230 dirh. a. | *Sulūk*, 3:1116 |
| Beg. Raj. 806/ mid–Jan. 1404 | 200 dirh. a. | *Nuzhat*, 2:184 |
| Raj 806/ Jan.–Feb. 1404 | ca. 250 dirh. a. | *Inbā'*, 2:261 |
| End Raj 806/ Feb. 1404 | 250 dirh. a. | *Nuzhat*, 2:186 |
| Shaʿb 806/ Feb.–Mar. 1404 | 250 dirh. a. | *Sulūk*, 3:1122 |
| Ṣaf 807/ Aug.–Sept. 1404 | 140 dirh. a. | Ibid., p. 1133[k] |
| 807/1404 | 320 dirh. a. | Ibid., p. 1134 |
| End Jum I 807/ beg. Dec. 1404 | 360 dirh. a. | Ibid., p. 1135 |
| Muḥ 808/ June–July 1405 | 150 dirh. a. | Ibid., p. 1170 |
| Rab I 808/ Aug.–Sept. 1405 | 120 dirh. a. | Ibid., 4:3 |

[j] The Nile-level was very low.
[k] The previous price was over 200 dirhams of account.

## *APPENDIX FIVE*

# *Bean Prices*

(PRICE PER *IRDABB*)

| Date | Price | Source |
|---|---|---|
| End Muḥ 784/ mid-Apr. 1382 | 22 dirhams | *Sulūk*, 3:466 |
| 787/1385–86 | 18 dirh. | Ibid., p. 538; *Nuzhat*, 1:123 |
| 6 Dhū'l-Q 796/ 2 Sept. 1394 | 20 dirh. | *Sulūk*, 3:818[a] |
| Dhū'l-Ḥ.I 796/ Sept.–Oct. 1394 | 20 dirh. | *Nuzhat*, 1:391; *Furāt*, 9:387 |
| 12 Ṣaf 797/ Dec. 1394 | 40 dirh. | Ibid., p. 399; *Sulūk*, 3:826 |
| 6 Rab I 797/ 30 Dec. 1394 | 33 dirh. | *Nuzhat*, 1:403 |
| 16 Rab II 797/ 8 Feb. 1395 | 33 dirh. | *Furāt*, 9:401; *Sulūk*, 3:831 |
| 27 Dhū'l-Q 797/ 13 Sept. 1395 | 54 dirh. | Ibid., p. 842 |
| End 797/ Sept.–Oct. 1395 | 54 dirh. | *Furāt*, 9:416; *Inbā'*, 1:487[b] |
| Beg. 798/ Oct.–Nov. 1395 | 50 dirh. | *Furāt*, 9:428 |
| Mid-Jum II 798/ Mar.–Apr. 1396 | 30 dirh. | *Sulūk*, 3:859 |
| End Jum II 798/ beg. Apr. 1396 | 30 dirh. | *Nuzhat*, 1:429[c] |

Note: Compare this table with Ashtor, *Histoire des prix et des salaires*, pp. 296–97.
[a]The Nile-level was receding quickly.
[b]The Nile-level was very high, thus creating a great demand for seed in anticipation of a good crop.
[c]Import of beans.

| Date | Price | Source |
|---|---|---|
| Beg. Muḥ 799/ Oct. 1396 | 35 dirh. | Ibid., p. 439 |
| Mid-Rab I 799/ mid-Dec. 1396 | 25 dirh. | Ibid., p. 446 |
| Beg. Muḥ 802/ beg. Sept. 1399 | 27 dirh. | *Sulūk*, 3:977 |
| Mid-Muḥ 802/ mid-Sept. 1399 | 35 dirh. | Ibid., p. 912[d] |
| Rab II–Jum I 802/ Dec.–Jan. 1399–1400 | General decrease in prices | *Inbā'*, 2:93 |
| Muḥ 803/ Aug.–Sept. 1400 | 30 dirh. | *Sulūk*, 3:1027 |
| Raj 805/ Jan–Feb. 1403 | 90 dirhams of account | Ibid., p. 1100; *Inbā'*, 2:235[e] |
| Dhū'l-Ḥ 805/ June–July 1403 | 80 dirh. a. | *Sulūk*, 3:1107 |
| Muḥ 806/ July–Aug. 1403 | 70 dirh. a. | Ibid., p. 1111 |
| 6 Rab I 806/ 23 Sept. 1403 | 120 dirh. a. | *Nuzhat*, 2:180[f] |
| 20 Rab I 806/ 7 Oct. 1403 | 130 dirh. a. | Ibid., p. 181[g] |
| 20 Rab I 806/ 7 Oct. 1403 | 230 dirh. a. | *Sulūk*, 3:1116[h] |
| Beg. Raj 806/ Jan.–Feb. 1404 | 200 dirh. a. | *Nuzhat*, 2:184 |

[d]The previous price was 25 dirhams per *irdabb*.
[e]Prices increased as a result of the official decision to decrease the volume of the basket (*quffah*) of *fulūs*, while keeping its price constant.
[f]The price mentioned is 28 dirhams of account. This is an obvious mistake, since barley sold for 110 dirhams and beans and barley prices are generally at the same price level. This correction is made in light of the price of barley as well as the possibility that it might have been a copyist's mistake that rendered *mi'ah* as *thamāniyah*.
[g]There is an obvious discrepancy between the prices quoted in *Nuzhat* and *Sulūk*. See the following entry.
[h]The Nile-level was very low.

| Date | Price | Source |
|---|---|---|
| Raj 806/ Jan.–Feb. 1404 | 180 dirh. a. | *Sulūk*, 3:1120 |
| Raj 806/ Jan.–Feb. 1404 | ca. 250 dirh. a. | *Inbā'*, 2:261 |
| End Raj 806/ mid-Feb. 1404 | 250 dirh. a. | *Nuzhat*, 2:186 |
| Shaʿb 806/ Feb.–Mar. 1404 | 250 dirh. a. | *Sulūk*, 3:1122 |
| Muḥ 807/ July–Aug. 1404 | 250 dirh. a. | Ibid., p. 1130 |
| 807/1404 | 320 dirh. a. | Ibid., p. 1134 |
| End Jum I 807/ beg. Dec. 1404 | 400 dirh. a. | Ibid., p. 1135 |
| Muḥ 808/ June–July 1405 | 150 dirh. a. | Ibid., p. 1170 |
| Rab I 808/ Aug.–Sept. 1405 | 120 dirh. a. | Ibid., 4:3 |

*APPENDIX SIX*

# *Flour Prices*

(PRICE PER *BAṬṬAH*)

| Date | Price | Source |
|---|---|---|
| Muḥ 784/ Mar.–Apr. 1382 | 30 dirhams | *Sulūk*, 3:466 |
| End Muḥ 784/ mid-Apr. 1382 | 11 dirh. | Ibid. |
| 6 Dhū'l-Q 796/ 2 Sept. 1394 | 12 dirh. | Ibid., p. 818; *Furāt*, 9:387 |
| 12 Ṣaf 797/ 7 Dec. 1394 | 18⅓ dirh. | *Sulūk*, 3:826[a] |
| 27 Dhū'l-Q 797/ 13 Sept. 1395 | 22 dirh. | Ibid., p. 842; *Furāt*, 9:416 |
| 9 Muḥ 798/ 24 Oct. 1395 | 26 dirh. | Ibid., p. 428; *Sulūk*, 3:849 |
| Rab II 798/ Jan. 1396 | 44 dirh. | Ibid., p. 856 |
| Prior to 9 Rab I 799/ 11 Dec. 1396 | 11 dirh. | Ibid., p. 872; *Furāt*, 9:457 |
| After 9 Rab I 799/ 11 Dec. 1396 | 14 dirh. | Ibid.; *Sulūk*, 3:872[b] |
| Dhū'l-Q 799/ Jul.–Aug. 1397 | 12 dirh. | Ibid., p. 882 |
| Mid-Muḥ 802/ mid-Sept. 1399 | 16⅔ dirh. | Ibid., p. 982[c] |
| 12 Shaᶜb 802/ 8 Apr. 1400 | 20 dirh. | Ibid., p. 1013[d] |

Note: Compare this table with Ashtor, *Histoire des prix et des salaires*, p. 305.
[a]Price given as 110 dirhams per *ḥamlah*.
[b]This date corresponded with the appointment of a new *muḥtasib*.
[c]Price given as 100 dirhams per *ḥamlah*.
[d]Price given as 120 dirhams per *ḥamlah*.

| Date | Price | Source |
|---|---|---|
| 6 Rab I 806/ 23 Sept. 1403 | 50 dirhams of account | *Nuzhat*, 2:180 |
| End Raj 806/ Feb. 1404 | 110 dirh. a. | Ibid., p. 186 |
| 807/1404–5 | 110 dirh. a. | *Sulūk*, 3:1134 |

*APPENDIX SEVEN*

# *Bread Prices*

(PRICE PER *RAṬL)*

| Date | Price | Source |
|---|---|---|
| Muḥ 784/ Mar.–Apr. 1382 | ½ dirham | *Sulūk*, 3:466 |
| End Muḥ 784/ mid-Apr. 1382 | ½ dirh. | Ibid. |
| 12 Ṣaf 797/ 7 Dec. 1394 | ⅓ dirh. | Ibid., p. 826 |
| End Shaw 797/ mid-Aug. 1395 | ⅖ dirh. | *Nuzhat*, 1:414 |
| 27 Dhū'l-Q 797/ 13 Sept. 1395 | ⅖ dirh. | *Sulūk*, 3:842 |
| End 797/ Sept.–Oct. 1395 | ⅖ dirh. | *Furāt*, 9:416 |
| 9 Muḥ 798/ 24 Oct. 1395 | ⅖ dirh. | *Sulūk*, 3:849 |
| 798/1395 | ⅖ dirh. | *Furāt*, 9:428 |
| Rab II 798/ Jan.–Feb. 1396 | ⅘ dirh. | *Sulūk*, 3:856 |
| 7 Jum I 798/ 17 Feb. 1396 | ⅘ dirh. | *Nuzhat*, 1:427 |
| Jum I 798/ Feb.–Mar. 1396 | ½ dirh. | *Sulūk*, 3:856[a] |
| 22 Jum II 798/ 2 Apr. 1396 | ¼ dirh. | Ibid., p. 859 |
| 25 Jum II 798/ 5 Apr. 1396 | ¼ dirh. | Ibid., p. 860[b] |

Note: Compare this table with Ashtor, *Histoire des prix et des salaires,* pp. 307–8.
[a]This price slightly decreased later.
[b]Official price. The source states that this price was per loaf, but in light of the preceding and the following entries, it is assumed that the loaf was one *raṭl*.

| Date | Price | Source |
|---|---|---|
| End Jum II 798/ Apr. 1396 | ¼ dirh. | *Nuzhat*, 1:429 |
| Before 9 Rab 799/ 11 Dec. 1396 | ⅙ dirh. | *Furāt*, 9:457; *Sulūk*, 3:872 |
| After 9 Rab I 799/ 11 Dec. 1396 | ⅕+ dirh. | Ibid.; *Furāt*, 9:457[c] |
| Dhū'l-Ḥ 800/ Aug.–Sept. 1398 | ⅛ dirh. | *Sulūk*, 3:909[d] |
| Mid-Muḥ 802/ mid-Sept. 1399 | ¼ dirh. | Ibid., p. 982 |
| End Muḥ 802/ beg. Oct. 1399 | ¼ dirh. | Ibid.[e] |
| Rab II–Jum 802/ Dec.–Jan. 1399–1400 | General decrease in prices | *Inbā'*, 2:93 |
| Jum I–Jum II 802/ Jan.–Feb. 1400 | 3/10 dirham of account | *Sulūk*, 3:1003[f] |
| 12 Shaʿb 802/ 8 Apr. 1400 | ⅓ dirh. a. | Ibid., p. 1013 |
| Raj 806/Jan.–Feb. 1404 | 1½ dirh. a. | Ibid., p. 1120[g] |
| Rab I 807/ Sept.–Oct. 1404 | 1 5/7 dirh. a. | Ibid., pp. 1133–34[h] |
| 807/1404–5 | 1⅕ dirh. a. | Ibid., p. 1155[i] |
| 807/1404–5 | 4/7 dirh. a. | Ibid.[j] |
| Dhū'l-Ḥ 808/ May–June 1406 | ⅔ dirh. a. | Ibid.[k] |

[c]This date corresponded to the appointment of a new *muḥtasib*.
[d]According to al-Maqrīzī, this price was the lowest in six years.
[e]Based on ⅛ dirham per 7 *ūqīyahs*.
[f]Epidemics. The price is based on ⅛ dirham per 5 *ūqīyahs*.
[g]Based on 1 dirham of account per 8 *ūqīyahs*.
[h]Based on 1 dirham of account per 7 *ūqīyahs*.
[i]Based on 1 dirham of account per 10 *ūqīyahs*.
[j]Based on 1 dirham of account per 1¾ *raṭls*.
[k]Based on ⅓ dirham of account per ½ *raṭl*.

## APPENDIX EIGHT

# Mutton Prices

(PRICE PER *RAṬL*)

| Date | Price | Source |
|---|---|---|
| 785/1383–84 | 4/5 dirham | *Sulūk*, 3:509; *Nuzhat*, 1:88; *Inbā'*, 1:279 |
| 788/1386 | ½ dirh. | *Sulūk*, 3:543.[a] |
| Rab I 788/ Apr. 1386 | ½ dirh. | *Inbā'*, 1:315 |
| Rab I 788/ Apr. 1386 | ½ dirh. | *Nuzhat*, 1:130[a] |
| 12 Ṣaf 797/ 7 Dec. 1394 | 1½ dirh. | Ibid, p. 399; *Sulūk*, 3:826[b] |
| 27 Dhū'l-Q 797/ 13 Sept. 1395 | 1¼ dirh. | Ibid., p. 842 |
| End 797/ Sept.–Oct. 1395 | 1¼ dirh. | *Furāt*, 9:416 |
| Rab I 802/ Nov. 1399 | 2 dirh. | *Sulūk*, 3:993[c] |
| Rab II–Jum I 802/ Dec.–Jan. 1399/1400 | General decrease in prices | *Inbā'*, 2:93 |
| Raj 805/ Jan.–Feb. 1403 | 3 dirhams of account | *Sulūk*, 3:1101[d] |

Note: Compare this table with Ashtor, *Histoire des prix et des salaires*, pp. 311–12.
[a]Price of boiled lamb.
[b]The previous price was ¾ dirham per *raṭl*.
[c]Civil strife in Cairo.
[d]The price was ¾ dirham per *raṭl*. Prices increased as a result of the official decision to decrease the volume of the basket (*quffah*) of *fulūs*, while keeping its price constant.

| Date | Price | Source |
|---|---|---|
| Shaw 805/ Apr.–May. 1403 | 1½ dirh. a. | *Inbā'*, 2:238 |
| Shaʿb 806/ Feb.–Mar. 1404 | 2½ dirh. a. | *Nuzhat*, 2:186; *Sulūk*, 3:1122 |
| Dhū'l-Q 806/ May–June 1404 | 5 dirh. a. | Ibid., p. 1124 |
| Ṣaf 807/ Aug.–Sept. 1404 | 5½ dirh. a. | Ibid., p. 1133 |
| Rab I 807/ Sept.–Oct. 1404 | 12 dirh. a. | Ibid. |
| Muḥ 808/ June–July 1405 | 7 dirh. a. | Ibid., p. 1170 |
| Rab I 808/ Aug.–Sept. 1405 | 8 dirh. a. | Ibid., 4:3; *Nuzhat*, 2:209 |
| Jum I 808/ Oct.–Nov. 1405 | 12 dirh. a. | *Sulūk*, 4:5 |
| Jum I 808/ Oct.–Nov. 1405 | 15 dirh. a. | Ibid., p. 6[e] |

[e]Epidemics in Cairo.

## *APPENDIX NINE*

# *Beef Prices*

(PRICE PER *RAṬL*)

| Date | Price | Source |
|---|---|---|
| 785/1383–84 | ½ dirham | *Inbā'*, 1:279 |
| 785/1383–84 | ½ dirh. | *Nuzhat*, 1:88; *Sulūk*, 3:509 |
| Beg. 788/ Feb.–Mar. 1386 | ⅖ dirh. | Ibid., p. 543 |
| 12 Ṣaf 797/ 7 Dec 1394 | 1 dirh. | Ibid., p. 826 *Nuzhat*, 1:399 |
| 27 Dhū'l-Q 797/ 13 Sept 1395 | 1 dirh. | *Sulūk*, 3:842 |
| End 797/ Sept.–Oct. 1395 | 1 dirh. | *Furāt*, 9:416 |
| Rab I 802/ Nov. 1399 | 1⅛ dirh. | *Sulūk*, 3:993[a] |
| Rab II–Jum I 802; Dec.–Jan. 1399–1400 | General decrease in prices | *Inbā'*, 2:93 |
| Raj 805/ Jan.–Feb. 1403 | 2 dirhams of account | *Sulūk*, 3:1101[b] |
| Shaw 805/ Apr.–May. 1403 | 1 dirh. a. | *Inbā'*, 2:238 |
| Dhū'l-Q 806/ May–June 1404 | 3 dirh. a. | *Sulūk*, 3:1124 |
| Ṣaf 807/ Aug.–Sept. 1404 | 3½ dirh. a. | Ibid., p. 1133 |

Note: Compare this table with Ashtor, *Histoire des prix et des salaires*, pp. 311–12.
[a]Civil strife in Cairo.
[b]The previous price was ½ dirham. Prices increased as a result of the decision to decrease the volume of the basket (*quffah*) of *fulūs*, while keeping its price constant.

| Date | Price | Source |
|---|---|---|
| Rab I 807/ Sept.–Oct. 1404 | 4¼ dirh. a. | Ibid. |
| Muḥ 808/ June–July 1405 | 4 dirh. a. | Ibid., p. 1170 |
| Ṣaf-Rab I 808/ Aug.–Sept. 1405 | 5 dirh. a. | *Nuzhat*, 2:209 |
| Rab I 808/ Aug.–Sept. 1405 | 5 dirh. a. | Sulūk, 4:3 |
| Jum I 808/ Oct.–Nov. 1405 | 6 dirh. a. | Ibid., p. 5 |

# *Abbreviations*

| | |
|---|---|
| *BIE* | *Bulletin de l'institut d'Egypte*. Cairo. |
| *BIFAO* | *Bulletin de l'institut français d'archéologie orientale*. Cairo. |
| *BSOAS* | *Bulletin of the School of Oriental and African Studies*. University of London, London. |
| *EI* | *Encyclopedia of Islam*. 1st ed. London, 1913–34. |
| $EI^2$ | *Encyclopedia of Islam*, 2d ed. Leiden, 1960–. |
| *Furāt* | Ibn al-Furāt. *Tārīkh Ibn al-Furāt*. Vols. 7–9. Beirut, 1936–38. |
| *Ighāthah* | al-Maqrīzī. *Ighāthat al-ummah bi-kashf al-ghummah*. Cairo, 1940. |
| *IJMES* | *International Journal of Middle East Studies*. Cambridge University Press. |
| *Inbā'* | Ibn Ḥajar al-ʿAsqalānī. *Inbā' al-ghumr bi-anbā' al-ʿumr*. 3 vols. Cairo, 1969–72. |
| ITL | Ibn Taghrī Birdī's List of the Nile-levels. In Omar Toussoun, *Mémoire sur les anciennes branches du Nil*, pt. 2, pp. 135–45. Cairo, 1923. |
| *Ittiʿāẓ* | al-Maqrīzī. *Ittiʿāẓ al-ḥunafā' bi-akhbār al-a'immah al-fāṭimīyīn al-khulafā'*. 3 vols. Cairo, 1967–73. |
| *JA* | *Journal Asiatique*. Paris. |
| *JAOS* | *Journal of the American Oriental Society*. |
| *JARCE* | *Journal of the American Research Center in Egypt*. |
| *JESHO* | *Journal of the Economic and Social History of the Orient*. Leiden. |
| *JRAS* | *Journal of the Royal Asiatic Society of Great Britain and Ireland*. London. |
| *Khiṭaṭ* | al-Maqrīzī. *Kitāb al-mawāʿiẓ wa'l-iʿtibār bi-dhikr al-khiṭaṭ wa'l-āthār*. Bulaq ed. 2 vols. Reprint: Baghdad, 1970. |
| *Nuqūd* | al-Maqrīzī. *al-Nuqūd al-islāmīyah*. Najaf, 1967. |
| *Nuzhat* | al-Ṣayrafī. *Nuzhat al-nufūs wa'l-abdān fī tawārīkh al-zamān*. 3 vols. Cairo, 1970–74. |
| *REI* | *Revue des études islamiques*. Paris. |
| *Shudhūr* | al-Maqrīzī. *Shudhūr al-ʿuqūd fī dhikr al-nuqūd*. Alexandria, 1933. |
| *Ṣubḥ* | al-Qalqashandī. *Ṣubḥ al-aʿshā*. 14 vols. Cairo, 1913–19. |
| *Sulūk* | al-Maqrīzī. *Kitāb al-sulūk li-maʿrifat duwal al-mulūk*. 4 vols. Cairo, 1956–73. |

# Notes

## TRANSLATOR'S INTRODUCTION

[1] A general survey of the Baḥrī Mamluks is found in P. M. Holt, *The Age of the Crusades: The Near East from the Eleventh Century to 1517* (London and New York: Longman, 1986), pp. 82–154. *See also* David Ayalon, "Baḥrī Mamlūks, Burjī Mamlūks: Inadequate Names for Two Reigns of the Mamlūk Sultanate," in *Tārīḫ: A Volume of Occasional Papers in Near Eastern Studies*, ed. Leon Nemoy and Vera B. Moreen (Philadelphia: Annenberg Research Institute, 1990), 1:53.

[2] P. M. Holt, *Age of Crusades*. For a summary of the destabilization of Asia Minor and Syria after Tīmūr's campaigns, see Adel Allouche, *The Ottoman-Ṣafavid Conflict (906–962/1500–1555)* (Berlin: Klaus Schwarz Verlag, 1983), pp. 15–20.

[3] An overview of these sources is given by Jere L. Bacharach, "Circassian Mamluk Historians and Their Quantitative Data," *JARCE* 12 (1975): 75–87. Bacharach states that the economic data contained in these sources pertain to the years 1382–1479; however, the data that I have collected do not show a significant value beyond the year 1473.

[4] Apart from the early studies of W. Heyd and his contemporaries, the most comprehensive work is Subhi Y. Labib, *Handelsgeschichte Ägyptens in Spätmittelalter (1171–1517)*. The series of articles by Eliyahu Ashtor, beginning with his "Prix et salaires à l'époque mamlouke: Une étude sur l'état économique de l'Egypte et de la Syrie à la fin du moyen âge," *REI* 17 (1949): 49–94, culminated in his two monographs: *Histoire des prix et des salaires dans l'Orient médiéval* and *Les métaux précieux et la balance des payements du Proche-Orient à la basse époque*, as well as his later articles and monograph on Levantine trade. Special mention should be made of a monograph on the social history of the Mamluks by Ira M. Lapidus entitled *Muslim Cities in the Later Middle Ages*. Other articles by David Ayalon, Claude Cahen, Jere Bacharach, and other specialists are listed in the bibliography.

[5] This trend was followed by Eliyahu Ashtor in a number of articles and in his *Levant Trade in the Later Middle Ages*. An overview of previous scholarship is found in the preface to Ashtor's book.

[6] In addition to existing catalogs of Islamic coinage, the works of Paul Balog on Ayyubid and Mamluk coinage merit special mention, especially *The Coinage of the Ayyubids*, with the article by Norman D. Nicol, "Paul Balog's *The Coinage of the Ayyubids*: Additions and Corrections," *Numismatic Chronicle* 146 (1986): 119–54; *The Coinage of the Mamluk Sultans of Egypt and Syria*; "A Hoard of Late Mamluk Copper Coins and Observations on the Metrology of the Mamluk Fals," *Numismatic Chronicle*, 7th series, 2 (1962): 243–73; and "History of the Dirhem in Egypt from the Fatimid Conquest until the Collapse of the Mamluk

Empire," *Revue numismatique*, 6th series, 3 (1961): 109–46. A number of articles by Andrew S. Ehrenkreutz focusing primarily on the period of the Crusades and on the Ayyubids are also relevant (see bibliography).

[7] Balog, "History of the Dirhem"; and Jere Bacharach and Adon A. Gordus, "Studies on the Fineness of Silver Coins," *JESHO* 11 (1968): 298–317. For the early Islamic period, see Andrew S. Ehrenkreutz, "Studies in the Monetary History of the Near East in the Middle Ages," *JESHO* 2 (1959): 128–61; 6 (1963): 243–77.

[8] Data contained in *waqf* documents, especially those related to stipends paid to teachers and students of religious institutions, are very important. However, only a few of these documents have been published so far. The most comprehensive catalog of Mamluk *waqf* documents has been published by Muḥammad Muḥammad Amīn in his *Fihrist wathā'iq al-Qāhirah ḥattā nihāyat ʿaṣr al-mamālīk* (Cairo: al-Maʿhad al-ʿilmī al-faransī lil-āthār al-sharqīyah, 1981) and in his edition of Ibn Ḥabīb, *Tadhkirat al-nabīh fī ayyām al-manṣūr wa banīh*. Separate studies of *waqf* deeds have been made by Muḥammad Muḥammad Amīn, Aḥmad Darrag, Leonor Fernandes, Ulrich Haarmann, and ʿAbd al-Laṭīf Ibrāhīm.

[9] This came to be a trait of the Circassian administration. Cases of appointment to the *ḥisbah* and other high positions because of money are recorded in contemporary chronicles. For the *ḥisbah*, see *Sulūk*, 3:566 (A.H. 789), 3:748 (A.H. 793), 3:879 (A.H. 799), 3:901 (A.H. 800), 3:1013 (A.H. 802); *Inbā'*, 1:371 (A.H. 791). Other instances involve the supervision of the treasury (*Sulūk*, 3:468 [A.H. 784]), the vizirate (*Sulūk*, 3:767 [A.H. 794]), and governorships (*Sulūk*, 3:377 [A.H. 781], 3:922 [A.H. 801]). Protection money (*ḥimāyah*) was paid to influential fief-holders and high officials. In 830/1427, Sultan Barsbāy tried to do away with this exemption, an attempt that was also made by later sultans; see *Sulūk*, 4:735.

[10] A good example consists of a discussion of the causes of the pneumonic plague of 833/1430, during the rule of Barsbāy, held by a group of theologians and reported by Ibn Ḥajar in *Inbā'*, 3:438–39. They agreed that this plague was a divine punishment for the injustice of the sultan toward merchants and for other oppressive economic measures. Other examples are given by Michael W. Dols, *The Black Death in the Middle East*, p. 115.

[11] Ibn Taghrī Birdī, *History of Egypt, 1382–1469 A.D.*, tr. William Popper (hereafter cited as Ibn Taghrī Birdī/Popper), 14:80. A similar comment by Ibn Taghrī Birdī is quoted by Susan Jane Staffa, *Conquest and Fusion: The Social Evolution of Cairo, A.D. 642–1850* (Leiden: E. J. Brill, 1977), p. 205.

[12] Aḥmad ʿAbd ar-Rāziq, "La ḥisba et le muḥtasib en Égypte au temps des Mamluks," *Annales islamologiques* 13 (1977): 148–49, 153. There is sufficient evidence that al-Maqrīzī may have held this position on four (and not three) occasions. Information gathered from al-Maqrīzī (*Sulūk*, 3:930, 969–70), Ibn Ḥajar (*Inbā'*, 2:54), and al-Ṣayrafī (*Nuzhat*, 1:486) tends to support the fact that the duration of the first appointment (11 Rajab to 1 Dhū'l Ḥijjah 801) actually corresponded to two separate appointments: from 11 Rajab to 1 Dhū'l-Qaʿdah 801 and from 17 Dhū'l-Qaʿdah to 1 Dhū'l-Ḥijjah 801.

[13] *Sulūk*, 3:1155.

[14] He was appointed *muḥtasib* of Cairo on seven occasions from 801/1399 to 847/1443. See ʿAbd ar-Raziq, "La ḥisba et le muḥtasib," pp. 148–68; Bacharach, "Circassian Mamluk Historians," pp. 78–79.

[15] Ibn Khaldūn, *The Muqaddimah: An Introduction to History*, 2d ed., tr. Franz Rosenthal, 1:462–63. A French translation of al-Maqrīzī's definition of the *ḥisbah* was made by ʿAbd ar-Rāziq, "La ḥisba et le muḥtasib," p. 121. See also R. P. Buckley, "The Muḥtasib," *Arabica* 39 (1992): 59–117.

[16] ʿAbd ar-Rāziq, "La ḥisba et le muḥtasib."

[17] *Nuzhat*, 2:206–19.

[18] *Collection complète des mémoires relatifs à l'histoire de France*, ed. Claude B. Petitot (Paris: 1819), series 1, 3:1–58. See also M. M. Ziyādah's introduction to vol. 1 of *Sulūk*.

[19] *Magasin encyclopédique* (1796): 472–502, (1797): 38–39; published as a monograph in 1797. This translation was reprinted in *Bibliothèque des arabisants français* (Cairo: Institut français d'archéologie orientale, 1905), 1:9–66. References in the text are to this edition.

[20] Hereafter cited as de Sacy, *Poids*.

[21] *Traité des monnoies musulmanes*, p. 46.

[22] *Histoire des sultans mamelouks de l'Egypte* 1:xv–xvi.

[23] "Le traité des famines de Maqrīzī," *JESHO* 5 (1962): 1.

[24] *Ighāthah*, p. 43.

[25] *Ighāthah*, introduction; "Traité des famines," p. 1.

[26] *Ighāthah*, p. 83.

[27] *Sulūk*, 4:5–6.

[28] *Ighāthah*, p. 77 (or section 6 of this translation); *Sulūk*, 4:6.

[29] *Sulūk*, 4:19 and 3–4, respectively.

[30] Ibid., 4:28; Ibn Taghrī Birdī/Popper, 14:129.

[31] *Ighāthah*, p. 76.

[32] Ibid., p. 81.

[33] *Sulūk*, 4:3 and 30, respectively.

[34] Ibid., 3:1170 and 4:30, respectively.

[35] Ibid., 4:28.

[36] Ibid., 3:930, 969–70, 999, 1013, 1155.

[37] Ibid., 4:858 (*Imtāʿ al-asmāʿ*, in A.H. 834) and 4:953 (*Durar al-ʿuqūd al-farīdah*, in A.H. 838).

[38] Ibid., 4:993.

[39] William Popper, *Egypt and Syria under the Circassian Sultans 1382–1468 A.D.: Systematic Notes to Ibn Taghrî Birdî's Chronicles of Egypt*, 2:61.

[40] *Ighāthah*, p. 72.

[41] Ibid., p. 76.

[42] See examples in *Ighāthah*, pp. 12, 18, 24, 29, 32; *Inbā'*, 2:324; *Sulūk*, 3:97, 223, 235.

[43] *Sulūk*, 3:854–55; *Inbā'*, 1:507–8.

[44] Abū Yūsuf, *Kitāb al-kharāj*, ed. Muḥammad Ibrāhīm al-Bannā, p. 110.

[45] Ibid., p. 111.

[46] Ibn Manẓūr, *Lisān al-ʿarab*, 15 vols. (Beirut: Dār Ṣādir, 1956), 15:131–32. E. W. Lane, *Arabic-English Lexicon*, 8 vols. (London: Williams and Norgate, 1877), 6:2287, defines it as "the price or rate at which a thing was to be sold, was or became high or exceeded the usual limit."

[47] Muḥammad ibn Muḥammad ibn Khalīl al-Asadī, *al-Taysīr wa'l-iʿtibār wa'l-taḥrīr wa'l-ikhtibār fīmā yajibu min ḥusn al-tadbīr wa'l-taṣarruf wa'l-ikhtiyār*, ed. ʿAbd al-Qādir Aḥmad Ṭulaymāt, pp. 134–45.

[48] Ibn Khaldūn, *The Muqaddimah*, 2:339.

[49] Ibid., 2:340. For the Arabic text, see *Prolégomènes d'Ebn Khaldoun*, ed. M. Quatremère, vol. 17, 2:299–301.

[50] Examples in *Sulūk*, 3:1119; *Ighāthah*, p. 43; Ibn Muyassar, *Akhbār miṣr*, ed. Henri Massé, p. 20.

[51] *The Muqaddimah*, 2:136; *Prolégomènes*, 2:125.

[52] I have avoided quoting Rosenthal's translation of this sentence because it is inadequate. See *Prolégomènes*, 2:125.

[53] *The Muqaddimah*, 2:136; *Prolégomènes*, 2:125. The addition of the Arabic in the text is mine.

[54] *The Muqaddimah*, 2:136–37; *Prolégomènes*, 2:125–26.

[55] *Khiṭaṭ*, 1:57–61.

[56] Amīn Sāmī, *Taqwīm al-Nīl*, 1:41. A complete list of the annual minimum and maximum levels of the Nile, covering the Hijrī years 20 to 855 (641 to 1452), is given by Ibn Taghrī Birdī and has been reproduced by Omar Toussoun in his *Mémoire sur les anciennes branches du Nil*, pt. 2, pp. 135–45.

[57] Such was the decrease in the price of bread in 800/1397–98. See *Sulūk*, 3:903, 909.

[58] *Nuzhat*, 3:262.

[59] During the drought of 806/1403–4, wheat prices increased from 100 dirhams of account the *irdabb* to 400 in seven months. See *Sulūk*, 3:1113–19; *Nuzhat*, 2:181–86.

[60] *Ighāthah*, p. 42.

[61] See Ira M. Lapidus, "The Grain Economy of Mamluk Egypt," *JESHO* 12 (1969): 1–15. Taking advantage of an increase in grain prices in 787/1385–86, the Mamluk administration forced millers to purchase wheat from the royal silos at the highest price; *Sulūk*, 3:538.

[62] In 787/1385–86, Sultan Barqūq ordered that wheat be sent to Mecca, where famine conditions existed; *Sulūk*, 3:536. He also distributed food and money among the poor of Cairo during the grain shortage of 798/1395–96; *Sulūk*, 3:853–55; *Nuzhat*, 1:424–25.

[63] See, for example, Ibn Taymīyah, *Public Duties in Islam: The Institution of the Ḥisba*, ed. Muhtar Ed. Holland and Khurshid Ahmad; and al-Shayzarī, *Kitāb nihāyat al-rutbah fī ṭalab al-ḥisbah*, ed. al-Bāz al-ʿArīnī.

[64] *Ighāthah*, p. 4.

[65] Ibid., pp. 14–15.

[66] Ibid., pp. 32–38.

[67] Ibid., p. 43.

[68] Ibid.

[69] This was Shams al-Dīn al-Ikhnā'ī. See *Nuzhat*, 2:178.

[70] See *Inbā'*, 1:318, 402–3, 470–75; *Sulūk*, 3:668–69, 810, 838, 853; *Nuzhat*, 1:386.

[71] See Mohammad Abdullah Enan, *Ibn Khaldun: His Life and Work*, pp. 91–102.

[72] *Sulūk*, 3:1111–4:11.

[73] Ibid., 3:1112.

[74] Ibid., 3:1117. This was in Rabīʿ I.

[75] Ibid., 3:1111, 1133, 4:51.

[76] Ibid., 3:1111, 1132.

[77] Ashtor, *Les métaux précieux*, pp. 43–44.

[78] Paul Balog, *The Coinage of the Mamluk Sultans of Egypt and Syria*, p. 42.

[79] Ashtor, *Les métaux précieux*, pp. 65–96.

[80] Eliyahu Ashtor, "The Venetian Supremacy in the Levantine Trade: Monopoly or Pre-Colonialism?" *Journal of European Economic History* 3, no. 1 (Spring 1974): 5–53; idem, "Levantine Sugar Industry in the Later Middle Ages—An Example of Technological Decline," *Israel Oriental Studies* 7 (1977): 226–80.

[81] Karl Jahn, "Paper Currency in Iran: A Contribution to the Cultural and Economic History of Iran in the Mongol Period," *Journal of Asian History* 4, no. 2 (1970): 101–35.

[82] Michael Dols, *The Black Death in the Middle East*. The total of twenty plagues is tabulated from *Sulūk*.

[83] See David Ayalon, "Regarding Population Estimates in the Countries of Medieval Islam," *JESHO* 28 (1985): 1–19.

[84] Subhi Labib, *Handelsgeschichte Ägyptens in Spätmittelalter*, pp. 269–70.

[85] *Sulūk*, 2:379–494, where frequent cases of purchases, confiscations, and borrowing are mentioned.

[86] Al-Shujāʿī, *Tārīkh al-malik al-Nāṣir Muḥammad ibn Qalāwūn*, ed. Barbara Schafer, 1:66–67.

[87] Cemal Kafadar, "Les troubles monétaires à la fin du XVIᵉ siècle et la prise de conscience ottomane du déclin," *Annales, E.S.C.* 46 (1991): 385. It is worth mentioning that a Turkish translation of al-Maqrīzī's *Shudhūr* was made during this crisis.

[88] Unfortunately, focused studies on the relationship between the structure of Mamluk *iqṭāʿ* and the economy are still lacking. The reader may find useful information in Lapidus, "The Grain Economy of Mamluk Egypt"; idem, *Muslim Cities in the Later Middle Ages*; M. Hassanein Rabie, *The Financial System of Egypt, A.H. 564–741/1169–1341*; and pertinent articles by Claude Cahen.

[89] *Sulūk*, 4:27.

[90] On the views of the four Sunnī schools of Islamic jurisprudence regarding specie, see the interesting article by Robert Brunschvig, "Conceptions monétaires chez les juristes musulmans (VIIIᵉ–XIIIᵉ siècles)," *Arabica* 14 (1967): 113–43.

## PROLOGUE

[1] I took the liberty of translating *mā darasa min sharīʿatihi* as "revived legislation." The literal translation would be "that which had been obliterated of His legislation," an obvious reference to Islam as God's revived legislation.

## 2. THE [YEARS OF] *GHALĀʾ*

[1] A discussion regarding the identity of this author is found in Michael Cook, "Pharaonic History in Medieval Egypt," *Studia Islamica* 57 (1983): 67–103.

[2] This is a corrected version of the Arabic text, which reads "according to Harjīb son of Shahlūf, etc." The version given here is made in light of information contained in al-Qalqashandī's *Ṣubḥ al-aʿshā* (hereafter cited as *Ṣubḥ*), 3:412, where it is mentioned that "Harjīb son of Shahlūq [*sic*] reigned for over seventy years, then was succeeded by his son Manāwash, . . . then by Afrawus son of Manāwash, during whose time occurred the Flood." Except for the variations in the spelling of these names, al-Nuwayrī, *Nihāyat al-arab fī funūn al-adab*, 15:35–38, gives a similar version.

[3] *Ṣubḥ*, 3:412; Nuwayrī, *Nihāyat al-arab*, 15:39–43.

[4] *Ṣubḥ*, 3:412; Nuwayrī, *Nihāyat al-arab*, 15:75–77. Both sources give his full name as Atrīb son of Qibṭīm son of Maṣrīm.

[5] *Ṣubḥ*, 3:413; Nuwayrī, *Nihāyat al-arab*, 15:45.

[6] The original "Coptic" is translated as "ancient Egyptian." For an explanation see Cook, "Pharaonic History in Medieval Egypt," p. 92.

[7] *Ṣubḥ*, 3:415; Nuwayrī, *Nihāyat al-arab*, 15:120–27.

[8] Qur'ān 12:43–57.

[9] Genesis 41.

[10] "Plague" is added in conformity with the Biblical tradition.

[11] Exodus 3–10.

[12] ʿAbd Allāh ibn ʿAbd al-Malik ibn Marwān was governor of Egypt from 11 Jumādā II 86/9 June 705 to 13 Rabīʿ I 90/30 January 709 (al-Kindī, *Kitāb al-wulāt wa kitāb al-quḍāt*, ed. Rhuvon Guest, pp. 58–64. He was appointed following the death of his uncle ʿAbd al-ʿAzīz, which occurred in 85/704 (al-Jahshiyārī, *Kitāb al-wuzarā' wa'l-kuttāb*, ed. Muṣṭafā al-Saqqā, p. 34. Al-Kindī mentions only this governor's corrupt practices and the widespread bribery that led to marked inflation, a statement confirmed by al-Maqrīzī in *Khiṭaṭ*, 1:302.

[13] Al-Kindī, *Kitāb al-wulāt*, pp. 294–96, does not mention this incident.

[14] Not mentioned ibid.

[15] ITL's maxima: sixteen cubits and seven fingers for A.H. 340, and sixteen cubits and ten fingers for A.H. 341.

[16] Kāfūr became *de facto* the ruler of Egypt and regent of the realm during the reign of ʿAlī (349–55/961–66), a minor. At the death of the latter, Kāfūr took over power until his own demise on 20 Jumādā I 357/22 April 968. Ibn Khallikān, *Wafayāt al-aʿyān*, ed. Iḥsān ʿAbbās (hereafter cited as Ibn Khallikān/ʿAbbās), 4:99–105, no. 545, places his death in A.H. 356. The correction to A.H. 357 is made in light of Kāfūr's biography in al-Kindī, *Kitāb al-wulāt*, pp. 296–97.

[17] ITL's maximum for A.H. 352: fifteen cubits and sixteen fingers.

[18] This level is identical with ITL's.

[19] ITL: sixteen cubits and fifteen fingers.

[20] ITL: fourteen cubits and nineteen fingers.

[21] ITL: twelve cubits and seventeen fingers.

[22] Al-Maqrīzī is correct. In ITL, prior to A.H. 356, the lowest maximum recorded was in A.H. 291 at thirteen cubits and four fingers.

[23] See note 16 above.

[24] See al-Kindī, *Kitāb al-wulāt*, pp. 297–98.

[25] The original *wa kathura al-irjāf bi-masīr al-qarāmiṭah ilā miṣr* implies the spread of false rumors. This is derived by the meaning of *irjāf* as found in Ibn Manẓūr, *Lisān al-ʿarab*, 15 vols. (Beirut: Dār Ṣādir, 1956), 9:113. Indeed the Carmathians captured al-Ramlah, defeated al-Ḥasan ibn ʿAbd Allāh ibn Ṭughj in 358/969, then made peace with him. In 362/971–72, the Carmathians engaged the Fatimid army in battle outside Cairo; *Ittiʿāẓ*, 1:130, 186; Ibn Ẓāfir, *Akhbār al-duwal al-munqaṭiʿah*, ed. André Ferré, pp. 24–25.

[26] Jawhar, the commander of the Fatimid expedition against Egypt, arrived there on 17 Shaʿbān 358/6 July 969; al-Kindī, *Kitāb al-wulāt*, p. 298; *Ittiʿāẓ*, 1:96–100, 110–11; Ibn Ẓāfir, *al-Duwal al-munqaṭiʿah*, p. 23; Ibn Khallikān, *Ibn Khallikān's Biographical Dictionary*, tr. M. G. de Slane (hereafter cited as Ibn Khallikān/de Slane), 1:340–47.

[27] Ibn ʿAzzah was appointed to the *ḥisbah* by Jawhar on the first of Rabīʿ II 359/11 February 970, then dismissed. He was later reappointed to the same office in Dhū'l-Qaʿdah of the same year/September 970. It seems that he was dismissed at the beginning of 363/October 973 when al-Muʿizz reorganized the financial administration of Egypt and appointed Abū'l-Faraj Yaʿqūb ibn Yūsuf and ʿAslūj

ibn al-Ḥasan to supervise all financial matters; *Itti*ᶜ*āẓ* 1:120–22, 132, 144–45. On the function of *muḥtasib*, see Ibn Khaldūn, *The Muqaddimah*, tr. Franz Rosenthal, 1:463; Claude Cahen and M. Talbi, "Ḥisba," *EI*², 3:485–89; N. Ziyādah, *al-Ḥisbah wa'l-muḥtasib fī'l-Islām*.

[28] Sāwīrus ibn al-Muqaffaᶜ, *History of the Patriarchs of the Coptic Church of Alexandria*, vol. 2, pt. 2, p. 90, mentions a seven-year famine, the beginning of which coincided with the Fatimid conquest in A.D. 969.

[29] During this period, the level of the Nile was above normal. ITL's maxima were seventeen cubits and nine fingers for A.H. 358 and 359, 17 cubits and twenty-one fingers for A.H. 360, and seventeen cubits and four fingers for A.H. 361. Political instability caused by the Fatimid conquest of Egypt and the invasion of this country by the Carmathians led to hoarding, which resulted in shortages and inflation.

[30] Abū Muḥammad al-Ḥasan ibn ᶜAmmār al-Kutāmī was the chief of the Maghribi faction in the army and administered Egypt from the beginning of al-Ḥākim's reign until Shaᶜbān 386/August 997, when he was overthrown by his successor Barjawān. He was killed in Shawwāl 390/September 1000; Ibn al-Ṣayrafī, *al-Ishārah ilā man nāla al-wizārah*, ed. ᶜAbd Allāh Mukhliṣ, pp. 26–27. The title he held was that of *wāsiṭah* (intermediary), since the institution of the vizirate did not exist under al-Ḥākim bi-Amr Allāh; *Khiṭaṭ*, 1:439–40, 2:3–4; Ibn Ẓāfir, *al-Duwal al-munqaṭiᶜah*, p. 60; Jamāl al-Dīn al-Shayyāl, *Majmūᶜat al-wathā'iq al-fāṭimīyah*, 1:131.

[31] ITL: sixteen cubits and seven fingers.

[32] This was the result of civil strife in Egypt, which was caused by the feuding between the Turkish and the Maghribi (mostly of the Berber tribe of Kutāmah) factions of the army. This led to the overthrow of Ibn ᶜAmmār and his replacement by Barjawān. It is interesting that al-Maqrīzī confirms this fact in *Ittiᶜāẓ*, 2:3–16, and *Khiṭaṭ*, 2:3–4, while he blames the low level of the Nile here, although the maximum for A.H. 387 was above average.

[33] Confirmed in *Ittiᶜāẓ*, 2:59.

[34] ITL: sixteen cubits and three fingers.

[35] *Ittiᶜāẓ*, 2:58, 69. The date is omitted in al-Maqrīzī, *Traité des monnoies musulmanes*, tr. Silvestre de Sacy (hereafter cited as de Sacy, *Monnoies*), p. 36, while in *Nuqūd*, p. 59, and *Shudhūr*, p. 27, it is A.H. 399.

[36] An identical version is found in *Shudhūr*, pp. 27–28; *Nuqūd*, p. 59; de Sacy, *Monnoies*, pp. 36–37.

[37] Confirmed in *Shudhūr*, p. 28; *Nuqūd*, p. 59; de Sacy, *Monnoies*, p. 37. In *Ittiᶜāẓ*, 2:69, the ratio is given as eighty new dirhams to the dinar: an obvious mistake that the editor failed to correct.

[38] In *Ittiᶜāẓ*, 2:71, this is mentioned among the events at the beginning of A.H. 398.

[39] al-Ḥākim presided over the opening of the canal in Dhū'l-Qaᶜdah 397/19 July–17 August 1007 when the level of the Nile was at fourteen cubits and a few fingers. Later, the Nile-level reached fourteen cubits and sixteen fingers; *Ittiᶜāẓ*, 2:70. This maximum is identical with the figure given in ITL.

[40] Al-Maqrīzī mistakenly refers to Masᶜūd al-Ṣaqlabī here as *mutawallī al-sitr* and in *Ittiᶜāẓ*, 2:30, as *ṣāḥib al-sitr*, because such a title did not exist under the Fatimids. However, two passages in vol. 2 of *Ittiᶜāẓ* shed some light on the position that al-Ṣaqlabī held during the reign of al-Ḥākim. On p. 30, it is stated that in A.H. 390 "Ḥusayn ibn Jawhar [the *wāsiṭah*] requested Masᶜūd al-Ṣaqlabī to

allow all people to reach al-Ḥākim and to forbid no one to do so." On p. 36, it is mentioned that later in the same year al-Ṣaqlabī "was awarded the command of the 'lower police' [*al-shurṭah al-suflā*], thus he came to be responsible for the two police [departments]" (*wa jumiᶜ at al-shurṭatān li-Masᶜūd al-Ṣaqlabī*). These two departments were those of Old Cairo, known as *al-shurṭah al-suflā*, and Cairo, known as *al-shurṭah al-ᶜulyā*. See Ibn al-Ṣayrafī, *Ishārah*, p. 24; ᶜAbd al-Munᶜim Mājid, *Nuẓum al-Fāṭimīyīn*, 2 vols. (Cairo: Maktabat al-anglū-miṣrīyah, 1953), 1:174–75. Hence, al-Ṣaqlabī was responsible for Cairo's police before he was awarded the command of those of Old Cairo as well. He was then *ṣāḥib al-shurṭah* or *wālī al-shurṭah* (i.e., commander of the police). It was common practice under the Fatimids to have *ṣāḥib al-shurṭah* simultaneously responsible for the *ḥisbah*; *Ṣubḥ*, 3:487. Masᶜūd al-Ṣaqlabī was the police commander and the *muḥtasib* for both Cairo and Old Cairo; *Ittiᶜāẓ*, 2:73.

[41] This was *maydān al-ghallah*, also called *maydān al-qamḥ*, "a place for grain at the time al-Maqs was Cairo's harbor on the Nile"; *Khiṭaṭ*, 2:124–25.

[42] In *Ittiᶜāẓ*, 2:74, this price is quoted for bread.

[43] These prices are also quoted in *Ittiᶜāẓ*, 2:74.

[44] ITL: fourteen cubits and nine fingers.

[45] *Ittiᶜāẓ*, 2:76; 9 Muḥarram 399/13 September 1008.

[46] In *Ittiᶜāẓ*, 2:77–78 and 81, there is no mention of famine or grain shortages, only of the spread of epidemics in Cairo.

[47] For its location, see Ibn Duqmāq, *Kitāb al-intiṣār*, 2:39; al-Maqrīzī, *Les marchés du Caire*, ed. A. Raymond and G. Wiet, pp. 217–21.

[48] For its location, see *Khiṭaṭ*, 1:433; *Ṣubḥ*, 3:350.

[49] This mosque was completed in 395/1004–5 and located south of Old Cairo close to the Nile; Ibn Duqmāq, *Kitāb al-intiṣār*, 1:78–7; *Khiṭaṭ*, 2:282–83; *Ṣubḥ*, 3:345.

[50] He was appointed vizir on 7 Muḥarram 442/1 June 1050 and dismissed in Muḥarram 450/March 1058, then killed the following month. See Ibn al-Ṣayrafī, *Ishārah*, pp. 40–45; Ibn Muyassar, *Akhbār miṣr*, ed. Henri Massé, pp. 8–10.

[51] According to ITL, the Nile-level was above average in the 440s, and the maximum for A.H. 444 was seventeen cubits and five fingers.

[52] Al-Yāzūrī "was first appointed to the service of al-Mustanṣir's mother, a position that allowed him great influence, since al-Mustanṣir's mother was the real power behind her son"; *Khiṭaṭ*, 1:355. The vizir Abū'l-Barakāt (see note 53 below) devised the scheme of appointing al-Yāzūrī to the judgeship as a way to make him lose his position at the service of the caliph's mother. But this scheme did not succeed and al-Yāzūrī was able to keep both positions. See Ibn Muyassar, *Akhbār misr*, p. 9; Ibn al-Ṣayrafī, *Ishārah*, p. 40.

[53] Abū'l-Barakāt al-Ḥusayn ibn ᶜImād al-Dawlah Muḥammad al-Jarjarā'ī was appointed vizir in 440/1048–49 and dismissed in Shawwāl 441/March 1050; Ibn al-Ṣayrafī, pp. 38–39.

[54] ᶜArīf.

[55] *Ṣaᶜlūk*.

[56] Correct title: caliph. In *Khiṭaṭ*, 1:109, al-Maqrīzī mistakenly ascribes these events to the rule of al-Mustaᶜīn.

[57] ITL: sixteen cubits and four fingers. Ibn Muyassar, *Akhbār miṣr*, pp. 6–7, mentions no cause but states that in 446/1054–55 and 447/1055–56 famines, epidemics, and deaths were on the increase.

[58] *Jirāyāt*. See notes 95 and 96 below for details.

[59] Confirmed by Ibn al-Ṣayrafī, *Ishārah*, p. 43.

[60] *Jahbadh* (plural: *jahābidhah*) is an Arabized form of the Persian word *kahbad*. Ibn Mammātī, *Kitāb qawānīn al-dawāwīn*, ed. A. S. Atiya, p. 304, defines the duties of the *jahbadh* as follows: "He imposes and collects taxes and writes receipts for the amounts he receives. It is incumbent upon him to keep daily accounts and he is required to send [to the authorities] the amounts he receives." See also *Ṣubḥ*, 5:466.

[61] *Rūznāmaj* (plural: *rūznamājat*) is an Arabized form of the Persian *rūznāmchah*, a daily book or a ledger.

[62] Ibn Muyassar, *Akhbār miṣr*, pp. 6–7, mentions that in 446/1054–55 the Byzantines withheld grain destined for Egypt. He states that the Byzantine emperor agreed to send 400,000 *irdabb*s of grain but died meanwhile and was succeeded by an empress (probably Theodora [1042–55]) who decided not to abide by the agreement because she failed in her attempt to secure the agreement of al-Mustanṣir to back her if challenged for power. This version is also found in *Khiṭaṭ*, 1:335.

[63] On 22 Ṣafar 450/20 April 1058 in Tinnīs; Ibn al-Ṣayrafī, *Ishārah*, p. 45, note 9; Ibn Muyassar, *Akhbār miṣr*, p. 8.

[64] Ibn al-Ṣayrafī, *Ishārah*, pp. 46–54, lists thirty appointments to the vizirate from Muḥarram 450/March 1058 to Rabīᶜ II 466/ December 1073. Ibn Muyassar, *Akhbār miṣr*, pp. 10–19, mentions a minimum of fifty appointments between 450/1058 and 461/1069. Less detailed information is found in Ibn Ẓāfir, *al-Duwal al-munqaṭiᶜah*, pp. 79–81; and *Ittiᶜāẓ*, 2:332–34.

[65] The same information is given by Ibn Muyassar, *Akhbār miṣr*, pp. 13–14; Ibn Ẓāfir, *al-Duwal al-munqaṭiᶜah*, p. 74; and Ibn al-Ṣayrafī, *Ishārah*, p. 55. This paragraph is found almost verbatim in *Ittiᶜāẓ*, 2:262–63.

[66] From 457/1064–65 to 464/1071–72: Ibn Muyassar, *Akhbār miṣr*, p. 34; *Khiṭaṭ*, 1:337; Ibn Ẓāfir, *al-Duwal al-munqaṭiᶜah*, p. 74. *Ittiᶜāẓ*, 2:300, states that these seven years were from 459 to 464, a period of only five years.

[67] Sāwīrus ibn al-Muqaffaᶜ, *History of the Patriarchs*, vol. 2, pt. 2, states that famine was so widespread that people resorted to eating corpses. Ibn Muyassar, *Akhbār miṣr*, p. 20, gives the impression that a pneumonic plague ravaged Egypt.

[68] A quarter for the wealthy in Cairo; Ibn Duqmāq, *Kitāb al-intiṣār*, 1:13–14.

[69] Fourteen (not fifteen) dinars in *Ittiᶜāẓ*, 2:297; *Khiṭaṭ*, 1:337; and Ibn Muyassar, *Akhbār miṣr*, p. 34.

[70] Same price quoted in *Ittiᶜāẓ*, 2:297, and *Khiṭaṭ*, 1:337. Ibn Muyassar, *Akhbār miṣr*, p. 34, quotes the price of two hundred dinars.

[71] Almost verbatim in Ibn Muyassar, *Akhbār miṣr*, p. 34; and *Ittiᶜāẓ*, 2:297.

[72] Ibn Muyassar, *Akhbār miṣr*, pp. 21, 31–34; and *Ittiᶜāẓ*, 2:280–96.

[73] Built by Jawhar, the commander of the Fatimid expedition, in Ramaḍān 358/July–August 969 outside Bāb al-Naṣr in Old Cairo. It was first known as Muṣallā al-ᶜĪd, where collective prayer was attended by the caliph on religious holidays, but later came to be known as Muṣallā al-Amwāt, a place where prayer was performed over the deceased prior to burial in the nearby cemetery. See *Khiṭaṭ*, 1:451, 2:106, and 463–64.

[74] Verbatim in *Ittiᶜāẓ*, 2:298. Ibn Ẓāfir, *al-Duwal al-munqaṭiᶜah*, p. 75, mentions that in 462/1069–70 al-Mustanṣir's mother and daughters arrived in Baghdad to escape the famines in Egypt.

[75] Ibn Ẓāfir, *al-Duwal al-munqaṭiᶜah*, p. 74, mentions the daughter of Bābshād, a grammarian and official of the Correspondence Bureau.

[76] Verbatim in *Itti<sup>c</sup>āẓ*, 2:298; summarized in Ibn Ẓāfir, *al-Duwal al-munqaṭiʿah*, p. 74.

[77] Verbatim in *Ittiʿāẓ*, 2:299. A slightly different version is given by Ibn Muyassar, *Akhbār miṣr*, p. 33.

[78] Ibn Muyassar, *Akhbār miṣr*, pp. 37–39, makes no mention of a famine during the rule of al-Āmir, but records a famine in A.H. 490 and a famine and epidemics in A.H. 493. Both dates fall during the rule of al-Mustaʿlī Billāh (487–95/1094–1101), al-Āmir's predecessor.

[79] Al-Afḍal Abū'l-Qāsim Shāhanshāh was the only vizir of al-Mustaʿlī Billāh, then of his successor al-Āmir bi-Aḥkām Allāh. He was killed while still in office at the end of Ramaḍān 515/December 1121; Ibn al-Ṣayrafī, *Ishārah*, p. 60; Ibn Muyassar, *Akhbār miṣr*, pp. 57–59; Ibn Ẓāfir, *al-Duwal al-munqaṭiʿah*, pp. 82–88; *Ittiʿāẓ*, 3:60–74.

[80] He was entrusted with all important tasks by al-Āmir bi-Aḥkām Allāh and appointed vizir following the death of al-Afḍal. He was killed and crucified on al-Āmir's orders of 19 Rajab 522/19 July 1128; Ibn Muyassar, *Akhbār miṣr*, p. 69; *Khiṭaṭ*, 1:462–63; *Ittiʿāẓ*, 3:121–22. Edward Zambaur, *Manuel de généalogie et de chronologie pour l'histoire de l'Islam*, p. 96, dates his death 4 Ramaḍān 519/4 October 1125.

[81] Al-Afḍal ibn Walakhshī was invested with the vizirate on 13 Jumādā I 531/6 February 1137. After fleeing to Syria on 13 Shawwāl 533/13 June 1139, he returned to Egypt on 1 Ṣafar 534/27 September 1139, where he was apprehended and imprisoned on 4 Rabīʿ II 534/28 November 1139 but escaped on 23 Dhū'l-Qaʿdah 542/14 April 1148, the date on which he appeared in Cairo and appointed himself vizir. He was killed three days later by a rebellious faction of the army; Ibn Ẓāfir, *al-Duwal al-munqaṭiʿah*, pp. 94–99; Ibn Muyassar, *Akhbār miṣr*, pp. 79–84, 87; *Ittiʿāẓ*, 3:161–84.

[82] In *Ittiʿāẓ*, 3:161–84, al-Maqrīzī lists two periods of grain shortages during the rule of al-Ḥāfiẓ: one in the years 532–33/1137–39 and another from mid-536 to the end of 537/1142–43. Al-Maqrīzī refers here to the first one, since it coincides with the vizirate of Ibn Walakhshī.

[83] He was only five at the start of his "reign," having been born on 21 Muḥarram 544/31 May 1149; Ibn Ẓāfir, *al-Duwal al-munqaṭiʿah*, p. 109; *Ittiʿāẓ*, 3:213.

[84] While governor of al-Ashmūnayn and al-Bahnasā, Ibn Ruzzīk marched on Cairo on 19 Rabīʿ I 549/3 June 1154 and took the vizirate. Vizir of al-Fā'iz and of his successor al-ʿĀḍid, he was wounded and died on 19 Ramaḍān 556/11 September 1161, as a result of a plot engineered against him by al-ʿĀḍid, who was also his son-in-law; Ibn Ẓāfir, *al-Duwal al-munqaṭiʿah*, pp. 108–13; *Ittiʿāẓ*, 3:213–55; Ibn Khallikān/de Slane, 1:657–61; 2:526–30.

[85] Mentioned in *Ittiʿāẓ*, 3:238, as one of the army commanders.

[86] This took place in 551/1156–57; Ibn Muyassar, *Akhbār miṣr*, p. 96; *Ittiʿāẓ*, 3:229.

[87] Ibn al-Athīr, *al-Kāmil fi'l-tārīkh*, 13 vols. (Beirut: Dār Ṣādir, 1966), 12:170, dates it 597/1200–1201, the same as Abū Shāmah, *Kitāb al-rawḍatayn*, 2:239. According to Sāwīrus ibn al-Muqaffaʿ, *History of the Patriarchs*, vol. 3, pt. 2, drought and famine struck Egypt from A.H. 597 to 599. An eyewitness account is given by ʿAbd al-Laṭīf al-Baghdādī (d. 629/1231) in *Kitāb al-ifādah wa'l-iʿtibār fi'l-umūr al-mushāhadah wa'l-ḥawādith al-muʿāyanah bi-arḍ miṣr*.

[88] Abū Shāmah, whose source is the well-known al-ʿImād al-Iṣfahānī (d. 597/

1201), states in *Kitāb al-rawḍatayn*, 2:239, that the Nile-level was twelve cubits and twenty-one fingers, the same level ITL gives.

[89] Added in light of information contained in the next note.

[90] The same maximum is given in ITL for A.H. 597.

[91] The maxima given in ITL are twelve cubits and twenty-one fingers for A.H. 596, fifteen cubits and sixteen fingers for A.H. 597, and fifteen cubits and twenty-three fingers for A.H. 598.

[92] The famine of 597/1200–1201 was as disastrous in Syria. Abū Shāmah, *Kitāb al-rawḍatayn*, 2:244–45, cites cases of anthropophagy.

[93] Ibn al-Dawādārī, *Kanz al-durar wa jāmiʿ al-ghurar*, ed. Ulrich Haarmann, 8:363–65, dates this 695/1295–96, the same date given by other contemporary chronicles: al-Nuwayrī, in Shah Morad Elham, *Kitbuġā und Lāǧīn: Studien zur Mamluken-Geschichte nach Baibars al-Manṣūrī und an-Nuwairī* (Freiburg im Bresgau: Klaus Schwarz Verlag, 1977), pp. 47–48 of the Arabic text; K. V. Zetterstéen, ed., *Beiträge zur Geschichte der Mamlukensultane in den Jahren 690–741 der Hiǧra nach arabischen Handschriften*, pp. 37–38; Ibn Ḥabīb, *Tadhkirat al-nabīh fī ayyām al-manṣūr wa banīh*, ed. M. M. Amīn, 1:184.

[94] Ibn al-Dawādārī, *Kanz al-durar*, 8:358, states that the Nile waters reached sixteen cubits then receded quickly, causing prices to rise. ITL lists the same maximum given by al-Maqrīzī.

[95] *Jirāyah* (plural: *jirāyāt*). *Ṣubḥ*, 4:51: "The persons who were entitled to receive rations were in addition to the sultan's own mamluks, those who were at the service of the sultan in the palace. A ration consists of meat, spices, bread, oil, and fodder."

[96] *Buyūt* or *buyūtāt* consists of the several departments at the personal service of the sultan and of his immediate entourage. Morphologically, their names are compounds, the second part of which is the noun *khānah*, the Persian word for "house." Ibn Mammātī, *Qawānīn al-dawāwīn*, p. 354, states that they consist of the *ḥawā'ijkhānah* and the like. Al-Ẓāhirī, *Zubdat kashf al-mamālik*, ed. Paul Ravaisse, pp. 124–28, writes that they consist of (a) *shurbkhānah* for drinks and sweets; (b) *ṭishtkhānah* for clothing and apparel; (c) *rakbkhānah* for horses and riding; (d) *firāshkhānah* for tents and banquets; (e) *ṭablkhānah* for drums and musical instruments; (f) *maṭbakh* or royal kitchen; (g) *shikārkhānah* for the hunt and falcons. He also adds (h) *al-isṭablāt al-sulṭānīyah* or royal stables, although they seem to have been part of the *rakbkhānah*. Al-Qalqashandī in *Ṣubḥ*, 4:9–13, gives a slightly different list: (a) *sharābkhānah* (same as *shurbkhānah*); (b) *ṭisht-khānah*; (c) *firāshkhānah*; (d) *rikābkhānah* (same as *rakbkhānah*); (e) *maṭbakh*; (f) *ṭablkhānah*; services that correspond to those mentioned by al-Ẓāhirī. To these he adds (g) *silāḥkhānah* (armory) and (h) *ḥawā'ijkhānah*. The latter is the most important: it is placed under the supervision of the vizir and provides for the needs of the royal kitchens and for the distribution of rations among the commanders. For a brief description of these services, see D. Ayalon, "The System of Payment in Mamluk Military Society," *JESHO* (1957–58): 275.

[97] See note 96 above.

[98] In modern Libya.

[99] Al-Buḥayrah, al-Gharbīyah, and al-Sharqīyah correspond today fairly closely to the provinces bearing the same names in Egypt.

[100] These seem to be items commonly used as a cure for epidemics. Ibn al-Dawādārī, *Kanz al-durar*, 8:365, mentions that, at this time, his mother pawned a pair of gold bracelets worth fifty dinars to buy four pullets.

[101] Ibn al-Dawādārī, *Kanz al-durar*, 8:365: one hundred eighty dirhams.
[102] Ibid.: eighty dirhams.
[103] Ibid.: eighty dirhams.
[104] A town along the Red Sea littoral between Mecca and Jayzan; Yāqūt, *Muʿjam al-buldān*, 2:297.
[105] Ibn al-Dawādārī lived through this epidemic and wrote that his brother died upon returning from Barqah. He also mentioned cases of anthropophagy. See his *Kanz al-durar*, 8:363–65.
[106] Vizir from 694/1295 to 697/1297–98; Ibn al-Dawādārī, *Kanz al-durar*, 8:360–68.
[107] In *Shudhūr*, p. 41; *Nuqūd*, p. 71; de Sacy, *Monnoies*, p. 48; al-Maqrīzī states that it was in A.H. 806 that copper coins were measured by weight for the first time in the history of Egypt.
[108] A detailed account by Mufaḍḍal ibn Abī'l-Faḍā'il is given in Samira Kortantamer, *Ägypten und Syrien zwischen 1317 und 1341 in der Chronik des Mufaḍḍal b. Abīl-Faḍā'il* (Freiburg im Bresgau: Klaus Schwarz Verlag, 1973).
[109] Al-Maqrīzī omits to mention the Black Death of 749/1348, which swept over the Middle East and Europe.
[110] The date should be corrected to 775/1373–74 in light of information given by Ibn Ḥajar al-ʿAsqalānī, *Inbā'*, 1:59, 71.
[111] Michael W. Dols, *The Black Death in the Middle East*, p. 230, thinks that this was a pneumonic plague.
[112] Al-Maqrīzī was less than ten years of age, having been born in 766/1364.

## 3. THE CAUSES OF OUR ORDEALS

[1] This is a clear allusion to Qur'ān 41:27.
[2] The year 796/1393–94 was not as catastrophic as al-Maqrīzī leads the reader to believe. In *Sulūk*, 3:816–18, he states that the Nile-level reached sixteen cubits then eighteen cubits and eleven fingers but rapidly receded, thus shortening the period of irrigation and causing a diminished crop. This is corroborated by Ibn Ḥajar in *Inbā'*, 1:476–77, who adds that prices started to rise immediately, obviously in anticipation of a diminished crop the next year. An identical version is given by *Furāt*, 9:385–87.
[3] No such price is found in *Sulūk* for the year 796/1393–94. It seems that in A.H. 796 the highest price for one *irdabb* of wheat was only forty dirhams. The price of seventy dirhams is quoted for the year 797/1394–95 (*Sulūk*, 3:826) and confirmed by Ibn Ḥajar in *Inbā'*, 1:486, while *Furāt*, 9:403, quotes the price of sixty-six dirhams.
[4] The date is added in light of information found in *Sulūk*, 3:841–42; *Inbā'*, 1:494; and *Furāt*, 9:412–13.
[5] The price of one *irdabb* of wheat came down to fifty dirhams following the harvest of the year 798/1395–96. See *Sulūk*, 3:859; *Inbā'*, 1:508; *Furāt*, 9:438–39.
[6] Al-Ẓāhir Barqūq died on 15 Shawwāl 801/20 June 1399. He was the first Mamluk sultan of the Burjī Mamluk line, also known as the Circassian Mamluks. He put an end to the Turkish line of the Mamluks (known as the Baḥrī Mamluks) in 784/1382 after a long series of conspiracies. He ruled from 784/1382 to 801/1399, except for a number of months between 791/1389 and 792/1390, when the former Baḥrī Mamluks were able momentarily to reinstate their leader Amīr Ḥājjī as sultan. See ʿĀshūr, *al-ʿAṣr al-mamālīkī fi miṣr wa'l shām*, pp. 145–85, and

Stanley Lane-Poole, *A History of Egypt in the Middle Ages*, pp. 322–32. For a biography of Barqūq, see Ibn Khaldūn, *Kitāb al-ʿibar*, 5:997–1093. A Latin biography of Barqūq, written by Mignanello in 1416, has been rendered into English by W. J. Fischel, "Ascensus Barcoch," *Arabica* 6 (1959): 59–74, and 152–72.

[7] In *Sulūk*, 3:982, al-Maqrīzī states that the price of one *irdabb* of wheat was twenty-five dirhams or less at the time of Barqūq's death.

[8] *Sulūk*, 3:982.

[9] Ibid., 3:993.

[10] Ibid., 3:1113–27.

[11] The failure of the Nile to flood in 806/1403–4 contributed to the worsening agricultural conditions in Egypt and created a food shortage that led to famine. During this same year, plague struck Cairo. Contemporary sources estimate at 12,000 the number of persons who died of starvation. See *Sulūk*, 3:1120–26; *Khiṭaṭ*, 2:236–37; *Inbā'*, 2:260–61; Ibn Taghrī Birdī, *History of Egypt 1382–1469 A.D.*, ed. and tr. William Popper, 14:80.

[12] A list of prices and wages that supports this assertion is given by al-Maqrīzī in *Sulūk*, 3:1133–34, 1145. See also Eliyahu Ashtor, *Histoire des prix et des salaires dans l'Orient médiéval*, pp. 283–300.

[13] The royal silos were under the supervision of an official who was also responsible for the bureau of escheats and held the title *nāẓir al-mawārīth wa'l-ahrā'*. See *Sulūk*, 3:925; *Inbā'*, 2:42.

[14] Al-Maqrīzī fails to mention the effect of the plague. See references in note 11 above.

[15] In *Sulūk*, 3:1145, al-Maqrīzī states that a calf sold for 7,000 dirhams of account although its regular price was only 500; one pair of geese sold for 2,200, and one egg cost 2 dirhams of account. Here he fails to mention that, in the same year, the rate of the dinar jumped, in two months, from 100 dirhams of account in mid-Jumādā I (*Sulūk*, 3:1134) to 310 in Rajab (*Sulūk*, 3:1145).

[16] See the discussion regarding the date of the composition of *Ighāthah* in the translator's introduction.

[17] The currency situation worsened dramatically in the year 806/1403–4 when orders were issued that all transactions would henceforth be calculated only in *fulūs*. For further details, see *Sulūk*, 3:1117, 1131; and *Nuzhat*, 2:178–400. See also Ashtor, *Histoire des prix et des salaires*, pp. 276–77; idem, *Les métaux précieux et la balance des payements du Proche-Orient à la basse époque*, pp. 43–44; Jere L. Bacharach, "Circassian Monetary Policy: Silver," *Numismatic Chronicle*, 7th Series, 11 (1971): 267–81; idem, "Circassian Monetary Policy: Copper," *JESHO* 19 (1976): 32–47.

[18] One example was that of the governor of Tripoli, in modern Lebanon, who was appointed to the same office in Aleppo after promising one million silver dirhams to the sultan (*Sulūk*, 3:922). This became common practice during the reign of the Circassian Mamluks: the increased expenses of the state, coupled with diminishing revenues—not to mention the corruption of government officials—led to this practice. It gradually developed into an accepted norm.

[19] In 801/1399, a newly appointed chief judge secured this post upon payment of 100,000 dirhams, the greater part of which was borrowed; *Sulūk*, 3:934.

[20] In 798/1395–96, Sultan Barqūq's charities consisted mostly of the distribution of money among the poor to help them meet the rising cost of food. See

*Sulūk*, 3:854–55, *Inbā'*, 1:507–8; and *Nuzhat*, 1:424–25. Al-Maqrīzī mentions that when the sultan realized that the people were selling the bread they were given, he decided to distribute money instead. Some took advantage of this situation to the point that, in al-Maqrīzī's words, "some paupers struck it rich"; *Sulūk* 3:857.

[21] No known monograph by al-Maqrīzī deals separately with this question. The author probably refers to *Sulūk*.

[22] Rural rebellions were on the increase during the last years of Barqūq's reign as well as that of Faraj (801–15/1399–1412, except for a number of months in 808/1405). For a general survey, see A. N. Poliak, "Les révoltes populaires en Egypte à l'époque des mamelouks et leurs causes économiques," *REI* 8 (1934): 251–73. The reader may find further details in *Sulūk*, 3:925, 1006–7, 1067, 1082, 1089; *Inbā'*, 2:140, 200, 207; and *Nuzhat*, 2:145.

[23] This is corroborated by al-Qalqashandī, who, in *Ṣubḥ*, 3:454, states that by A.H. 790, the rent of one *faddān* of fertile land was about forty dirhams. By 810, the rent increased to four hundred and even to six hundred dirhams. The latter amounts should be read as dirhams of account, but at the rate of five dirhams of account per *kāmilī* silver dirham in A.H. 810, they represent—respectively—a twofold and threefold increase.

## 4. CURRENCY

[1] Of this work, which is believed to comprise eighty parts, only a few fascicules have been published so far under the auspices of the Arab Academy of Damascus. A translation of the topographical part was published by Nikita Elisséeff under the title *La description de Damas d'Ibn ʿAsākir* (Damascus: Institut français de Damas, 1959).

[2] *Al-sawdā' al-wāfiyah.*

[3] It is worth noting that al-Maqrīzī follows the erroneous tradition that the *ṭabarī*, with half the weight of the dirham, is pre-Islamic. See appendix 1.

[4] See appendix 1 under *qayṣarī*; al-Balādhurī, *Kitāb futūḥ al-buldān*, ed. Ṣalāḥ al-Dīn al-Munajjid, p. 571: *danānīr Hirqil*; al-Maqrīzī, *Traité des poids et des mesures légales des musulmans*, tr. Silvestre de Sacy (hereafter cited as de Sacy, *Poids*), p. 155: *al-danānīr al-hiraqlah*, attributed to Heraclius.

[5] The same version is found in *Shudhūr*, p. 4, *Nuqūd*, pp. 24–25, and al-Maqrīzī, *Traité des monnoies musulmanes*, tr. Silvestre de Sacy (hereafter cited as de Sacy, *Monnoies*), p. 13.

[6] *Al-wāfī.*

[7] I took some liberty in translating *wa kānat al-mawāzīn innamā hiya al-shawāhīn*. A literal translation would be awkward in English.

[8] Slightly different versions of these sayings are indexed by Wensinck, *Concordance et indices de la tradition musulmane*, 8 vols. (Leiden: E. J. Brill, 1936–88), 7:202.

[9] See al-Māwardī, *al-Aḥkām al-sulṭānīyah*, p. 119.

[10] The different copies of the manuscript state that this took place during the eighth year of ʿUmar's rule, which is an obvious error since he was elected caliph in 13/634. This inaccuracy was corrected by the editors of the 1940 Cairo edition but still exists in *Shudhūr*, p. 7, and *Nuqūd*, p. 31.

[11] His real name was al-Ḍaḥḥāk ibn Qays al-Tamīmī. See al-Balādhurī, *Futūḥ al-buldān*, pp. 383, 437; and Ibn Khallikān, *Ibn Khallikān's Biographical Dictionary*, tr. M. G. de Slane (hereafter cited as Ibn Khallikān/de Slane), 1:635–42.

[12] This is only one version among others. See al-Balādhurī, *Futūḥ al-buldān*, pp. 437–40.

[13] In the original text: *al-dirhamayn al-wazinah*, which Gaston Wiet, "Le traité des famines de Maqrīzī," p. 53, translated as "deux dirhams-poid." The editors of the Arabic text (p. 51) noted that two copies of the manuscript contained a word that they were unable to decipher. This could be read either as *al-darīyah* or *al-dhurrīyah*. Grammatically, *al-dhurrīyah*, being a noun, cannot follow *al-dirhamayn*. "Sasanian" is based on the *al-darīyah* reading, an Arabized form of the Persian word *darī*, meaning "of the royal court," probably a reference to Darius. This adjective is omitted in *Shudhūr*, pp. 7–8; *Nuqūd*, p. 31; de Sacy, *Monnoies*, p. 17. At any rate, these were Sasanian coins.

[14] *Al-Ḥamdu lillāh*. Same in *Shudhūr*, p. 8; *Nuqūd*, p. 32; de Sacy, *Monnoies*, p. 17.

[15] *Rasūl Allāh*. The more complete formula *Muḥammad rasūl Allāh* is mentioned in *Shudhūr*, p. 8; *Nuqūd*, p. 32; de Sacy, *Monnoies*, p. 17.

[16] *Lā ilāha illā Allāh waḥdahu*. *Nuqūd*, p. 32; *Shudhūr*, p. 8; de Sacy, *Monnoies*, p. 17.

[17] This same weight is mentioned in *Shudhūr*, p. 8; *Nuqūd*, p. 32; de Sacy, *Monnoies*, p. 17.

[18] *Allāhu akbar*. Identical with *Shudhūr*, p. 8; *Nuqūd*, p. 32; de Sacy, *Monnoies*, pp. 17–18. George C. Miles, *The Numismatic History of Rayy*, pp. 5–6, lists for the period A.H. 23–35, which corresponds to ʿUthmān's tenure as caliph, six Arab-Sasanian silver coins minted in A.H. 29, 30, 32, 35, 35 (two coins). The common inscription was *Bism Allāh rabbī* (In the name of God, my Lord).

[19] Ziyād ibn Abī Sufyān, known as Ziyād ibn Abīh. Al-Jahshiyārī, *Kitāb al-wuzarā'*, pp. 24–26, states that he died on 4 Ramaḍān 53/23 August 673.

[20] The reading of this sentence is difficult. The present version is based on the weight of the *dānaq*. Wiet, "Famines," p. 53, states that the black dirhams were "weighing six *dānaq*s less," which is erroneous in view of the weight of the *dānaq*. See also John Walker, *A Catalogue of the Arab-Sassanian Coins*, pp. 25–27.

[21] *Bism Allāh rabbī*. The inscription is not mentioned in the Arabic text and is added here in light of specimens contained in Walker, *Arab-Sassanian Coins*, pp. 36–46 and plates 6–8; Miles, *Rayy*, p. 6; Michael Mitchiner, *The Oriental Coins and Their Value*, p. 57, plates 27–28.

[22] See Walker, *Arab-Sassanian Coins*, pp. 25–27; idem, *A Catalogue of the Arab-Byzantine and Post-Reform Umaiyad Coins*, pp. xxxi–xxxii, for a discussion of al-Maqrīzī's statement. See also Heinz Gaube, *Arabosasanidische Numismatik*.

[23] He was killed and crucified by al-Ḥajjāj; Ibn Khallikān, *Wafayāt al-aʿyān*, ed. Iḥsān ʿAbbās (hereafter cited as Khallikān/ʿAbbās), 3:716, no. 340; al-Yaʿqūbī, *Tārīkh al-Yaʿqūbī*, 2:255–67.

[24] *Muḥammad rasūl Allāh*.

[25] *Amara Allāh bi'l-wafā' wa'l-ʿadl*. George C. Miles, *Rare Islamic Coins*, p. 4, lists two dirhams, nos. 11 and 12, minted at Darabjird in A.H. 65 and Kirman in A.H. 67, respectively. Walker, *Arab-Sassanian Coins*, pp. xli–xlii and 29–36, lists thirty-one specimens from A.H. 62 to 69, among these fourteen bear ʿAbd Allāh's name only, seventeen bear his name and his title as "Commander of the Faithful."

[26] He was appointed governor of Iraq by his brother ʿAbd Allāh in 68/687–88. He died in Dhū'l-Qaʿdah 72/April 692; al-Yaʿqūbī, *Tārīkh*, 2:263–65; Ibn Shākir al-Kutubī, *Fawāt al-wafayāt*, ed. Iḥsān ʿAbbās, 4:143–44. The latter source dates his death in 71/690–91.

[27] Walker, *Arab-Sassanian Coins*, pp. 102–4, lists nine specimens minted in Iraq and Iran for this period.

[28] *Qul huwa Allāhu aḥad*; Qur'ān 112:1.

[29] The first postreform gold dinar listed by Walker, *Arab-Byzantine Coins*, p. 84, and Stanley Lane-Poole, *Catalogue of Oriental Coins in the British Museum*, 1:1, no., 1, was minted in 77/696–97. The first silver dirham listed by Walker, *Arab-Byzantine Coins*, p. 104, was minted in 79/698–99. This dirham is identical with the one minted in 81/700–701 at Rayy and listed by Miles, *Rayy*, p. 8, and with the one mentioned by Lane-Poole, *Catalogue*, 1:7, and minted at Abrashahr in 93/711–12. On Syria's coinage in the Umayyad period, see Michael L. Bates, "History, Geography, and Numismatics in the First Century of Islamic Coinage," *Revue suisse de numismatique* 65 (1986): 231–62; idem, "The Coinage of Syria under the Umayyads, 692–750," in *The Fourth International Conference on the History of Bilād al-Shām during the Umayyad Period: Proceedings of the Third Symposium, 2–7 Rabīʿ I 1408 A.H./24–29 October 1987*, ed. M. Adnan Bakhit and Robert Schick, vol. 2 (English section), pp. 195–228.

[30] *Qul huwa Allāhu aḥad*. It is doubtful that such an inscription existed. It seems that the inscription was the standard *Allāhu aḥad, Allāhu al-ṣamad, lam yalid wa lam yūlad* (Qur'ān 112:1–3). See Walker, *Arab-Byzantine Coins*, p. 104.

[31] "Standard weights" is the translation of *ṣanaj* (sing.: *ṣanajah*), which in numismatic terminology correspond to "coin weights."

[32] For samples of such a coin, see Walker, *Arab-Byzantine Coins*, pp. 42–43.

[33] A legist of Medina, who died ca. 95/713–14. Ibn Khallikān/ʿAbbās, 2:375–78, no. 262; Ibn Khallikān/de Slane, 1:568–70.

[34] *Qul huwa Allāhu aḥad*.

[35] *Lā ilāha illā Allāh*.

[36] *Ḍuriba hādhā al-dirham bi-madīnat kadhā* . . . The blank space in this translation corresponds to the name of the city. Most coins bear the date or the mint and the date. *Bismillāh* is added from numismatic evidence. See Walker, *Arab-Byzantine Coins*, pp. 104ff.

[37] *Muḥammad rasūl Allāh arsalahu bi'l-hudā wa dīni al-ḥaqq li-yuẓhirahu ʿalā al-dīni kullih, wa law kariha al-mushrikūn*. This is a paraphrase of Qur'ān 9:33 and 61:8. The inscription mentioned by al-Maqrīzī is the full text found on some dirhams of that period. A number of dirhams bear a shortened form of this verse. See Walker, *Arab-Byzantine Coins*, pp. 104ff.

[38] These are the ratios of the legal dirham and of the legal dinar; see appendix 1 and al-Māwardī, *al-Aḥkām al-sulṭānīyah*, p. 119.

[39] *Dirham al-kayl*.

[40] *Qul huwa Allāhu aḥad*. See the correction in note 30 above. Dirhams of good alloy are usually called white dirhams.

[41] He is the founder of the Mālikite school of jurisprudence.

[42] Born ca. 23/643–44 and died on 9 Shawwāl 110/15 January 730 in Baṣrah; Ibn Khallikān/ʿAbbās, 4:181–83, no. 565.

[43] He was appointed governor of Iraq at the beginning of Yazīd's reign and was later replaced by Khālid ibn ʿAbd Allāh al-Qasrī on orders of Hishām, Yazīd's successor; al-Jahshiyārī, *Kitāb al-wuzarā'*, pp. 58–60; al-Balādhurī, *Futūḥ al-buldān*, p. 575.

[44] He was appointed governor of Iraq and Khurasan by Hishām ibn ʿAbd al-Malik in Shawwāl 105/March 724 and dismissed in Jumādā I 120/April–May 738. He died in 126/743–44; al-Jahshiyārī, *Kitāb al-wuzarā'*, pp. 60–64.

[45] See Walker's discussion of this passage in *Arab-Byzantine Coins*, p. lxiii.

[46] He was a cousin of al-Ḥajjāj ibn Yūsuf. Appointed governor of Iraq in 120/737–38 and dismissed in 126/743–44, he was killed in the same year or the following year. Ibn Khallikān/ʿAbbās, 7:101–12; Ibn Khallikān/de Slane, 4:435–48.

[47] This same version is to be found in Ibn Khallikān/ʿAbbās, 7:107–8.

[48] The Arabic text mentions a weight of seven. The correction to "six" is made in light of Walker, *Arab-Byzantine Coins*, p. lxiii. For silver dirhams minted at Wāsit between A.H. 120 and 126, see Walker, *ibid.*, pp. 198–99; Lane-Poole, *Catalogue*, 1:31; and A. S. DeShazo and Michael L. Bates, "The Umayyad Governors of al-ʿIrāq and the Changing Annulet Patterns on Their Dirhams," *Numismatic Chronicle*, 7th series, 14 (1974): 107–15.

[49] Same as al-Balādhurī, *Futūḥ al-buldān*, p. 576.

[50] Near Balkh; Yāqūt, *Muʿjam al-buldān*, 1:257–58.

[51] *Al-Sikkah al-ʿabbāsīyah.* Lane-Poole, *Catalogue*, 1:34, lists one gold dinar minted in A.H. 132. On page 35, he lists one silver dirham minted in A.H. 133. Neither bears "Abbasid coinage" as stated by al-Maqrīzī. For an overview of the inscriptions on Abbasid coins, see Miles, *Rare Coins*, p. 35.

[52] Lane-Poole, *Catalogue*, 1:37, lists the earliest dinar minted in A.H. 136. On page 41 (no. 32), he lists the earliest dirham of al-Manṣūr minted in A.H. 136 at Baṣrah.

[53] *Fīhā niqāṭ* is translated as "had points." Al-Maqrīzī refers to the secret markings on the coins. For silver dirhams and copper *fulūs* minted during al-Mahdī's rule, see Miles, *Rayy*, pp. 38–49.

[54] Al-Maqrīzī's statement is erroneous. Gold, silver, and copper coins from the reign of Mūsā al-Hādī are listed in several sources: Lane-Poole, *Catalogue*, 1:61–63, 208–9; Miles, *Rayy*, pp. 49–50; idem, *Rare Coins*, p. 60; Mitchiner, *Oriental Coins*, p. 72, no. 171.

[55] Jaʿfar's name appears on a large number of coins. Contrary to al-Maqrīzī's statement, none were minted in Baghdad; most were minted in Egypt (where Jaʿfar was the nominal governor) and some in Rayy. See Miles, *Rayy*, pp. 60, 67–68, 70–81; Lane-Poole, *Catalogue*, 1:64–66, 77–78; Mitchiner, *Oriental Coins*, p. 72. See also the overview by Michael L. Bates in "Coins and Money in the Arabic Papyri," in *Documents de l'Islam médiéval: Nouvelles perspectives de recherche*, ed. Yousef Ragheb, pp. 43–64.

[56] Al-Muḥammadīyah and Rayy refer to the same mint. From 148/765–66 onward, al-Muḥammadīyah appears on most coins instead of Rayy. See Lane-Poole, *Catalogue*, 1:43; Miles, *Rayy*, p. 30.

[57] The correction to 101 *mithqāls* instead of 100 (mentioned in the Arabic text) is made in light of the following verse and of information provided by al-Jahshiyārī, *Kitāb al-wuzarā'*, p. 241. Nawrūz is the Persian New Year. It corresponds to the spring equinox, although its date differed in the Middle Ages. Mihrajān (Persian: Mihragān) means "the Festival of Mithra" and corresponds to the autumn equinox. It is celebrated on the 16th of the month of Mihr (seventh month of the Persian calendar) and is still celebrated by Zoroastrians. See M. Boyce, "Mihragan among the Irani Zoroastrians," in *Mithraic Studies*, ed. John R. Hinnels, 2 vols. (Manchester: Manchester University Press, 1975), 1:106–18; S. H. Taqizadeh, *Old Iranian Calendars*, (London: Royal Asiatic Society, 1938).

[58] Al-Jahshiyārī, *Kitāb al-wuzarā'*, p. 241, states that each verse was inscribed on one side of the coin. For a discussion of this medallion, see Nahidh A. R. Daftar, "The Medallion of Jaʿfar al-Barmakī," *Numismatic Chronicle*, vol. 140 (7th series, vol. 20), (1980): 191–92.

[59] *Ḍarb al-ḥasanī li-kharīṭat amīr al-mu'minīn.*

[60] Al-Maqrīzī's statement is erroneous. This palace was built by Jaʿfar al-Barmakī, who donated it to the young al-Ma'mūn during the rule of Hārūn al-Rashīd. Upon the return of al-Ma'mūn from Khurasan to Baghdad, al-Ḥasan ibn Sahl took up residence there and the palace became known as al-Ḥasanī Palace. See Guy Le Strange, *Baghdad during the Abbasid Caliphate* (Oxford: Clarendon Press, 1900), pp. 242–46, where its location is shown on the map between pp. 262 and 263. For a biography of al-Ḥasan ibn Sahl, see Dominique Sourdel, *Le vizirat ʿabbaside*, 2 vols. (Damascus: Institut français de Damas, 1959), 1:215–18.

[61] A number of sources state that he managed the affairs of state without holding the title of vizir. He held this position from the death of Jaʿfar al-Barmakī in 187/802 until the death of Hārūn al-Rashīd in 193/809. He continued in the same position under al-Amīn (193–98/809–13), went into hiding at the advent of al-Ma'mūn, and died in retirement in Dhū'l-Ḥijjah 208/April–May 824; al-Jahshiyārī, *Kitāb al-wuzarā'*, pp. 265, 289–90; Sourdel, *Vizirat ʿabbaside*, 1:184–94.

[62] On al-Sindī ibn Shāhaq, see al-Jahshiyārī, *Kitāb al-wuzarā'*, p. 236; Sourdel, *Vizirat ʿabbaside*, 1:187, note 7. On the mintage, see Mile's remarks in *Rayy*, p. 84.

[63] *Rabbī Allāh.*

[64] *Al-ʿAbbās ibn al-Faḍl.* This is questioned by Miles, *Rayy*, pp. 91–92; however, a dinar minted in A.H. 196 and mentioned in Lane-Poole, *Catalogue*, 1:86, no. 234, partially supports al-Maqrīzī's assertion, but instead of the full name, only "al-ʿAbbās" appears at the bottom of the reverse of the coin. A similar coin is listed by Mitchiner, *Oriental Coins*, p. 74. These are Baghdad dinars and it seems that the legend on the coins varied over the few years when al-ʿAbbās supervised the mint.

[65] It is impossible to check the validity of al-Maqrīzī's statement regarding the introduction of the weight indicator. On Ibn ʿĀmir, see al-Yaʿqūbī, *Tārīkh*, 2:166ff.; Walker, *Arab-Sassanian Coins*, pp. xlvi–xlvii.

[66] On the coinage of al-Ma'mūn, see Lane-Poole, *Catalogue*, 1:91–107; Miles, *Rayy*, pp. 99–115. Al-Maqrīzī's statement is erroneous. Al-Ma'mūn introduced major changes: see the very recent study by Tayeb El-Hibri, "Coinage Reform under the ʿAbbāsid Caliph al-Ma'mūn," *JESHO* 36 (1993): 58–83.

[67] His own military commanders.

[68] *Ghashsh al-darāhim.*

[69] *Al-Maqrīzī's statement about ʿUbayd Allāh ibn Ziyād's coinage is disputed by Walker, Arab-Sassanian Coins*, pp. xlvii–xlix.

[70] *Duwal al-aʿājim.*

[71] Al-Maqrīzī is probably referring to *Khiṭaṭ*.

[72] A companion of Muḥammad and narrator of *ḥadīth*.

[73] Wensinck, *Concordance*, 6:274, mentions this *ḥadīth* on the authority of Muslim and Ibn Ḥanbal.

[74] A traditionist who compiled the *Ṣaḥīḥ*, a collection of *ḥadīth*; Ibn Khallikān/ʿAbbās, 5:194–96, no. 717.

[75] A traditionist who compiled the *Kitāb al-sunan*, a collection of *ḥadīth*; Ibn Khallikān/de Slane, 1:589–91.

[76] See also al-Balādhurī, *Futūḥ al-buldān*, p. 330.

[77] Al-Balādhurī, ibid., pp. 252–53, estimates the total amount at only two

million dinars. Another version is found in Ibn ʿAbd al-Ḥakam, *Futūḥ miṣr wa akhbāruhā*, ed. Charles Torrey (New Haven: Yale University Press, 1922), pp. 152–53.

[78] "Protected people", i.e., the status of non-Muslims living under Muslim rule.

[79] See other versions in al-Balādhurī, *Futūḥ al-buldān*, pp. 332–33; and al-Yaʿqūbī, *Tārīkh*, 2:152.

[80] Several historians of the Mamluk period have relied on al-Musabbiḥī's work. In addition to al-Maqrīzī, one may mention Ibn Ḥajar al-ʿAsqalānī and Ibn Iyās. The remaining fragment of this work has been discussed by Carl Becker (1977) and edited twice by Ayman Fu'ād Sayyid and Thierry Bianquis (1978) and William Milward (1980).

[81] Paul Balog, "History of the Dirhem in Egypt from the Fatimid Conquest until the Collapse of the Mamluk Empire," *Revue numismatique*, 6th Series, 3 (1961): 130, ascertains that the degree of fineness of these dirhams fluctuates between 23 and 30 percent, the average being around 27 percent. He calls the "reform" of A.H. 622 "nothing but a huge fraud." More recent studies show that the reform of 622 is no "fraud" and that silver content was about 30 percent. Claude Cahen ascribes this to a possible scribal error resulting in this version of the figures (i.e., ⅔ silver). Moreover, the problem is complicated by the fact that the term *kāmilī* was used in Mamluk sources not necessarily for the Ayyubid coin, but for the current silver coin. See Claude Cahen, "Monetary Circulation in Egypt at the Time of the Crusades and the Reform of al-Kāmil," in *The Islamic Middle East, 700–1900: Studies in Economic and Social History*, ed. A. L. Udovitch, pp. 327–28; and Michael L. Bates, "Crusader Coinage with Arabic Inscriptions," in *A History of the Crusades*, ed. Kenneth M. Sutton, 6:433, note 36.

[82] Same version in *Nuqūd*, p. 30; de Sacy, *Monnoies*, p. 38. This proves that the *kāmilī* dirham was not the only circulating silver coin in Egypt. See the analysis of Hassanein Rabie, *The Financial System of Egypt, A.H. 564–741/1169–1341*, pp. 182–83.

[83] The name of the Andalusian Ibn Saʿīd should be corrected to Abū'l-Ḥasan ʿAlī ibn Mūsā ibn Saʿīd al-Maghribī. The title of the work that al-Maqrīzī mentions here appears with several variations in Ibn Saʿīd, *Kitāb al-jughrāfiyā*, ed. Ismāʿīl al-ʿArabī (Beirut: al-Maktab al-tijārī lil-ṭibāʿah wa'l-nashr wa'l-tawzīʿ, 1970), p. 23; and in *Ṣubḥ*, 2:93, 14:391.

[84] The Arabic version gives the impression that both copper coins have the same exchange value. This passage is found almost verbatim in *Sulūk*, 3:1131.

[85] According to the published version of *Ighāthah*, this took place in A.H. 650. The editors of the Arabic text mentioned that the majority of manuscripts contain the date 750, which they thought was erroneous, because it did not fall within the period preceding the rule of Kitughā (A.H. 694–96). The exact year of this event is 759, as mentioned in *Sulūk*, 3:1131–32, and *Ṣubḥ*, 3:443–44, 467, and as corrected here.

[86] In some of his other works, al-Maqrīzī gives a totally different version; see section 2, note 107. The Cairene *raṭl* is a weight of 144 dirhams; therefore, one silver dirham was exchanged for a weight of 72 dirhams (about 214 grams) of copper *fulūs*.

[87] Almost verbatim in *Nuqūd*, p. 39; de Sacy, *Monnoies*, pp. 46–47. See also *Sulūk*, 3:1132; and Jere L. Bacharach, "Circassian Monetary Policy: Copper," *JESHO* 19 (1976): 32–37.

[88] *Sulūk*, 3:1132–33; Jere L. Bacharach, "Monetary Movements in Medieval Egypt, 1171–1517," in *Precious Metals in the Later Medieval and Early Modern Worlds*, ed. J. F. Richards, pp. 159–81.

[89] Here al-Maqrīzī informs the reader that one dinar equals one hundred and fifty dirhams of account; one silver dirham equals five dirhams of account; and one dirham of account equals a weight of twenty-four dirhams of copper *fulūs*. Keeping in mind that the silver dirham has ceased to circulate, its rate will be a multiple of the dirham of account. The conversion of these monetary units into weights of copper coins is as follows:

1 dinar = 150 × 24 = 3,600 dirhams (weight) of copper coins (approx. 10.710 kg);
1 silver dirham = 5 × 24 = 120 dirhams (weight) of copper coins (approx. 357 g);
1 dirham of account = 24 dirhams (weight) of copper coins (approx. 71.4 g).

The addition in the text of the value of the *raṭl* of copper is based on the following:

1 dirham of account = a weight of 24 dirhams of copper coins;
1 *raṭl* = a weight of 144 dirhams;
1 *raṭl* of copper coins = 144 ÷ 24 = 6 dirhams of account.

## 5. A DESCRIPTION OF THE POPULATION

[1] It is impossible to translate *fuqarā'* as poor or paupers. This term is occasionally applied to the Ṣūfis of the *khānqahs*, a meaning that does not fit here because of the inclusion of the *ajnād al-ḥalqah* and in light of further information given by al-Maqrīzī later in this section. I have preferred to render it as "those who receive a stipend," based on my reading of *Sulūk* 4:27, where al-Maqrīzī mentions the worsening economic condition of those who receive a stipend, either from religious endowments (*awqāf*), such as legists and the like, or from the sultan.

[2] These were the non-Mamluk cavalry and the sons of mamluks. They were born and bred in Egypt and thus could not aspire to be part of the Mamluk elite. They usually held a small fief and were required to participate in the expeditions if ordered to do so. See *Ṣubḥ*, 4:16; David Ayalon, "Studies on the Structure of the Mamluk Army," *BSOAS* 15 (1953): 448–59; Ulrich Haarmann, "The Sons of Mamluks as Fief-holders in Late Medieval Egypt," in *Land Tenure and Social Transformation in the Middle East*, ed. Tarif Khalidi, pp. 141–68.

[3] This statement indicates the rate of the silver dirham in terms of money of account, i.e., in dirhams of account. In light of note 89 in section 4, one silver dirham is equivalent to 5 dirhams of account. Here al-Maqrīzī confirms this ratio when he states that 20,000 silver dirhams are now equal to 100,000 dirhams of account (100,000 = 5 × 20,000).

[4] The average market rate was 30 to 32 silver dirhams per dinar. Based on a more realistic exchange rate of 1:30, 20,000 silver dirhams would be 666.6 dinars, not 1,000 as al-Maqrīzī claims. Here he uses the rate of 1:20 instead of the market rate that existed prior to the adoption of the dirham of account as money of account.

[5] The sum of 666.6 dinars is obtained by dividing 100,000 dirhams of account by 150, the rate of the dinar in dirhams of account. The ratio of the dinar to the silver dirham would therefore be 1:30 (150 ÷ 5 = 30).

[6] Here al-Maqrīzī gives the impression that prices have doubled.

[7] 3,000 ÷ 20 = 150.

[8] Obviously, al-Maqrīzī is choosing a bad example. If one considers that the silver dirham is equivalent to 5 dirhams of account, 1,000 silver dirhams will equal 5,000 dirhams of account, a sum that is much higher than the 3,000 dirhams of account that al-Maqrīzī mentions here.

[9] At the rate of 5 dirhams of account per silver dirham, the 100 dirhams of account will equal the 20 silver dirhams that al-Maqrīzī mentions.

## 6. CURRENT PRICES AND PRESENT ORDEALS

[1] See appendix 1 for a definition of these measures. Throughout this section, al-Maqrīzī adopts the rate of the dirham of account as explained in note 89 of section 4.

[2] This passage gives the general formula for the conversion of dirhams of account into weights of minted copper. The *raṭl* (approx. 1 lb or 428.4 g) is used to determine the value of the dirham of account. Hence:

1 *raṭl* (428.4 g) = a weight of 144 dirhams = 6 dirhams of account;
1 dirham of account = 144 ÷ 6 = a weight of 24 dirhams = (71.4 g) = 2 *ūqīyahs* (one *ūqīyah* = 12 dirhams);
1 dirham (weight) = 2.975 g.

[3] Notice the ratio 1:30 between gold and silver currencies in Cairo. In the Arabic text the silver dirham is referred to as *dirham al-muʿāmalah* (the dirham of transaction) to distinguish it from unminted silver.

[4] A sum equivalent to 4 *mithqāls* of gold at the rate of 1:150.

[5] 100 *mithqāls* of gold × 150 = 15,000 dirhams of account.

[6] See appendix 8, where this price for mutton is quoted (in *Sulūk*) for the end of Jumādā I 808/October–November 1405. Appendix 9 shows that the price of beef was 6 dirhams of account earlier in the same month. This is further evidence that the completion of *Ighāthah* was later than the stated date of Muḥarram 808; see the translator's introduction.

[7] The Arabic text states that "a chicken sold for 100 dirhams, i.e., 20 dirhams of *fulūs*." The correction is made in light of the value of the silver dirham (5 dirhams of account).

[8] The original Arabic text states that "the price of a goose ranged from 200 dirhams to 50 dirhams of *fulūs*." This is inconsistent with the style of medieval chronicles. First, the lower price is usually mentioned first; second, the margin between the two prices is unrealistically wide. The 200 are dirhams of *fulūs* (dirhams of account), while the 50 must be silver dirhams.

[9] A sum equivalent to almost 15 *mithqāls* of gold.

[10] Al-Maqrīzī correctly points out that, if these prices are calculated in gold dinars or in silver dirhams at the rate of 150 and 5 dirhams of account respectively, they do not show an increase. See my comments on grain prices in the translator's introduction.

## 7. THE MEANS TO ERADICATE THIS DISEASE

[1] "5" in the Arabic text. This correction is explained in note 3 below.

[2] "5¼" in the Arabic text. See note 3 below.

[3] Unfortunately, al-Maqrīzī gives a flawed example. Simply put, the numbers he gives do not add up. Without the corrections (notes 1 and 2), the reader is left with the following:

1. The price of 100 dirhams of silver = 5 *mithqāls*.
2. The mint fee, plus 50 dirhams of copper = ¼ *mithqāl*.
3. The final product (150 silver dirhams) = 5¼ *mithqāls*.

Therefore, 1 *mithqāl* = 150 silver dirhams divided by 5.25 = 28.57.

This ratio does not coincide to the ratio 1:24 that al-Maqrīzī mentions. By correcting items 1 and 2, one *mithqāl* will equal 24 silver dirhams. With the corrections, we will have the following figures:

1. The price of 100 dirhams of silver = 6 *mithqāls*.
2. The mint fee = ¼ *mithqāl*.
3. The final product (150 silver dirhams) = 6¼ *mithqāls*.

Therefore, to calculate the rate of one *mithqāl* in silver dirhams, one must divide 150 silver dirhams by 6.25. The result is 24, the same rate that al-Maqrīzī mentions. Another alternative is to put the mint fee at 1¼ *mithqāl*, but this is unlikely because it leads to the conclusion that the fee to cover the expenses for the alloy and the mint represents 20 percent of the final amount, an impossible percentage in light of the price of copper and of labor. In Ayyubid times, according to the mint manual of Ibn Baʿrah, this cost amounted to 5 percent only; A. Ehrenkreutz, "The Standard of Fineness of Gold Coins Circulating in Egypt at the Time of the Crusades," *JAOS* 74 (1954): 163. In mid-fifteenth century, the fee was 5½ percent; see al-Asadī, *al-Taysīr*, p. 129.

[4] A weight of 23⅓ *raṭls* of copper *fulūs* is equivalent to 3,360 dirhams, since one *raṭl* equals 144 dirhams. This is valued at one *mithqāl* of gold or at 140 dirhams of account. Therefore, one *raṭl* of *fulūs* is worth 6 dirhams of account and one dirham of account corresponds to a weight of 24 dirhams of copper coins. It is clear here that al-Maqrīzī bases his calculation on the exchange rate of 140 dirhams of account per dinar. If one *raṭl* of *fulūs* is 6 dirhams of account, 23⅓ *raṭls* will be 140 dirhams of account, the rate quoted earlier for the dinar.

[5] If one dinar is 3,360 dirhams of copper coins, one silver dirham (1/24 of one dinar) will be equal to a weight of 140 dirhams of copper coins.

## 8. THE MERITS OF THIS PROPOSAL

[1] See *Sulūk*, 4:6.

[2] See Eliyahu Ashtor, "Levantine Sugar Industry in the Later Middle Ages—An Example of Technological Decline," *Israel Oriental Studies* 7 (1977): 226–80, especially pp. 257–59.

[3] 100 *qinṭārs* = 10,000 *raṭls* = 60,000 dirhams of account. Therefore, one *raṭl* of *fulūs* is valued at 6 dirhams of account.

[4] "66⅓ *qintārs*" in the Arabic text. See note 5 below.

[5] "700 dirhams" in the Arabic text. These corrections are necessitated by the fact that 66⅓ *qinṭārs* of meat at 700 dirhams of account each add up to 46,433⅓ dirhams of account, and not to 60,000. Later, al-Maqrīzī quotes the price of 9 dirhams of account per *raṭl* of mutton (or 900 per *qinṭār*); see note 9 below.

[6] Or at ⅖ of a silver dirham per *raṭl*. This is an indication that al-Maqrīzī tries to prove his point regardless of the facts by choosing the lowest suitable price.

This price is for the beginning of A.H. 788. Later, the average price was one silver dirham. See appendix 9.

[7] Same comment as in note 6. The price of ⅔ of a silver dirham per *raṭl* is much lower than the average price of mutton quoted in appendix 8.

[8] Or a weight of 240 dirhams. The rate of the *raṭl* (or 12 *ūqīyahs*) of *fulūs* is then 6 dirhams of account.

[9] This price (9 dirhams of account per *raṭl*) confirms the correction that has been made in the text; see note 5 above.

[10] The Arabic text states that "this is based on the rate that 5 dirhams of account, a weight of 10 *ūqīyahs*, are worth one silver dirham." At the rate of 5 dirhams of account per silver dirham, the 37 dirhams of account mentioned in the preceding sentence will be equivalent to 7.4 silver dirhams and not 6⅙ as stated by al-Maqrīzī. This type of error is another instance where al-Maqrīzī revises the original manuscript and forgets to adjust relevant data.

# Bibliography

ʿAbd ar-Rāziq, Ahmad. 1982. "Les gouverneurs d'Alexandrie au temps des Mamlūks." *Annales islamogiques* 18: 123–69.

———. 1980. "Le vizirat et les vizirs d'Egypte au temps des Mamlūks." *Annales islamologiques* 16: 183–239.

———. 1978. "Les muḥtasibs de Fusṭāṭ au temps des Mamlūks." *Annales islamologiques* 14: 127–46.

———. 1977. "La ḥisba et le muḥtasib en Egypte au temps des Mamlūks." *Annales islamologiques* 13: 115–78.

———. 1970. "Un document concernant le mariage des esclaves au temps des Mamlūks." *JESHO* 13: 309–14.

Abū'l-Fidā, ʿImād al-Dīn. 1965. *Kitāb al-mukhtaṣar fī akhbār al-bashar.* 7 vols. Beirut: Dār al-kitāb al-lubnānī.

Abū Shāmah, Shihāb al-Dīn. 1871. *Kitāb al-rawḍatayn fī akhbār al-dawlatayn.* 2 vols. Cairo: Maṭbaʿat wādī al-nīl.

Abū Yūsuf. 1981. *Kitāb al-kharāj.* Ed. Muḥammad Ibrāhīm al-Bannā. Cairo: Dār al-iṣlāḥ.

ʿAlī Mubārak. 1886–89. *al-Khiṭaṭ al-tawfīqīyah al-jadīdah li-miṣr al-qāhirah wa muduniha wa bilādiha al-qadīmah wa'l-shahīrah.* 2 vols. Bulaq: al-Maṭbaʿah al-amīrīyah.

Amīn, Muḥammad Muḥammad. 1981. *Fihrist wathā'iq al-qāhirah ḥattā nihāyat ʿaṣr al-mamālīk.* Cairo: al-Maʿhad al-ʿlmī al-faransī lil-āthār al-sharqīyah.

———. 1980. *al-Awqāf wa'l-ḥayāt al-ijtimāʿīyah fī miṣr. 648–923/1250–1517.* Cairo: Dār al-nahḍah al-ʿarabīyah.

al-Asadī, Muḥammad ibn Muḥammad ibn Khalīl. 1967. *al-Taysīr wa'l-iʿtibār wa'l-taḥrīr wa'l-ikhtibār fīmā yajibu min ḥusn al-tadbīr wa'l-taṣarruf wa'l-ikhtiyār.* Ed. ʿAbd al-Qādir Aḥmad Ṭulaymāt. Cairo: Dār al-fikr al-ʿarabī.

Ashtor, Eliyahu. 1992. *Technology, Industry and Trade: Levant versus Europe, 1250–1500.* London: Variorum Reprints.

———. 1986. *East-West Trade in the Medieval Mediterranean.* London: Variorum Reprints.

———. 1985. "Investments in Levant Trade in the Period of the Crusades." *Journal of European Economic History* 14, no. 3 (Winter): 427–41.

———. 1984. "The Wheat Supply of the Mamluk Kingdom." *Asian and African Studies* 18: 283–95.

———. 1983a. *The Jews and the Mediterranean Economy, 10th–15th Centuries.* London: Variorum Reprints.

———. 1983b. *Levant Trade in the Later Middle Ages.* Princeton: Princeton University Press.

———. 1980. "The Volume of Medieval Spice Trade." *Journal of European Economic History* 9: 753–63.

———. 1978. *The Medieval Near East: Social and Economic History*. London: Variorum Reprints.
———. 1977a. "The Development of Prices in the Medieval Near East." In *Wirtschaftsgeschichte des Vorderen Orients in islamischer Zeit*, pt. 1, pp. 98–115. Leiden: E. J. Brill.
———. 1977b. "Levantine Sugar Industry in the Later Middle Ages—An Example of Technological Decline." *Israel Oriental Studies* 7: 226–80.
———. 1977c. "Quelques problèmes que soulève l'histoire des prix dans l'Orient médiéval." In *Studies in the Memory of Gaston Wiet*, ed. M. Rosen-Ayalon, pp. 203–27. Jerusalem: Hebrew University of Jerusalem.
———. 1976a. "Etudes sur le système monétaire des Mamlouks Circassiens." *Israel Oriental Studies* 6: 264–87.
———. 1976b. *A Social and Economic History of the Near East in the Middle Ages*. Berkeley and Los Angeles: University of California Press.
———. 1976c. "Spice Prices in the Near East in the 15th Century." *JRAS*: 26–41.
———. 1975. "Profits from the Trade with the Levant in the Fifteenth Century." *BSOAS* 38: 250–75.
———. 1974. "The Venetian Supremacy in the Levantine Trade: Monopoly or Pre-Colonialism?" *Journal of European Economic History* 3, no. 1 (Spring): 5–53.
———. 1971a. "Etude sur quelques chroniques mamloukes." *Israel Oriental Society* 1: 272–97.
———. 1971b. *Les métaux précieux et la balance des payements du Proche-Orient à la basse époque*. Paris: SEVPEN.
———. 1970a. "The Diet of the Salaried Classes in the Medieval Near East." *Journal of Asian History* 4, no. 1: 1–24.
———. 1970b. "Quelques observations d'un orientaliste sur la thèse de Pirenne." *JESHO* 13: 166–94.
———. 1969a. "Débat sur l'évolution économico-sociale de l'Egypte au moyen-âge, à propos d'un livre récent." *JESHO* 12: 102–9.
———. 1969b. *Histoire des prix et des salaires dans l'Orient médiéval*. Paris: SEVPEN.
———. 1963. "Matériaux pour l'histoire des prix dans l'Egypte médiévale." *JESHO* 6: 158–89.
———. 1961. "L'évolution des prix dans le Proche-Orient à la basse époque." *JESHO* 4: 15–46.
———. 1960. "Le coût de la vie dans l'Egypte médiévale." *JESHO* 3: 56–77, 240.
———. 1959. "Quelques indications sur les revenus dans l'Orient musulman au haut moyen-âge." *JESHO* 2: 262–80.
———. 1949. "Prix et salaires à l'époque mamlouke: Une étude sur l'état économique de l'Egypte et de la Syrie à la fin du moyen-âge." *REI* 17: 49–94.
ʿĀshūr, Saʿīd ʿAbd al-Fattāḥ. 1965. *al-ʿAṣr al-mamālīkī fī miṣr wa'l-shām*. Cairo: Dār al-nahḍah al-ʿarabīyah.
Attman, Artur. 1981. *The Bullion Flow between Europe and the East, 1000–1750*. Göteborg: Kungl. Vetenskaps-och Vitterhets-Samhallet.
Ayalon, David. 1990. "Baḥrī Mamlūks, Burjī Mamlūks: Inadequate names for the two Reigns of the Mamlūk Sultanate." In *Tārīḫ: A Volume of Occasional*

*Papers in Near Eastern Studies*. Ed. Leon Nemoy and Vera B. Moreen, 1:3:53. Philadelphia: Annenberg Research Institute.

———. 1987. "The End of the Mamluk Sultanate (Why did the Ottomans spare the Mamluks of Egypt and wipe out the Mamluks of Syria?)." *Studia Islamica* 65: 125–48.

———. 1985. "Regarding Population Estimates in the Countries of Medieval Islam." *JESHO* 28: 1–19.

———. 1979. *The Mamluk Military Society: Collected Studies*. London: Variorum Reprints.

———. 1977. *Studies on the Mamluks of Egypt (1250–1517)*. London: Variorum Reprints.

———. 1968. "The Muslim City and the Mamluk Military Aristocracy." In *Proceedings of the Israel Academy of Sciences and Humanities*, 2:311–29. Jerusalem: Israel Academy of Sciences and Humanities.

———. 1957–58. "The System of Payment in Mamluk Military Society." *JESHO* 1: 37–65, 257–96.

———. 1953, 1954. "Studies on the Structure of the Mamluk Army." *BSOAS* 15 (1953): 203–28, 448–76; 16 (1954): 57–90.

———. 1951. *L'esclavage du Mamelouk*. Jerusalem: Israel Oriental Society.

———. 1946. "The Plague and Its Effects upon the Mamluk Army." *JRAS*: 67–73.

al-ʿAynī, Badr al-Dīn. 1987. *ʿIqd al-jumān fī tārīkh ahl al-zamān*. Ed. Muḥammad Muḥammad Amīn. 2 vols. [A.H. 648–88]. Cairo: al-Hay'ah al-miṣrīyah lil-kitāb.

———. 1985, 1989. *ʿIqd al-jumān fī tārīkh ahl al-zamān*. Ed. ʿAbd al-Razzāq al-Ṭanṭāwī al-Qarmūṭ. Vol. 1 [A.H. 815–23]: Cairo: Maṭbaʿat al-ʿalā. Vol. 2 [A.H. 824–50]: Cairo: al-Zahrā' lil-iʿlām al-ʿarabī.

———. 1967. *al-Sayf al-muhannad fī sīrat al-malik al-mu'ayyad*. Ed. Faḥīm Muḥammad Shaltūt and Muṣṭafā Muḥammad Ziyādah. Cairo: Dār al-kitāb al-ʿarabī lil-ṭibāʿah wa'l-nashr.

Bacharach, Jere L. 1983. "Monetary Movements in Medieval Egypt, 1171–1517." In *Precious Metals in the Later Medieval and Early Modern Worlds*, ed. J. F. Richards, pp. 159–81. Durham, N.C.: Carolina Academic Press.

———. 1976. "Circassian Monetary Policy: Copper." *JESHO* 19: 32–47.

———. 1975. "Circassian Mamluk Historians and Their Quantitative Economic Data." *JARCE* 12: 75–87.

———. 1973. "The Dinar versus the Ducat." *IJMES* 4: 77–96.

———. 1971. "Circassian Monetary Policy: Silver." *Numismatic Chronicle*, 7th series, 11: 267–81.

Bacharach, Jere L., and H. A. Awad. 1973. "The Problem of the Obverse and the Reverse in Islamic Numismatics." *Numismatic Chronicle*, 7th series, 13: 183–91.

Bacharach, Jere L., and Adon A. Gordus. 1968. "Studies on the Fineness of Silver Coins." *JESHO* 11: 298–317.

al-Baghdādī, ʿAbd al-Laṭīf. 1983. *Kitāb al-ifādah wa'l-iʿtibār fī'l-umūr al-mushāhadah wa'l-ḥawādith al-muʿāyanah bi-arḍ miṣr*. Damascus: Dār Qutaybah.

al-Balādhurī, Aḥmad ibn Yaḥyā. 1956. *Kitāb futūḥ al-buldān*. Ed. Ṣalāḥ al-Dīn al-Munajjid. Cairo: Maktabat al-nahḍah al-miṣrīyah.

al-Balaṭunusī, Taqī al-Dīn. 1989. *Taḥrīr al-maqāl fīmā yaḥillu wa yaḥrumu min bayt al-māl*. Ed. Fatḥ Allāh Muḥammad Ghāzī al-Ṣabbāgh. Cairo: Dār al-wafā.

Balog, Paul. 1981. "Fatimid Glass Jetons: Token Currency or Coin Weights?" *JESHO* 24 (January): 93–109.

———. 1980. *The Coinage of the Ayyubids.* London: Royal Numismatic Society.

———. 1978–79. "Unusual Honorific Title on a Mamluk Coin." *Jahrbuch für Numismatik und Geldegeschichte* 28–29: 135–38.

———. 1970. "Islamic Bronze Weights from Egypt." *JESHO* 13: 233–56.

———. 1964. *The Coinage of the Mamluk Sultans of Egypt and Syria.* New York: American Numismatic Society.

———. 1962. "A Hoard of Late Mamluk Copper Coins and Observations on the Metrology of the Mamuluk Fals." *Numismatic Chronicle*, 7th series, 2: 243–73.

———. 1961. "History of the Dirhem in Egypt from the Fatimid Conquest until the Collapse of the Mamluk Empire." *Revue numismatique*, 6th series, 3: 109–46.

al-Baṭā'iḥī. See Ibn al-Ma'mūn al-Baṭā'iḥī, Jamāl al-Dīn.

Bates, Michael L. 1991. "Coins and Money in the Arabic Papyri." In *Documents de l'Islam médiéval: Nouvelles perspectives de recherche.* Ed. Yousef Ragheb. Actes de la table ronde organisée par le CNRS (Paris, 3–5 mars 1988), pp. 43–64. Cairo: Institut français d'archéologie orientale.

———. 1989a. "The Coinage of Syria under the Umayyads, 692–750." In *The Fourth International Conference on the History of Bilād al-Shām during the Umayyad Period: Proceedings of the Third Symposium, 2–7 Rabīʿ I 1408 A.H./24–29 October 1987*, ed. M. Adnan Bakhit and Robert Schick, vol. 2 (English section), pp. 195–228. Amman: University of Jordan.

———. 1989b. "Crusader Coinage with Arabic Inscriptions." In *A History of the Crusades*, ed. Kenneth M. Sutton, 6:421–82. 6 vols. Madison: University of Wisconsin Press.

———. 1989c. "The Dirham Mint of the Northern Provinces of the Umayyad Caliphate." In *Studies in Honor of Dr. Paul Z. Badoukian*, ed. Y. T. Nercessian. *Armenian Numismatic Journal* 15: 89–111.

———. 1986. "History, Geography, and Numismatics in the First Century of Islamic Coinage." *Revue suisse de numismatique* 65: 231–62.

———. 1984–. "Arab-Sasanian Coins." In *Encyclopaedia Iranica*, ed. Ehsan Yarshater, 2:225–29. 6 vols. London and Boston: Routledge and Kegan Paul.

———. 1981. "The Function of Fatimid and Ayyubid Glass Weights." *JESHO* 24: 63–92.

———. 1978–79. "Islamic Numismatics." *MESA Bulletin* 12, no. 2 (1978): 1–16; 12, no. 3 (1978): 2–18; 13, no. 1 (1979): 3–21; 13, no. 2 (1979): 1–9.

———. 1976. "The Arab-Byzantine Bronze Coinage of Syria: An Innovation by ʿAbd al-Malik." In *A Colloquium in Memory of George Carpenter Miles (1904–1975)*, pp. 16–27. New York: American Numismatic Society.

Bautier, Robert-Henri. 1970. "Les relations économiques des occidentaux avec les pays d'Orient au moyen-âge: Points de vue et documents." In *Sociétés et compagnies de commerce en Orient et dans l'océan indien: Actes du huitième colloque international d'histoire maritime (Beyrouth, 5–10 septembre 1966)*, ed. Michel Mollat, pp. 263–331. Paris: SEVPEN.

Bean, J. M. W. 1963. "Plague, Population and Economic Decline in England in the Later Middle Ages." *Economic History Review* 15, no. 3 (April): 423–37.

Becker, Carl H. 1977. *Beiträge zur Geschichte Ägyptens unter dem Islam.* 2 vols. in 1. Philadelphia: Porcupine Press. Reprint of the 1902–3 ed. published by K. J. Trubner, Strassburg.

Bianquis, Thierry. 1980. "Une crise frumentaire dans l'Egypte fatimide." *JESHO* 23: 67–101.

Blachère, R. 1969. "L'agglomération du Caire, vue par quatre voyageurs arabes du moyen-âge." *Annales islamologiques* 8: 1–26.

Blake, Robert P. 1937. "The Circulation of Silver in the Moslem East Down to the Mongol Epoch." *Harvard Journal of Asiatic Studies* 2, nos. 3–5 (December): 291–328.

Bosworth, C. Edmund. 1967. *The Islamic Dynasties.* Edinburgh: Edinburgh University Press.

Bowsky, William M., ed. 1971. *The Black Death: A Turning Point in History?* New York: Holt, Rinehart and Winston.

Brinner, William N. 1963. "The Significance of the Ḥarāfīsh and their Sultan." *JESHO* 6: 190–215.

Brunschvig, Robert. 1967. "Conceptions monétaires chez les juristes musulmans (VIII^e^–XIII^e^ siècles)." *Arabica* 14: 113–43.

Buckley, R. P. 1992. "The Muḥtasib." *Arabica* 39: 59–117.

Cahen, Claude. 1984. "La circulation monétaire en Egypte des Fatimides aux Ayyubides." *Revue numismatique*, 6th series, 26: 208–17.

———. 1981. "Monetary Circulation in Egypt at the Time of the Crusades and the Reform of al-Kāmil." In *The Islamic Middle East, 700–1900: Studies in Economic and Social History*, ed. A. L. Udovitch, pp. 315–33. Princeton: Darwin Press.

———. 1977. *Makhzūmiyyāt: Etudes sur l'histoire économique et financière de l'Egypte médiévale.* Leiden: E. J. Brill.

———. 1970. "Note sur l'esclavage musulman et le devshirme ottoman: à propos de travaux récents." *JESHO* 13: 211–18.

———. 1969. "Débat sur l'évolution économico-sociale de l'Egypte à la fin du moyen-âge, à propos d'un livre récent: Note additionnelle." *JESHO* 12: 109–11.

———. 1964. "Douanes et commerce dans les ports méditerranéens de l'Egypte médiévale." *JESHO* 7: 217–314.

———. 1962. "Contribution à l'étude des impôts dans l'Egypte médiévale." *JESHO* 5: 244–78.

Canard, Marius. 1935. "Le traité de 1281 entre Michel Paléologue et le sultan Qalā'ūn." *Byzantion* 10: 669–80.

Carpenter, David. 1987. "Gold and Gold Coins in England in the Mid-thirteenth Century." *Numismatic Chronicle* 147: 106–13.

Carpentier, Elisabeth. 1962. "La peste noire: Famines et épidémies au XIV^e^ siècle." *Annales, E.S.C.* 17 (November–December): 1062–92.

Cattenoz, Henri Georges. 1961. *Tables de concordance des ères chrétienne et hégirienne.* 3d ed. Rabat: Editions techniques nord-africaines.

Chapoutot-Remadi, Mounira. 1983. "Une grande crise à la fin du XIII^e^ siècle en Egypte." *JESHO* 26: 217–45.

Cipolla, Carlo M. 1967. *Money, Prices, and Civilization in the Mediterranean World.* New York: Gordian Press.

———. 1963. "Currency Depreciation in Medieval Europe." *Economic History Review* 15, no. 3 (April): 413–22.

Cohen, M. R. 1984. "Jews in the Mamluk Environment: The Crisis of 1442 (A Geniza Study)." *BSOAS* 47: 425–48.

Conrad, L. I. 1982. "Ṭā'ūn and wabā': Conceptions of Plague and Pestilence in Early Islam." *JESHO* 25: 268–307.

Cook, Michael A., ed. 1970. *Studies in the Economic History of the Middle East from the Rise of Islam to the Present Day*. London: Oxford University Press.
Curiel, R., and R. Gyselin. 1980–81. "Une collection de monnaies de cuivre sasanides tardives et arabo-sasanides." *Studia Iranica* 9 (1980): 165–84; 10 (1981): 61–83.
Daftar, Nahidh A. R. 1980. "The Medallion of Jaᶜfar al-Barmakī." *Numismatic Chronicle*, vol. 140 (7th series, vol. 20): 191–92.
Darrāj (Darrag), Aḥmad. 1968. "al-Ḥisbah wa atharuhā ᶜalā al-ḥayāt al-iqtiṣādīyah fī miṣr al-mamlūkīyah." *al-Majallah al-tārīkhīyah al-miṣrīyah* 14: 109–41.
———. 1963. "Les relations commerciales entre l'état mamlouk et la France." *Cairo University: Bulletin of the Faculty of Arts* 25 (December): 1–22.
———. 1961. *L'Egypte sous le règne de Barsbay*. Damascus: Institut français de Damas.
Day, John. 1978. "The Great Bullion Famine of the Fifteenth Century." *Past and Present* 79 (May): 3–54.
De Boüard, Michel. 1939. "Sur l'évolution monétaire de l'Egypte médiévale." *L'Egypte contemporaine* 30: 427–59.
DeShazo, A. S., and Michael L. Bates. 1974. "The Umayyad Governors of al-ᶜIrāq and the Changing Annulet Patterns on Their Dirhams." *Numismatic Chronicle*, 7th series, 14: 107–15.
Dols, Michael W. 1977. *The Black Death in the Middle East*. Princeton: Princeton University Press.
———. 1974. "Plague in Early Islamic History." *JAOS* 94: 371–83.
Duplessy, J. 1956. "La circulation des monnaies arabes en Europe occidentale du VIIIᵉ au XIIIᵉ siècle." *Revue numismatique*, 5th series, 18: 103–63.
al-Dūrī, ᶜAbd al-ᶜAzīz. 1969. *Muqaddimah lil-tārīkh al-iqtiṣādī al-ᶜarabī*. Beirut: Dār al-ṭalīᶜah.
"Early Islamic Mint Output: A Preliminary Inquiry into the Methodology and Application of the 'Coin-Die Count' Method." 1966. Prepared by a seminar at the University of Michigan. *JESHO* 9: 212–41.
Ehrenkreutz, Andrew S. 1992. *Monetary Change and Economic History in the Medieval Muslim World*. London: Variorum Reprints.
———. 1970. "Monetary Aspects of Medieval Near Eastern Economic History." In *Studies in the Economic History of the Middle East*, ed. M. A. Cook, pp. 37–50. London: Oxford University Press.
———. 1959, 1963. "Studies in the Monetary History of the Near East in the Middle Ages." *JESHO* 2 (1959): 128–61; 6 (1963): 243–77.
———. 1956. "The Crisis of Dinar in the Egypt of Saladin." *JAOS* 76: 178–84.
———. 1954a. "Contributions to the Knowledge of the Fiscal Administration of Egypt in the Middle Ages." *BSOAS* 16: 504–14.
———. 1954b. "The Standard of Fineness of Gold Coins Circulating in Egypt at the time of the Crusades." *JAOS* 74: 162–66.
———. 1953. "Extracts from the Technical Manual on the Ayyubid Mint in Cairo: The Manuscript of Ibn Baᶜra." *BSOAS* 15: 423–47.
Ehrenkreutz, Andrew S., with Theresa K. Toman Emington and Salih Kh. Sari. 1988. "Contributions to the Knowledge of the Standard of Fineness of Silver Coinage Struck in Egypt and Syria during the Period of the Crusades." *JESHO* 31: 301–3.
El-Hibri, Tayeb. 1993. "Coinage Reform under the ᶜAbbāsid Caliph al-Ma'mūn." *JESHO* 36: 58–83.

Elham, Shah Morad. 1977. *Kitbuġā und Lāǧīn: Studien zur Mamluken-Geschichte nach Baibars al-Manṣūrī und Nuwairī*. Freiburg im Bresgau: Klaus Schwarz Verlag.

Elisséeff, Nikita. 1959. *La description de Damas d'Ibn ʿAsākir*. Damascus: Institut français de Damas.

Enan, Mohammad Abdullah. 1962. *Ibn Khaldun: His Life and Work*. Lahore: Sh. Muhammad Ashraf.

Escovitz, J. H. 1983. "Patterns of Appointment to the Chief Judgeships of Cairo during the Baḥrī Mamluk Period." *Arabica* 30: 147–68.

Fernandes, Leonor. 1988. *The Evolution of a Ṣūfī Institution in Mamluk Egypt: The Khānqāh*. Berlin: Schwarz.

Fischel, Walter J. 1967. *Ibn Khaldun in Egypt*. Berkeley and Los Angeles: University of California Press.

———. 1959. "Ascensus Barcoch." *Arabica* 6: 59–74, 152–72.

———. 1957–58. "The Spice Trade in Mamluk Egypt." *JESHO* 1: 157–74.

Foster, Benjamin. 1970. "Agoranomos and Muḥtasib." *JESHO* 13: 128–44.

Garcin, Jean-Claude. 1978. "Note sur les rapports entre bédouins et fellahs à l'époque mamluke." *Annales islamologiques* 14: 147–63.

———. 1976. *Un centre musulman de la Haute-Egypte médiévale: Qūṣ*. Cairo: Institut français d'archéologie orientale.

———. 1973–74. "La 'méditerranisation' de l'empire mamelouk sous les sultans baḥrides." *Rivista degli studi orientali* 48: 109–16.

———. 1969. "Le Caire et la province: Constructions au Caire et à Qūṣ sous les mamlouks baḥrides." *Annales islamologiques* 8: 47–61.

Gaube, Heinz. 1973. *Arabosasanidische Numismatik*. Braunschweig: Klinkhardt and Biermann.

Gaudefroy-Demombynes, Maurice. 1923. *La Syrie à l'époque des mamelouks d'après les auteurs arabes*. Paris: Paul Geuthner.

Ghānim, Ḥamīd Zayyān. [1976?] *al-Azamāt wa'l-awbi'ah fī miṣr: ʿAṣr salāṭīn al-mamālīk*. Cairo: al-Maktabah al-ʿālamiyah.

Goitein, S. D. 1967–88. *A Mediterranean Society*. 5 vols. Berkeley and Los Angeles: University of California Press.

———. 1965, 1966, 1969. "The Exchange Rate of Gold and Silver Money in Fatimid and Ayyubid Times." *JESHO* 8 (1965): 1–46; "Appendix." *JESHO* 9 (1966): 67–68; "Erratum to *JESHO* VIII, 1965, p. 35." *JESHO* 12 (1969): 112.

———. 1957–58. "New Light on the Beginnings of the Kārimī Merchants." *JESHO* 1: 175–84.

Grierson, Ph. 1960. "The Monetary Reforms of ʿAbd al-Malik: Their Metrological Basis and Their Financial Repercussions." *JESHO* 3: 241–64.

Haarmann, Ulrich. 1984. "The Sons of Mamluks as Fief-holders in Late Medieval Egypt." In *Land Tenure and Social Transformation in the Middle East*, ed. Tarif Khalidi, pp. 141–68. Beirut: American University of Beirut.

al-Ḥakīm, ʿAlī ibn Yūsuf. 1960. *al-Dawḥah al-mushtabikah fī ḍawābiṭ dār al-sikkah*. Ed. Ḥusayn Mu'nis. Madrid: Maʿhad al-dirāsāt al-islāmīyah.

Halm, Heinz. 1979–82. *Ägypten nach den Mamlukischen Lehenregistern*. 2 parts. Wiesbaden: Ludwig Reichert.

Harīdī, Aḥmad ʿAbd al-Majīd. 1983–84. *Index des Ḫiṭaṭ: Index analytique des ouvrages d'Ibn Duqmāq et de Maqrīzī sur le Caire*. 3 vols. Cairo: Institut français d'archéologie orientale.

Ḥasan, Ḥasan Ibrāhīm. 1932. *al-Fāṭimīyūn fī Miṣr wa aʿmāluhum al-siyāsīyah wa'l-dīnīyah bi-wajh khāṣṣ*. Cairo: al-Maktabah al-amīrīyah.

Hendy, Michael F. 1985. *Studies in the Byzantine Monetary Economy. c. 300–1450.* Cambridge: Cambridge University Press.
Hennequin, Gilles. 1977. "Nouveaux aperçus sur l'histoire monétaire de l'Egypte à la fin du moyen-âge." *Annales islamologiques* 13: 179–215.
———. 1974a. "Mamlouks et métaux précieux, à propos de la balance des paiements de l'état syro-égyptien à la fin du moyen-âge: Questions de méthode." *Annales islamologiques* 12: 37–44.
———. 1974b. "Points de vue sur l'histoire monétaire de l'Egypte musulmane au moyen-âge." *Annales islamologiques* 12: 1–36.
Heyd, W. 1959. *Histoire du commerce du Levant au moyen-âge.* 2 vols. Amsterdam: Adolf M. Hakkert.
Hinz, Walther. 1955. *Islamische Masse und Gewichte.* Leiden: E. J. Brill.
Hirschleifer, Jack. 1987. *Economic Behaviour in Adversity.* Chicago: University of Chicago Press.
Ibn ʿAbd al-Ḥakam, ʿAbd al-Raḥmān. 1922. *Futūḥ miṣr wa akhbāruhā.* Ed. Charles Torrey. New Haven: Yale University Press.
Ibn Ajā, Muḥammad ibn Maḥmūd. 1974. *Tārīkh al amīr Yashbak al-Ẓāhirī.* Ed. ʿAbd al-Qādir Aḥmad Ṭulaymāt. Cairo: Dār al-fikr al-ʿarabī.
Ibn al-Athīr, ʿIzz al-Dīn. 1966. *al-Kāmil fī'l-tārīkh.* 13 vols. Beirut: Dār Ṣādir.
Ibn al-Dawādārī, Abū Bakr. 1960, 1971. *Kanz al-durar wa jāmiʿ al-ghurar.* Vol. 8, ed. Ulrich Haarmann; vol. 9, ed. Hans Robert Roemer. Cairo: Deutsches Archäologisches Institut.
Ibn Duqmāq, Ibrāhīm ibn Muḥammad. 1966. *Kitāb al-intiṣār li-wāsiṭat ʿaqd al-amṣār.* Beirut: al-Maktab al-tijārī lil-ṭibāʿah wa'l-nashr wa'l-tawzīʿ.
Ibn al-Furāt, Muḥammad ibn ʿAbd al-Raḥīm. 1936–38. *Tārīkh Ibn al-Furāt.* Vols. 7–9. Ed. Q. Zurayq and N. ʿIzz al-Dīn. Beirut: al-Maṭbaʿah al-amrīkānīyah.
Ibn al-Fuwaṭī, Kamāl al-Dīn. 1932. *al-Ḥawādith al-Jāmiʿah wa'l-tajārib al-nāfiʿah fī'l-mi'ah al-sābiʿah.* Baghdad: al-Maktabah al-ʿarabīyah.
Ibn Ḥabīb, al-Ḥasan ibn ʿUmar. 1976–86. *Tadhkirat al-nabīh fī ayyām al-manṣūr wa banīh.* Ed. M. M. Amīn. 3 vols. Cairo: al-Hay'ah al-miṣrīyah al-ʿāmmah lil-kitāb.
Ibn Ḥajar al-ʿAsqalānī, Aḥmad ibn ʿAlī. 1969–72. *Inbā' al-ghumr bi-anbā' al-ʿumr.* Ed. Ḥasan Habashī. 3 vols. Cairo: al-Majlis al-aʿlā lil-shu'ūn al-islāmīyah.
———. 1966–67. *al-Durar al-kāminah fī aʿyān al-mi'ah al-thāminah.* Ed. M. S. Jādd al-Ḥaqq. 5 vols. Cairo: Dār al-kutub al-ḥadīthah.
Ibn al-ʿImād, ʿAbd al-Ḥayy ibn Aḥmad. 1966. *Shadharāt al-dhahab fī akhbār man dhahab.* 8 vols in 4. Beirut: al-Maktab al-tijārī lil-ṭibāʿah wa'l-nashr wa'l-tawzīʿ.
Ibn Iyās, Muḥammad ibn Aḥmad. 1960–75. *Badā'iʿ al-zuhūr fī waqā'iʿ al-duhūr.* Ed. Muḥammad Muṣṭafā. 5 vols. Cairo: Dār iḥyā al-kutub al-ʿarabīyah.
———. 1951. *Ṣafaḥāt lam tunshar min badā'iʿ al-zuhūr fī waqā'iʿ al-duhūr.* Ed. Muḥammad Muṣṭafā. Cairo: Dār al-maʿārif.
Ibn al-Jīʿān, Aḥmad. 1974. *al-Tuḥfah al-sanīyah bi-asmā' al-bilād al-miṣrīyah.* Cairo: Maktabat al-kullīyah al-azharīyah.
Ibn Khaldūn. 1967. *The Muqaddimah: An Introduction to History.* 2d ed. Tr. Franz Rosenthal. 3 vols. Princeton: Princeton University Press.
———. 1959. *Kitāb al-ʿibar.* 7 vols. Beirut: Dār al-kitāb al-lubnānī.
———. 1858. *Prolégomènes d'Ebn-Khaldoun.* Ed. M. Quatremère. Notices et extraits des manuscrits de la bibliothèque impériale, vol. 17. Paris: Firmin Didot.

Ibn Khallikān, Aḥmad. 1969–72. *Wafayāt al-aʿyān*. Ed. Iḥsān ʿAbbās. 8 vols. Beirut: Dār al-thaqāfah.

———. 1842–71. *Ibn Khallikān's Biographical Dictionary*. Tr. M. G. de Slane. 4 vols. Paris: Oriental Translation Fund of Great Britain and Ireland.

Ibn Mammātī, Asʿad ibn al-Muhadhdhab. 1943. *Kitāb qawānīn al-dawāwīn*. Ed. Aziz S. Atiya. Cairo: al-Jamʿīyah al-zirāʿīyah al-malakīyah.

Ibn al-Ma'mūn al-Baṭā'iḥī, Jamāl al-Dīn. 1983. *Passages de la chronique d'Egypte*. Ed. Ayman Fu'ād Sayyid. Cairo: Institut français d'archéologie orientale.

Ibn al-Muqaffaʿ, Sāwīrus. 1943–. *History of the Patriarchs of the Coptic Church of Alexandria*. 4 vols. Cairo: Jamʿīyat al-āthār al-qibṭīyah.

Ibn Muyassar, Muḥammad. 1919. *Akhbār miṣr*. Ed. Henri Massé. Cairo: Institut français d'archéologie orientale.

Ibn Qāḍī Shuhbah, Abū Bakr ibn Aḥmad. 1977. *Tārīkh*. Ed. ʿAdnān Darwīsh. Vol. 1. Damascus: Institut français de Damas.

Ibn al-Ṣayrafī, ʿAli ibn Munjib. 1924. *al-Ishārah ilā man nāla al-wazārah*. Ed. ʿAbd Allāh Mukhliṣ. Cairo: Maṭbaʿat al-maʿhad al-ʿilmī al-faransī.

Ibn Shaddād, Bahā al-Dīn. 1903. *Sīrat Ṣalāḥ al-Dīn al-Ayyūbī*. Cairo: Manṣūr ʿAbd al-Mutaʿāl.

Ibn al-Shiḥnah, Muḥibb al-Dīn Muḥammad ibn Muḥammad. 1909. *al-Durr al-muntakhab fī tārīkh mamlakat ḥalab*. Ed. Y. Sarkīs al-Dimashqī. Beirut: al-Maṭbaʿah al-kāthūlīkīyah.

Ibn Taghrī Birdī, Abū'l-Maḥāsin. 1963–72. *al-Nujūm al-zāhirah fī mulūk miṣr wa'l-qāhirah*. 16 vols. Cairo: al-Mu'assasah al-miṣrīyah lil-ta'līf wa'l-tarjamah wa'l-ṭibāʿah wa'l-nashr.

———. 1954–63. *History of Egypt, 1382–1469 A.D.* Tr. William Popper. 8 vols. University of California Publications in Semitic Philology, vols. 13–14, 17, 18, 19, 22–23; indices, vol. 24. Berkeley and Los Angeles: University of California Press.

———. 1942. *Extracts from Abû l-Maḥâsin ibn Taghrî Birdî's Chronicle Entitled Ḥawâdith ad-duhûr fî madâ 'l-ayyâm wash-shuhûr* [Years 845–74]. Ed. William Popper. University of California Publications in Semitic Philology, vol. 8. Berkeley and Los Angeles: University of California Press.

Ibn Taymīyah, Taqī al-Dīn. 1982. *Public Duties in Islam: The Institution of the Ḥisba*. Ed. Muhtar Ed. Holland and Khurshid Ahmad. Leicester: Islamic Foundation.

Ibn Ṭūlūn, Shams al-Dīn Muḥammad ibn ʿAlī. 1962–64. *Mufākahat al-khillān fī ḥawādith al-zamān*. Ed. Muḥammad Muṣṭafā. 2 vols. Cairo: al-Mu'assasah al-miṣrīyah lil-ta'līf wa'l-tarjamah wa'l-ṭibāʿah wa'l-nashr.

Ibn Ẓāfir. 1972. *Akhbār al-duwal al-munqaṭiʿah*. Ed. André Ferré. Cairo: Institut français d'archéologie orientale.

Ibrāhīm ʿAlī, ʿAbd al-Laṭīf. 1965–66. "Naṣṣān jadīdān min wathīqat al-amīr Ṣarghatmish." *Cairo University. Majallat kullīyat al-ādāb* 27 (May–December 1965): 121–58; 28 (May–December 1966): 143–210.

ʿInān, Muḥammad ʿAbd Allāh. 1969. *Miṣr al-islāmīyah wa tārīkh al-khiṭaṭ al-miṣrīyah*. 2d ed. Cairo: Maktabat al-khānjī.

Iskandar, Tawfīq. 1957. "Niẓām al-muqāyaḍah fī tijārat miṣr al-khārijīyah fī'l-ʿaṣr al-wasīṭ." *al-Majallah al-tārīkhīyah al-miṣrīyah* 6: 37–46.

Issawi, Charles. 1970. "The Decline of Middle Eastern Trade." In *Islam and the Trade of Asia*, ed. D. S. Richards, pp. 245–66. Philadelphia: University of Pennsylvania Press.

Jahn, Karl. 1970. "Paper Currency in Iran: A Contribution to the Cultural and Economic History of Iran in the Mongol Period." *Journal of Asian History* 4, no. 2: 101–35.

al-Jahshiyārī, Muḥammad ibn ʿAbdūs. 1938. *Kitāb al-wuzarāʾ waʾl-kuttāb*. Ed. Muṣṭafā al-Saqqā. Cairo: Muṣṭafā al-Bābī al-Ḥalabī.

Kafadar, Cemal. 1991. "Les troubles monétaires à la fin du XVIe siècle et la prise de conscience ottomane du déclin." *Annales, E.S.C.* 46: 381–400.

al-Khaṭīb al-Jawharī. See al-Ṣayrafī, ʿAlī ibn Dāwūd.

al-Kindī, Abū ʿUmar Muḥammad ibn Yūsuf. 1912. *Kitāb al-wulāt wa kitāb al-quḍāt*. Ed. Rhuvon Guest. Leiden: E. J. Brill.

Kortantamer, Samira. 1973. *Ägypten und Syrien zwischen 1317 und 1341 in der Chronik des Mufaḍḍal b. Abīl-Faḍāʾil*. Freiburg im Bresgau: Klaus Schwarz Verlag.

al-Kutubī, Muḥammad ibn Shākir. 1973–74. *Fawāt al-wafayāt waʾl dhayl ʿalayhā*. Ed. Iḥsān ʿAbbās. 5 vols. Beirut: Dār al-thaqāfah.

Labib, Subhi Y. 1974. "Medieval Islamic Maritime Policy in the Indian Ocean Area." *Recueils de la société Jean Bodin* 32: 225–41.

———. 1970. "Egyptian Commercial Policy in the Middle Ages." In *Studies in the Economic History of the Middle East*, ed. M. A. Cook, pp. 63–77. London: Oxford University Press.

———. 1969. "Capitalism in Medieval Islam." *Journal of Economic History* [New York] 29 (March): 79–96.

———. 1965a. "al-Asadī und sein Bericht über Verwaltungs und Geldreform im 15. Jahrhundert." *JESHO* 8: 312–16.

———. 1965b. *Handelsgeschichte Ägyptens im Spätmittelalter (1171–1517)*. Wiesbaden: Franz Steiner Verlag GMBH.

———. 1952. "al-Tujjār al-kārimīyah wa tijārat miṣr fīʾl-ʿuṣūr al-wusṭā." *al-Majallah al-tārīkhīyah al-miṣrīyah* 4: 5–63.

Lane-Poole, Stanley. 1967. *Catalogue of Oriental Coins in the British Museum*. 10 vols. Bologna: Forni Editore; reprint of the 1875–90 edition.

———. 1901. *A History of Egypt in the Middle Ages*. London: Methuen.

Laoust, Henri. 1952. *Les gouverneurs de Damas sous les mamlouks et les premiers ottomans: 658–1156/1260–1744*. French translation of the annals of Ibn Ṭūlūn and Ibn Jumʿah. Damascus: Institut français de Damas.

Lapidus, Ira Marvin. 1969. "The Grain Economy of Mamluk Egypt." *JESHO* 12: 1–15.

———. 1967. *Muslim Cities in the Later Middle Ages*. Cambridge, Mass.: Harvard University Press.

Levitzion, Nehemia. 1986. "Mamluk Egypt and Takrūr (West Africa)." In *Studies in Islamic History and Civilization in Honour of Professor David Ayalon*, ed. M. Sharon, pp. 183–207. Jerusalem: Cana; Leiden: E. J. Brill.

Little, Donald P. 1986. *History and Historiography of the Mamluks*. London: Variorum Reprints.

———. 1970. *An Introduction to Mamluk Historiography*. Wiesbaden: Franz Steiner Verlag GMBH.

Lopez, Robert S. 1986. *The Shape of Medieval Monetary History*. London: Variorum Reprints.

———. 1951. "The Dollar of the Middle Ages." *Journal of Economic History* 11, no. 3 (Summer): 209–34.

Lopez, Robert S., and Irwing W. Raymond. 1955. *Medieval Trade in the Mediterranean World*. New York: Columbia University Press.

Lowe, J. D. 1986. "A Medieval Instance of Gresham's Law: The Fatimid Monetary System and the Decline of Bimetallism." *Jusūr* 2: 1–24.

Lowick, Nicholas. 1990. *Islamic Coins and Trade in the Medieval World*. London: Variorum Reprints.

Mājid, ʿAbd al-Munʿim. 1953. *Nuẓum al-fāṭimīyīn*. 2 vols. Cairo: Maktabat al-anglū-miṣrīyah.

al-Maqrīzī, Aḥmad ibn ʿAlī. 1979. *Les marchés du Caire*. Tr. A. Raymond and G. Wiet. Cairo: Institut français d'archéologie orientale.

———. 1970–73. *Kitāb al-sulūk li-maʿrifat duwal al-mulūk*. Ed. Saʿīd ʿAbd al-Fattāḥ ʿĀshūr. Vols. 3–4. Cairo: Maṭbaʿat dār al-kutub.

———. 1970. *Kitāb al-mawāʿiẓ wa'l-iʿtibār bi-dhikr al-khiṭaṭ wa'l-āthār; al-maʿrūf bi'l-khiṭaṭ al-maqrīzīyah*. 2 vols. Baghdad: al-Muthannā.

———. 1967–73. *Ittiʿāẓ al-ḥunafā' bi-akhbār al-a'immah al-fāṭimīyīn al-khulafā'*. Ed. Jamāl al-Dīn al-Shayyāl and M. H. Muḥammad Aḥmad. 3 vols. Cairo: al-Majlis al-aʿlā lil-shu'ūn al-islāmīyah.

———. 1967. *al-Nuqūd al-islāmīyah; al-musammā bi-shudhūr al-ʿuqūd fī dhikr al-nuqūd*. Ed. Muḥammad al-Sayyid ʿAlī Baḥr al-ʿUlūm. Najaf: al-Maktabah al-ḥaydarīyah.

———. 1962. "Le traité des famines de Maqrīzī." Tr. Gaston Wiet. *JESHO* 5: 1–90.

———. 1961. *al-Bayān wa'l-iʿrāb ʿammā bi-arḍ miṣr min al-aʿrāb*. Ed. ʿAbd al-Majīd ʿAbduh. Cairo: ʿĀlam al-kutub.

———. 1956. *Kitāb al-sulūk li-maʿrifat duwal al-mulūk*. Ed. M. M. Ziyādah. Vols. 1–2. Cairo: Lajnat al-ta'līf wa'l tarjamah wa'l-nashr.

———. 1940. *Ighāthat al-ummah bi-kashf al-ghummah*. Ed. M. M. Ziyādah and Jamāl al-Dīn al-Shayyāl. Cairo: Lajnat al-ta'līf wa'l-tarjamah wa'l nashr; 2d ed., 1957.

———. 1933. *Shudhūr al-ʿuqūd fī dhikr al-nuqūd*. Ed. and tr. L. A. Mayer. Alexandria: Morris.

———. 1845–47. *Histoire des sultans mamelouks de l'Egypte*. Tr. E. Quatremère. 2 vols. Paris: Oriental Translation Fund.

———. 1799. *Traité des poids et des mesures légales des musulmans*. Tr. Silvestre de Sacy. Paris: Didot Jeune.

———. 1797. *Traité des monnoies musulmanes*. Tr. Silvestre de Sacy. Paris: Fuchs.

Mate, Mavis. 1978. "The Role of Gold Coinage in the English Economy, 1338–1400." *Numismatic Chronicle*, 7th series, 18, no. 138: 126–41.

al-Māwardī, ʿAlī ibn Muḥammad. 1966. *al-Aḥkām al-sulṭānīyah*. 2d ed. Cairo: Muṣṭafā al-Bābī al-Ḥalabī.

Michel, Bernard. 1925. "L'organisation financière de l'Egypte sous les sultans mamelouks d'après Qalqashandī." *BIE* 7: 127–47.

Miles, George C. 1958. *Contribution to Arabic Metrology*. New York: American Numismatic Society.

———. 1952. "Miḥrāb and ʿAnazah: A Study of Early Islamic Iconography." In *Archaeologica orientalia in memoriam Ernst Herzfeld*, pp. 156–71. Locust Valley, N.Y.: J. J. Augustin.

———. 1950. *Rare Islamic Coins*. New York: American Numismatic Society.

———. 1938. *The Numismatic History of Rayy*. New York: American Numismatic Society.

Minost, E. 1936–37. "Au sujet du traité des monnaies musulmanes de Makrîzî." *BIE* 19: 45–61.

Misikimin, Harry A. 1964. "Monetary Movements and Market Structure: Forces for Contraction in Fourteenth and Fifteenth Century England." *Journal of Economic History* 24: 470–90.
Mitchiner, Michael. 1977. *The Oriental Coins and Their Value*. London: Hawkins Publications.
Mochiri, Malek Iradj. 1983. *Etude de numismatique iranienne sous les sassanides et arabe-sassanides*. Louvain: Imprimerie Orientaliste.
———. 1981. "A Pahlavi Forerunner of the Umayyad Reformed Coinage." *JRAS*: 168–72.
Mollat, Michel. 1986. *The Poor in the Middle Ages: An Essay in Social History*. Tr. Arthur Goldhammer. New Haven: Yale University Press.
Morimoto, K. 1981. *The Fiscal Administration of Egypt in the Early Islamic Period*. Kyoto: Dohosha.
Mortel, Richard T. 1989. "Prices in Mecca during the Mamluk Period." *JESHO* 32: 279–334.
al-Musabbiḥī, Muḥammad ibn ʿUbayd Allāh. 1980. *Akhbār miṣr fi-sanatay 414–415 H*. Ed. William J. Milward. Cairo: al-Hay'ah al-miṣrīyah lil-kitāb.
———. 1978. *al-Juz' al-arbaʿūn min Akhbār miṣr*. Ed. Ayman Fu'ād Sayyid and Thierry Bianquis. Cairo: Institut français d'archéologie orientale.
Nicol, Norman D. 1986. "Paul Balog's *The Coinage of the Ayyubids*: Additions and Corrections." *Numismatic Chronicle* 146: 119–54.
Nicol, Norman D., and Raafat El-Nabarawy. 1984. "A Hoard of Mamluk Copper Coins ca. 770 A.H./1369 A.D. in the Collection of the Egyptian National Library." *JARCE* 21: 109–18.
Nicol, Norman D., with R. El-Nabarawy and J. L. Bacharach. 1982. *Catalog of the Islamic Coins, Glass Weights, Dies and Medals in the Egyptian National Library, Cairo*. Malibu: Undena.
Nohl, Johannes. 1924. *The Black Death*. Tr. C. H. Clarke. London: Harper and Brothers.
al-Nuwayrī, Aḥmad ibn ʿAbd al-Wahhāb. 1964. *Nihāyat al-arab fī funūn al-adab*. 21 vols. Cairo: al-Mu'assasah al-miṣrīyah al-ʿāmmah lil-ta'līf wa'l-tarjamah wa'l-ṭibāʿah wa'l-nashr.
al-Nuwayrī, Muḥammad ibn Qāsim. 1968–76. *Kitāb al-ilmām*. Ed. Aziz S. Atiya. 7 vols. Heydarabad, Deccan: Dā'irat al-maʿārif al-ʿuthmānīyah.
Oddy, W. A. 1980. "The Gold Contents of Fatimid Coins Reconsidered." In *Metallurgy in Numismatics*, ed. M. Metcalf and W. A. Oddy, 2 vols. 1: 99–118. London: Royal Numismatic Society.
Piloti, Samuel. 1950. *L'Egypte au commencement du quinzième siècle*. Ed. P. H. Dopp. Cairo: Université Fouad Ier.
Poliak, Abraham N. 1978. *Feudalism in Egypt, Syria, Palestine and the Lebanon: 1250–1900*. Philadelphia: Porcupine Press. Reprint of London: Royal Asiatic Society, 1939.
———. 1938. "The Demographic Evolution of the Middle East. Population Trends since 1348." *Palestine and the Middle East* 10: 201–5.
———. 1937. "Some Notes on the Feudal System of the Mamluks." *JRAS*: 97–107.
———. 1936. "La féodalité islamique." *REI* 10: 247–65.
———. 1934. "Les révoltes populaires en Egypte à l'époque des mamelouks et leurs causes économiques." *REI* 8: 251–73.
Popper, William. 1955–57. *Egypt and Syria under the Circassian Sultans 1382–1468*

A.D.: *Systematic Notes to Ibn Taghrî Birdî's Chronicles of Egypt*. 2 vols. University of California Publications in Semitic Philology, vols. 15–16. Berkeley and Los Angeles: University of California Press.

———. 1951. *The Cairo Nilometer*. Berkeley: University of California Press.

al-Qalqashandī, Aḥmad. 1913–19. *Ṣubḥ al-aʿshā*. 14 vols. Cairo: al-Maṭbaʿah al-amīrīyah.

Qāsim, ʿAbduh Qāsim. 1979. *Dirāsāt fī tārīkh miṣr al-ijtimāʿī: ʿAṣr salāṭīn al-mamālīk*. Cairo: Dār al-maʿārif.

Rabie, Hassanein M. 1972. *The Financial System of Egypt, A.H. 564–741/1169–1341*. London: Oxford University Press.

———. 1970. "The Size and Value of the Iqṭāʿ in Egypt. 564–741 A.H./1169–1341. A.D." In *Studies in the Economic History of the Middle East*, ed. M. A. Cook, pp. 129–38. London: Oxford University Press.

Raymond, A. 1984. "Cairo's Area and Population in the Early 15th Century." *Muqarnas* 2: 21–31.

Renouard, Yves. 1950. "Le commerce de l'argent au moyen-âge." *Revue historique* 103: 41–52.

Richards, D. S., ed. 1970. *Islam and the Trade of Asia*. Oxford: Bruno Cassirer; Philadelphia: University of Pennsylvania Press.

Richards, J. F., ed. 1983. *Precious Metals in the Later Medieval and Early Modern Worlds*. Durham, N.C.: Carolina Academic Press.

Robbert, Louise Buenger. 1983. "Monetary Flows—Venice 1150 to 1400." In *Precious Metals in the Later Middle Ages*, ed. J. F. Richards, pp. 53–77. Durham, N.C.: Carolina Academic Press.

Robbins, Helen. 1928. "A Comparison of the Effects of the Black Death on the Economic Organization of France and England." *Journal of Political Economy* 36: 447–79.

Russell, Josiah C. 1966. "The Population of Medieval Egypt." *JARCE* 5: 69–82.

al-Ṣafadī, Khalīl ibn Aybak. 1931–1959, 1970. *Kitāb al-wāfī bi'l-wafayāt*. Vols. 1–4. Istanbul: Milli Eğitim Basımevi. Vols. 5–8. Wiesbaden: Franz Steiner Verlag GMBH.

al-Sakhāwī, Muḥammad ibn ʿAbd al-Raḥmān. 1934–36. *al-Daw' al-lāmiʿ li-ahl al-qarn al-tāsiʿ*. 12 vols. Cairo: Maktabat al-Qudsī.

———. 1896. *al-Tibr al-masbūk fī dhayl al-sulūk*. Ed. Aḥmad Zakī. Cairo: al-Maṭbaʿah al-amīrīyah.

Salibi, M. K. 1957. "Listes chronologiques des grands cadis de l'Egypte sous les mamelouks." *REI* 25: 81–125.

Sāmī Bāshā, Amīn. 1916–36. *Taqwīm al-Nīl*. 3 vols. Cairo: al-Maktabah al-amīrīyah.

al-Saqaṭī, Abu ʿAbd Allāh Muḥammad. 1931. *Un manuel hispanique de ḥisba*. Ed. and tr. G. S. Colin and E. Lévi-Provençal. Paris: Ernest Leroux.

Sari, Salih Kh. 1988. "A Note on al-Maqrīzī's Remarks regarding the Silver Coinage of Baybars." *JESHO* 31: 298–301.

Sauvaire, M. H. 1887. "Matériaux pour servir à l'histoire de la numismatique et de la métrologie musulmanes. Complément." *JA*, 8th series, 10: 200–259.

———. 1886a. "Matériaux pour servir à l'histoire de la numismatique et de la métrologie musulmanes. Troisième partie—Mesures de capacité." *JA*, 8th series, 7 (1886): 124–77, 394–468; 8 (1886): 113–65, 272–97.

———. 1886b. "Matériaux pour servir à l'histoire de la numismatique et de la métrologie musulmanes. Quatrième et dernière partie—Mesures de longueur et de superficie." *JA*, 8th series, 8: 479–536.

———. 1884–85. "Matériaux pour servir à l'histoire de la numismatique et de la métrologie musulmanes. Deuxième partie—Poids." *JA*, 8th series, 3 (1884): 368–445; 4 (1884): 207–321; 5 (1885): 498–506.

———. 1879–82. "Matériaux pour servir à l'histoire de la numismatique et de la métrologie musulmanes." *JA*, 7th series, 14 (1879): 455–533; 15 (1880): 228–77, 421–78; 18 (1881): 499–516; 19 (1882): 23–77, 97–163, 281–327.

al-Ṣayrafī, ʿAlī ibn Dāwūd. 1970–74. *Nuzhat al-nufūs wa'l-abdān fī tawārīkh al-zamān*. 3 vols. Ed. Ḥasan Ḥabashī. Cairo: Maṭbaʿat dār al-kutub.

———. 1970. *Inbā' al-haṣr bi-abnā' al-ʿaṣr*. Ed. Ḥasan Ḥabashī. Cairo: Dār al-fikr al-ʿarabī.

al-Shayyāl, Jamāl al-Dīn. 1965. *Majmūʿat al-wathā'iq al-fāṭimīyah*. 2d ed. 2 vols. Cairo: Dār al-maʿārif.

al-Shayzarī, ʿAbd al-Raḥmān ibn Naṣr. 1946. *Kitāb nihāyat al-rutbah fī ṭalab al-ḥisbah*. Ed. al-Bāz al-ʿArīnī. Cairo: Lajnat al-ta'līf wa'l-tarjamah wa'l-nashr.

Shoshan, Boaz. 1986. "Exchange Rate Policies in Fifteenth-Century Egypt." *JESHO* 29: 28–51.

———. 1983. "Money Supply and Grain Prices in Fifteenth-Century Egypt." *Economic History Review*, 2nd series, 36: 47–67.

———. 1982. "From Silver to Copper: Monetary Changes in Fifteenth-Century Egypt." *Studia Islamica* 56: 97–116.

———. 1980a. "Fatimid Grain Policy and the Post of Muḥtasib." *IJMES* 13: 181–89.

———. 1980b. "Grain Riots and the 'Moral Economy' in Cairo: 1350–1517." *Journal of Interdisciplinary History* 10: 459–78.

———. 1978. "Money, Price and Population in Mamluk Egypt." Ph.D. dissertation. Princeton University.

al-Shujāʿī, Shams al-Dīn. 1977. *Tārīkh al-malik al-Nāṣir Muḥammad ibn Qalāwūn al-Ṣāliḥī wa awlāduh*. Ed. Barbara Schafer. Wiesbaden: Franz Steiner Verlag.

Smith, John Masson, Jr. 1969. "The Silver Currency of Mongol Iran." *JESHO* 12: 16–41.

Smith, John Masson, Jr., and Frances Plunkett. 1968. "Gold Money in Mongol Iran." *JESHO* 11: 275–97.

Sperber, Daniel. 1972. "Islamic Metrology from Jewish Sources II." *Numismatic Chronicle*, 7th series, 12: 275–82.

Staffa, Susan Jane. 1977. *Conquest and Fusion: The Social Evolution of Cairo, A.D. 642–1850*. Leiden: E. J. Brill.

Sublet, Jacqueline. 1971. "La peste prise aux rêts de la jurisprudence: Le traité d'Ibn Ḥağar al-ʿAsqalānī sur la peste." *Studia Islamica* 33: 141–49.

———. 1962. "ʿAbd al-Laṭīf al-takrītī et la famille des Banū Kuwayk, marchands Kārimī." *Arabica* 9, no. 2 (May): 193–96.

al-Suyūṭī, Jalāl al-Dīn. 1967–68. *Ḥusn al-muḥāḍarah fī tārīkh miṣr wa'l-qāhirah*. Ed. Muḥammad Abū'l-Faḍl Ibrāhīm. 2 vols. Cairo: ʿIsā Bābī al-Ḥalabī.

Toubert, Pierre. 1973. "Une des premières vérifications de la loi de Gresham: La circulation monétaire dans l'état pontifical vers 1200." *Revue numismatique*, 6th series, 15: 180–89.

Toussoun, Omar. 1926. *La géographie de l'Egypte à l'époque arabe*. 3 vols. Cairo: Institut français d'archéologie orientale.

———. 1922–23. *Mémoire sur les anciennes branches du Nil*. 2 parts. Cairo: Institut français d'archéologie orientale.

Tucker, W. F. 1981. "Natural Disasters and the Peasantry in Mamluk Egypt." *JESHO* 24: 215–24.

Udovitch, Abraham L., ed. 1981. *The Islamic Middle East, 700–1900: Studies in Economic and Social History*. Princeton: Darwin Press.

———. 1979. "Bankers without Banks: Commerce, Banking, and Society in the Islamic World in the Middle Ages." In *The Dawn of Modern Banking*, pp. 255–73. New Haven: Yale University Press.

Udovitch, Abraham L., Robert Lopez, and Harry Miskimin. 1970. "England to Egypt, 1350–1500: Long-term Trends and Long-Distance Trade." In *Studies in the Economic History of the Middle East*, ed. M. A. Cook, pp. 93–128. London: Oxford University Press.

Unvala, J. M. 1938. *Coins of Tabaristan and Some Sassanian Coins from Susa*. Paris: G. P. Maisonneuve.

Wake, C. H. H. 1979. "The Changing Pattern of Europe's Pepper and Spice Imports, ca. 1400–1700." *Journal of European Economic History* 8, no. 2 (Fall): 361–403.

Walker, John. 1967. *A Catalogue of the Arab-Sassanian Coins*. London: Trustees of the British Museum.

———. 1956. *A Catalogue of the Arab-Byzantine and Post-Reform Umaiyad Coins*. London: Trustees of the British Museum.

Watson, Andrew. 1967. "Back to Gold and Silver." *Economic History Review*, 2d series, 20, no. 1: 1–34.

Wensinck, Arent J. 1936–88. *Concordance et indices de la tradition musulmane*. 8 vols. Leiden: E. J. Brill.

Wiet, Gaston. 1955. "Les marchands d'épices sous les sultans mamlouks." *Cahiers d'histoire égyptienne* 7 (May): 81–147.

———. 1932. *Les biographies du "Manhal Sâfi"* [of Ibn Taghrī Birdī]. Mémoires de l'institut d'Egypte, vol. 19. Cairo: Institut français d'archéologie orientale.

———. 1915. "Kindî et Maqrîzî." *BIFAO* 12: 61–73.

al-Yaʿqūbī, Aḥmad. 1960. *Tārīkh al-Yaʿqūbī*. 2 vols. Beirut: Dār Ṣādir.

Yāqūt ibn ʿAbd Allāh al-Ḥamawī. 1955–57. *Muʿjam al-buldān*. 5 vols. Beirut: Dār Ṣādir.

al-Ẓāhirī, Ghars al-Dīn Khalīl ibn Shāhīn. 1894. *Zubdat kashf al-mamālik*. Ed. Paul Ravaisse. Paris: Ernest Leroux.

Zambaur, Edward. 1927. *Manuel de généalogie et de chronologie pour l'histoire de l'Islam*. Hanover: H. Lafaire.

Zetterstéen, K. V., ed. 1919. *Beiträge zur Geschichte der Mamlukensultane in den Jahren 690–741 der Hiğra nach arabischen Handschriften*. Leiden: E. J. Brill.

Ziegler, Philip. 1969. *The Black Death*. New York: John Day Company.

Ziyādah, Muḥammad Muṣṭafā, et al. 1971. *Dirāsāt ʿan al-Maqrīzī*. Cairo: al-Hay'ah al-miṣrīyah al-ʿāmmah lil-ta'līf wa'l-nashr.

Ziyādah, Niqūlah. 1962. *al-Ḥisbah wa'l-muḥtasib fī'l-Islām*. Beirut: al-Maṭbaʿah al-kāthūlīkīyah.

# Index